Brief Therapy With Couples and Families in Crisis

As the average length of therapy shortens, clinicians need a resource to lead them step-by-step through the goals and process of the opening sessions of brief therapy, and clear treatment maps for the most common presenting problems. This resource helps clinicians do just that and more, including doing a quick assessment and isolating and addressing the underlying emotional wounds that prevent families and couples from solving problems on their own. Readers will not only learn how to "think brief," they will also discover how to navigate the session process in an interactive and action-oriented way, even with clients who are in high-pressure, crisis situations.

Robert Taibbi is a licensed clinical social worker with forty-plus years' experience, primarily in community mental health working with couples and families as a clinician, supervisor and clinical director. He is the author of nine books.

Brief Therapy With Couples and Families in Crisis

Robert Taibbi

NEW YORK AND LONDON

First published 2018
by Routledge
711 Third Avenue, New York, NY 10017

and by Routledge
2 Park Square, Milton Park, Abingdon, Oxon, OX14 4RN

Routledge is an imprint of the Taylor & Francis Group, an informa business

© 2018 Taylor & Francis

The right of Robert Taibbi to be identified as author of this work has been asserted by him in accordance with sections 77 and 78 of the Copyright, Designs and Patents Act 1988.

All rights reserved. No part of this book may be reprinted or reproduced or utilized in any form or by any electronic, mechanical, or other means, now known or hereafter invented, including photocopying and recording, or in any information storage or retrieval system, without permission in writing from the publishers.

Trademark notice: Product or corporate names may be trademarks or registered trademarks, and are used only for identification and explanation without intent to infringe.

Library of Congress Cataloging-in-Publication Data
Names: Taibbi, Robert, author.
Title: Brief therapy with couples and families in crisis / by Robert Taibbi.
Description: New York, NY : Routledge, 2017. | Includes bibliographical
　references.
Identifiers: LCCN 2017028271| ISBN 9780415787802 (hardcover : alk. paper) |
　ISBN 9780415787819 (pbk. : alk. paper) | ISBN 9781315225715 (e-book)
Subjects: | MESH: Marital Therapy—methods | Psychotherapy, Brief—methods |
　Couples Therapy—methods | Family Therapy—methods
Classification: LCC RC488.5 | NLM WM 430.5.M3 | DDC 616.89/1562—dc23
LC record available at https://lccn.loc.gov/2017028271

ISBN: 978-0-415-78780-2 (hbk)
ISBN: 978-0-415-78781-9 (pbk)
ISBN: 978-1-315-22571-5 (ebk)

Typeset in Sabon
by Swales & Willis Ltd, Exeter, Devon, UK

Contents

1	The Landscape of Brief	1
2	Core Concepts	12
3	Treatment Maps for Common Couple Problems	45
4	Treatment Maps for Common Family Problems	73
5	First Session Goals	91
6	First Session Process	105
7	Second Session and Beyond	120
8	Couple and Family Therapy Techniques and Tools	143
9	Integrating the Brief Approach Into Your Own Therapeutic Style	162
	Index	179

1   The Landscape of Brief

Anne leaves a voice mail message. She just discovered that her husband Bill has been having an affair for the past six months, and he in fact admitted so last night. She is understandably distressed and would like an appointment as soon as possible, and Bill, though reluctant, has agreed to come in.

The couple is in crisis. While Anne and Bill are struggling with infidelity, they could have just as easily been reeling from a bigger-than-usual argument that resulted in the police being called. For families, crises may come in the form of parents learning that their 10-year-old son just got suspended from school for pushing a teacher, or that their 15-year-old daughter is pregnant. Their emotions are high and they want to be seen quickly. They need help putting out the fire.

This is what this book about—how to put out the emotional fire and effectively help those couples and families who come to you in crisis, using a brief treatment model. Our approach will be two-pronged. One is using tools and techniques to calm the emotional waters and put the couple's or family's presenting problems to rest. This is about hitting the ground running, demonstrating leadership, successfully shaping the content and process in those crucial opening sessions.

But we also want to go beyond simple crisis intervention, and our other focus, and larger focus on this book, is to help couples and families leave treatment not just feeling better, but with the awareness and tools they need to successfully manage future problems on their own. To do this you need to quickly diagnose the source of their problems and crises, repair the faulty infrastructure and teach them the communication and emotional skills that they lack. And to do this within a brief model demands an action- and process-oriented behavioral approach, one that keeps the clients in lockstep with you throughout. This is what we plan to provide.

But in order to get our bearings, let's begin by exploring in this chapter the broad landscape of brief therapy and the dynamics of those in crisis.

Brief World

You might be considering a brief model for a number of reasons. Perhaps you work in a setting where this is the clinical norm: a walk-in community clinic where crisis work is the bulk of what you do, or a community agency where there is always a strong demand for services, where waiting lists are common and where there may be a cap on the number of sessions that clients can receive. Or perhaps you want to be more flexible in your overall approach, your own clinical style already leans towards a short-term approach, and you are looking for new ideas and techniques that will enable you do such work better.

Or brief work may be less of a choice and more a reality, you realize, of how long clients stay. You're not alone if you think this way. When we look at the statistics of those in therapy, it turns out that most clients come to therapy once (Phillips, 1985) and the average length of treatment is five to eight sessions (Cooper, 2011). In spite of any cherished images we may have of the inward journey of therapy, the unraveling of the past and the unconscious, the reality check is that, in fact, most couples and families are in brief therapy. Both their expectations and actual involvement often limit you to a fairly short window of treatment. Crises only increase the challenge. You have to work fast, effectively and efficiently, in order to quell their high emotions, making sure that each and every session counts. If you don't—if your pace doesn't match their expectations—they're likely not coming back.

Thinking Brief

Imagine that you wake up one morning with a huge rash on your arm. Quickly you go on the internet, open up WebMD and begin looking at an array of ghastly pictures of various types of rashes—one from Africa that actually can rapidly spread mayhem all over your body and looks exactly like the rash on your arm, and another that is a form of Lyme disease that you remember your mother having many summers ago, which caused her much pain and months to recover from. Now you're feeling a bit panicky. You call your family doctor who (big relief!) schedules you for 2:00. Just having the appointment helps you calm down.

You show up a bit early, still worrying. In comes your doctor to the exam room, and what does she do? She asks you what is bothering you. You show her your arm. She looks at the rash under a magnifying glass. She asks you an assortment of questions—when did this start, does it itch, did you try any treatments on your own, have you been in the woods lately, has it gotten worse? She says she'd like to do some blood work to rule out any possible underlying infection, but she doubts that the case. It looks to her like simple contact dermatitis, probably some exposure from your hike last weekend. She gives you a sample of skin cream that you need to apply three times a day for the next five days. In the meantime, she will see what the blood work shows, and if the medication doesn't seem to be working in the next three days, you are to give her a call.

Do you feel better when you walk out of her office 15 minutes later? Absolutely! Why? Because you imagined that you had that rare African rash or your mother's Lyme disease, and she assures you it is neither. You have the prescription—something to do and try—which gives you a sense of control and relief. You feel more settled; you have a new perspective—this is fixable—and you're not dealing with this on your own.

If you're doing brief therapy with couples and families in crisis, you want to be like your doctor—assess quickly, counter and change the couples' or families' worse-case expectations, and provide a clear action-oriented plan that helps them feel that they are in good hands. And what the doctor does in 15 minutes you have 50 minutes to accomplish. Not bad.

But what are we exactly talking about when we talk about brief therapy and how is it different from longer-term models? It's less about time and more about how you think; namely, about being clear and decisive. Here is an overview of the basic elements of the brief model that we will be working from and discussing more fully in later chapters.

Focus on the Present Rather Than the Past

The psychodynamic tradition has made the exploring of a client's past and the unraveling core issues the foundation for treatment. In brief therapy your focus is on the present—the here and now, fixing the problems the clients present. Though you may dip into the past as part of an initial assessment, or address the past when pertinent issues arise, the present is your therapeutic footprint and arena.

Focus on Patterns and Behaviors Rather Than Insight

The psychodynamic deconstruction of the past seeks to provide clients with insights into their history that can help them better navigate the present. This is where the unconscious becomes conscious, where a clinician's interpretation hits its mark and creates an "Aha" experience or "breakthrough" for the client.

While clients in brief therapy can certainly have an "Aha" experience, insights are replaced with clients' recognition of patterns—the ways they act and react to each in other in set ways, enabling them to move from a "who has the problem" mindset to realize how natural human instincts and brain processes contribute the problems they are struggling with. Patterns are essentially problems in motion, and the goal becomes replacing dysfunctional patterns with healthier ones.

Alongside pattern recognition, and in contrast to most psychodynamic approaches, your focus is on planned behavioral change—stopping and reshaping the dysfunctional patterns, communicating in new ways, helping clients step outside of their comfort zones to increase their behavioral and emotional range. While many clients' attitudes are that they need to feel better before they can do anything different, your message to them is the opposite: that while you can't directly control how you feel, you can control what you do; if you keep doing the same thing, you will keep feeling the same way. This is where behavioral homework assignments become the means of putting treatment into everyday practice.

Focus on Process Rather Than Content

Most couples and families come to therapy essentially speaking a different language than that of the brief therapy clinician. Clients are usually speaking the language of content—the blow-by-blow argument over what the dog did and didn't do, what his brother really said at Christmas, how the spouse wasn't "tuning out" but "listening," how much debt in dollars and cents he put on the credit card—all important to each in presenting and defending his own version of reality. And as emotions rise, so too does the content.

Just as they erroneously believe that they need to feel better before they can act, their emotional brain is erroneously telling them they need to do a better job of lining up their facts in order to win an argument. While they believe that the issue in the room is about whose reality is right, the real issue, your issue, is about what keeps the couple or family from successfully solving their problems on their own. And that is about process—how they talk and manage their emotions—not content and facts.

But this is not what the couple or family expects from you. They expect you to enter into the sorting and sifting of facts. They are trying to drag you into the weeds of their stories so you can, at best, be an arbitrator and pass judgment on who is right after all or, if not, at least be a mediator and find a factual path out of their mess. You are neither. Instead, you want to focus on and speak to them about process—help them see that *how* they talk and problem-solve is more important than *what* they talk about. Help them see how the interactional dance unfolds in the room and how listening and problem-solving fall apart. Assess what missing skills or negative emotions keep them from moving forward. Make them curious about what gets in the way of their running their lives more effectively. While the content is ever-changing, the process is generally always the same. It is not the content, you say, that is faulty, but the process that carries the content.

Staying in Lockstep Throughout

This focus on process also means that you are always aware of what is unfolding moment by moment in the room. Good therapists are naturally attuned to this, but because you are dealing with crises in a limited amount of time, and because each session is critical, the need is greater and your focus needs to be sharper to ensure that the couple or family are always in lockstep with you. As you present your assessment, make an interpretation, educate them about the dynamics and recommend a course of action, you are always looking for solid agreement. This is what your doctor does after she explains to you why she believes you have contact dermatitis; she is looking for agreement—verbally or non-verbally—before marching ahead with a treatment plan. If she senses any objection—that you make a face, you become passive or you say "yes, but"—she is likely to stop and ask what are your hesitations or questions.

You always want to do the same. If you don't, and if the couple or family is not fully on board with your assessment or treatment, they will disregard it and not do what you suggest, or not return. You need track the process at each step along the way.

Focus on Specific Concrete Goals Rather Than Personality Overhaul

Because couples and families are in crisis and your time is limited, and because you're focusing on problem-solving specific issues rather than historical deconstruction, you are not expecting to overhaul personalities. That said, by focusing on the overall *how* of process, rather than the specific *what* of content, these new skills and behavioral changes can ripple out and affect other areas of clients' everyday lives. You are not only repairing this problem and this relationship but also enabling clients to carry these new skills and perspectives into other present and future relationships.

Focus on Rapid Assessment

While you will continue to assess and reassess as a means of fine-tuning treatment, the bulk of your assessment, like that of your doctor, occurs in the first session. Why? Because, like your doctor, you want to reduce the crisis, and the angst and anxiety that comes with it, by providing clear feedback and beginning treatment by the end of the first session. To this you need to be active and clear.

Focus on Having Treatment Maps in Place

Your family doctor is able to be efficient because she mentally has linked the common medical problems she sees with specific tried-and-true treatments. In order to hit the ground running, you want to do the same: mentally have your own treatment maps at the ready for common couple and family problems. While such maps, like all maps, are not the same as actually walking the terrain, they do provide you with a preliminary plan, a starting point for your assessment and treatment goals and tasks.

So when Anne leaves her message about Bill's affair, or a parent calls about her daughter's unexpected pregnancy, you are already mentally moving ahead and placing the problem within your clinical orientation, thinking about what information you need to gather in the first session, mentally sorting through your clinical repertoire of tools and techniques. Your treatment planning, in effect, begins even before your first contact with a client.

Focus on Changing the Emotional Climate

While behavioral change is the meat and potatoes of treatment, you also want to change the emotional climate, calm those emotional waters in the first session to ensure that the couple or family feels different when they walk out than when they walked in. If they don't—if they feel much the same as when they walked in—they are likely to dismiss you and your therapy and not return. While your feedback and treatment plan will do most of the heavy lifting in this area, you are looking for opportunities to change the emotional climate in the room throughout the session. We'll be talking about specific ways of doing this in Chapter 5.

The theme running throughout these points is clear—that a brief treatment model requires setting clear boundaries on the scope of treatment and making those first sessions focused, specific, and action-oriented so clients know what to do to relieve their anxiety and their problems. This will be our focus throughout.

When Not to Do Brief Therapy

Jake comes to therapy with his partner Teresa. Teresa has a history of anorexia, and though she had been stable for many years, the stress of having their first child has taken its toll and caused Teresa to relapse. Jake is frightened by her rapid loss of weight and frustrated at seeing the little she eats and the restrictive food patterns she has fallen back into. Jake believes she needs to go into residential treatment, but Teresa, not wanting to be separated from the baby, continually swears she will do better; in spite of her efforts, however, she is making no progress.

While a sizeable majority of couples and families usually come to therapy in some form of crisis and need crisis stabilization, not all such clients are appropriate for a brief therapy approach to treatment. While Jake and Teresa may benefit from having a safe place to discuss their worries, perspectives and possible options, it is obvious to you that

Teresa does indeed need either residential treatment or ongoing intensive outpatient treatment if she is to pull out of her relapse. Offering a limited number of sessions is an unrealistic and inappropriate level of treatment and is unethical.

Similarly, there are other such individuals who may be in a relationship crisis but also need ongoing or intensive support: those with psychotic disorders or with undiagnosed or untreated bipolar disorder; those with addictions or who easily fall into self-injurious behaviors such as cutting; or those who are struggling with severe environmental stressors or intellectual challenges, or are lacking family supports, need both therapy and case management. Like Jake and Teresa, they may benefit from an initial brief intervention to help stabilize the relationship, but the individual issues need to be more intensively addressed if both the individual is to improve and the relationship is to stay out of further crises.

And then there are those who are not appropriate for brief therapy because they do not want brief therapy; instead, they are looking for an insight-oriented, more in-depth approach. They may be wanting to untangle what they see as the knot of their past, or simply want a safe place and good listener who allows them to discover what makes them tick. They want less behavioral change and more of an opportunity for reflection.

Finally, there are those clients who are coming to appease someone in the family or a community agency, who believe that they have little or no problem, blame others for the ways things are or don't see any value in "talking to strangers." They may come for a few sessions, and while you do your best to engage them, they are basically going through the motions. Their lack of motivation undermines what brief therapy or, in fact, what any therapy at this time can provide.

Characteristics of Couples and Families in Crisis

To talk about crisis is to talk about a particular state of both mind and dynamic. Here are some of the characteristics of couples and families in crisis.

High Emotion

Anne and Bill may collapse into a shouting match within minutes of sitting on your couch, or Anne may fall apart and sink into heavy sobbing as Bill becomes ever more stoic. First sessions with other couples and families are less packed with open emotion, but instead are filled with a palpable anxiety—everyone is on edge, hypervigilant, both from the awkwardness of a first session and a bracing for what may come. Whatever shape or level their emotions may take, your immediate goal is to lower the temperature by building rapport and a sense of safety.

High Focus on Content

As mentioned, most clients speak the language of content, and just as first sessions with clients in crisis are packed with emotion, they are also packed with content. Here Anne launches into her semi-prepared speech: how she stumbled on his text messages while innocently checking out Bill's new phone app, what the messages said (underscored with her own voiced exclamation points), how she suspected something was awry between them ever since "that trip in April." Bill now counters: that she was reading into the tone of the texts, how she is always snooping behind him, how the affair wasn't an affair but a close collegial business relationship.

In a family therapy session, the opening remarks are much the same: One parent makes his case (supported by explicit examples) for how the other parent spoils the children, or there is a step-by-step breakdown of the Saturday's parent–teen meltdown, with multiple versions of dialogue and debates over who said what nasty comment first. And as the conversation escalates, more and more supporting evidence is brought out as ammunition.

They are deluging you with facts, and this is where, under the weight of it all, less-experienced therapists can begin to collapse. And if, like them, you do get swept up in their content, you not only become distracted from the process but also subtly reinforce and teach the couple or family that, in your form of therapy, facts are indeed important. Rather than learning to recognize their own process, they will spend their week preparing their stories, trying to get their facts straight, thinking that this is what you want to hear. This is not your aim and this is not the message you want to send to them. Instead, you want to help them learn how to stop the warring or open the discussion by changing their reactions so they can better solve their problems.

Playing Courtroom

Anne is probably expecting you to side with her in condemning Bill's behavior, while Bill is probably hoping that you will tell Anne that she is over-reacting, just as the parents of the pregnant teen are wishing you would absolve them of any blame.

The combination of high emotion and high content easily lead to the "playing courtroom" that we mentioned earlier. You don't want to dismiss their concerns or minimize their anxiety or hurt, but because it is not your role to arbitrate or mediate, you need to quickly reshape their expectations—that you don't see therapy as a courtroom, nor is it your job to pronounce judgment. Instead, you say, you want to help them find ways to make sense of what has happened and learn to solve their problems on their own.

Leaning In, Leaning Out

This is a concept developed by William Doherty (2015): the notion that there is always one person leaning in—in terms of being more invested in fixing the relationship and using therapy to do so—and one person leaning out—who is more ambivalent about the relationship problems and therapy as a solution. While those in crisis seem to have a more equal stake in the process than other couples and families might, it is helpful to assume that this dynamic is still in force, albeit perhaps more subtly. One of your goals, particularly in the first session, is that of bringing the "out" partner/family member "in," be it Bill who feels that Anne is over-reacting, or a dad who thinks that therapy is only for those who are crazy. Here is where you use your skills and work hard to build rapport, uncover and counter their reservations, and find a common ground on which to build treatment.

Need for Feedback, Next Steps, Leadership

Even if all of you are able to sidestep the couple's or family's deluge of content or need to play courtroom and are able to engage the "leaning out" partner or family member, the couple or family is still expecting to leave the first session with "something." Imagine if your family doctor, after hearing your complaints and asking a few preliminary questions said, "Well, I'm sorry, but we're actually out of time for today. Let's go ahead and schedule another appointment and see if next time we can figure out what is going on." You'd likely feel frustrated, at best, and angry and likely to not to return at worst.

Couples and families in crisis have the same need for clear feedback. This is not the time to spend the session marching through your agency's 20 pages of general info, HIPPA regs and social security numbers. Even if you do need more time for assessment, they need to know that you understand their crisis and have some thoughts about how you and they can go about fixing it—hence the importance of having treatment maps in place. Anything less will leave them frustrated and discouraged.

What you have undoubtedly noticed is that the characteristics of those couples and families in crisis underscore the key elements of brief therapy that we've already discussed: the importance of pre-planning and having your treatment model and goals firmly in place so you can hit the ground running in the first session; focusing on present and process rather than getting lost in the content and playing courtroom; and doing a rapid assessment so you can offer the family next steps and have something to leave the couple or family with by the end of the session. It's all about leadership, and for couples and families mired in crisis, this is exactly what they need most.

10   *The Landscape of Brief*

Book Overview

In our journey together we'll be looking at tools and techniques for putting out the fire, as well as clearing away some of the obstacles that prevent couples and families from solving problems on their own. The book is essentially divided into three parts.

In Chapter 2, we will lay down a foundation of core concepts that enable you to quickly assess and drill down to the source of problems, as well as provide a framework for treatment. We'll look at Bowen's differentiated self and Minuchin's structural family model—the standards that we can measure couples and families against for quick assessment. We also look at the three main obstacles to couple and parenting relationships—poor communication skills, triggering of childhood emotional wounds and differing visions. Alongside these will be a discussion of learning problems vs. problems about learning, the seven-year itch and the Big Six process skills.

In Chapter 3 we will look at treatment maps, including goals and challenges, for common couple problems: affairs, violence, addictions, attention-deficit disorder, sexual issues, control and criticism, ambivalent relationships, struggles with major decisions, stress of life transitions, conflicts with extended family. We'll also discuss guidelines for when to refer partners out for individual therapy and how to coordinate individual and couple work.

In Chapter 4 we'll do the same for common family issues: polarized parents; child behavioral issues; adolescent presenting problems such as oppositional defiant disorder, self-abuse and, depression; young adult failure-to-launch; cutoffs by adult children; adult children and elderly parent concerns. These maps, along with vignettes, will help you have treatment plans in place that you can offer the couples and families.

In the second section, Chapters 5–7, we'll talk about goals of that crucial first session, walk through the first-session process and map the landscape of the second and subsequent sessions—what you need to know to put out the emotional fire and engage the couple or family in the treatment plan. By the third session most couples and families are no longer in crisis, and you and they have a good idea of what they need to focus on to move forward and be able to solve their own problems in the future.

In Chapter 8, the start of our last section, we'll offer a range of techniques that you can add to your toolbox: guided imagery, sculpting, letter-writing for grief and closure, enactments, at-home business meetings, Emotional Freedom Technique (EFT), self-soothing techniques for anxiety and depression. Finally, in Chapter 9, our last chapter, we'll look at ways of integrating the elements of the brief therapy approach to your own clinical style.

Our journey is underway.

References

Cooper, G. (2011). New perspectives on termination. *Psychotherapy Networker, 35*(5), 10–11.

Doherty, W. (2015). Assessing our impact. *Psychotherapy Networker, 39*(3), 36–43.

Phillips, E. (1985). *Psychotherapy revised: New frontiers in research and practice.* Hillsdale, NJ: Erlbaum.

2 Core Concepts

What enables your family physician to make a quick diagnosis and ultimately prescribe treatment are several things: One is her ability to use tools and apply models that enable her to compare and contrast your symptoms and overall condition against those who are healthy. The lab tests performed on your blood sample let her know, for example, whether your white blood cell count is high, or if your liver values are off, alerting her to other possible underlying conditions. She also has her own knowledge of conditions common to your area and demographic, allowing her to quickly dismiss the African mange that you were so sure you had. Finally, once she settles on a likely diagnosis, she has from her training and experience an array of treatment protocols mentally in place. Contact dermatitis? She has a list of prescriptions at the ready.

We can take this same overall approach with couples and families in crisis. In this chapter we are going to discuss a variety of concepts that will enable you to look at your clients and their problems from several angles. By having these at your disposal to filter and frame the clients' content, you, too, can make rapid assessments and, together with treatment maps, quickly develop a preliminary treatment plan. Some concepts will provide the healthy standards that, like your doctor's blood test, you can compare and contrast your clients against; they save you time by allowing you to sidestep the traditional assessment tramp into the weeds of history. Others can help you place common problems within the normal developmental terrain, while still others provide tools for successfully shaping the process.

Some of these concepts you may already know; others may be new to you. There's plenty here to choose. Take the ones you find useful and that resonate with your own approach and style. The aim is to help you avoid having to reinvent the wheel with each and every new couple and family, but instead have a conceptual foundation in place upon which you can build treatment plans and guide the process in the crucial opening sessions.

Our Couple Model: The Adult

Let's start with our healthy standard for individual adults and their interactions with their partners. What we're calling the adult is essentially what Bowen defined as self-differentiation (1993). Here are some of the qualities of the adult stance (Gilbert, 1992; Taibbi, 2014):

- An ability to be emotionally calm
- An ability to observe yourself in a relationship pattern and make changes without expectations of the other
- An ability to view others as anxious or fearful rather than malicious or manipulative
- An ability to not react in kind to anger or anxiety of others
- An ability to make choices and be assertive even if this risks losing the approval or acceptance of others
- An ability to focus more on your personal responsibility and behavior than on the behavior of the other
- An ability to be thoughtful in decision-making

The theme here is clear—be deliberative, proactive and rational, rather than reactive and emotional; keep your head down and focus on you and what you can do, rather than the other guy and what he is doing. All this is the antithesis of what you usually see in couples in crisis, where such couples tend to see their partners and their behaviors as the source of their problems; rather than focusing on themselves, they try to find ways to get the other to change, and, more often than not, they see the other as malicious or manipulative rather than anxious.

The adult thinks like this: "I'm responsible for what I think, do, say. If something bothers me, it is *my* problem. Because you can't read my mind, I need to tell you what is bothering me, and if there is something you can do to help me with my problem, I need to tell you that as well. But if you decide, for whatever reason, not to help me with my problem, I need to decide what I'm going to do next because it is ultimately *my* problem. Similarly, if something bothers you, it is *your* problem; that doesn't mean that I don't care, but I don't need to take over and feel a responsibility to fix it for you. If there is something I can do to help you with your problem, you need to tell me and I will try to help if I can. If you want to handle it on your own, that's fine."

Adults in a relationship are then clear about who has the problem: If you feel it, it's yours; while you can ask for help, the ultimate responsibility for both having it and fixing it is yours. This is a key concept, one invaluable for couples to understand and incorporate. Acknowledging and owning their problems enables the partners to bypass the defensiveness, anxiety, control and manipulation that less-healthy couples feel. Better yet, such adults can be more intimate. By being able to be both responsible and strong, they can take the risks of being open, honest and vulnerable.

When you think about it, this way of being seems not only reasonable but even commonplace. Most of us are able, by and large, to act in such an adult manner outside of our intimate relationships—for example, on the job in our professional role. If a work colleague does something that bothers us—parks in our parking space, for example, or seems to be unexpectedly offended by a comment that we make—we're not likely to rise up and rail in response, but instead can stay calm, voice our concern, and work to resolve the issue, all simple courteous behavior. What makes this more difficult to do in close relationships is that we relax and drop the professional role; transference and everyday intimacy more easily trigger our sensitivities and old emotional wounds. While these can challenge our defenses and rational thinking, we still retain our ability to act reasonably. As clinicians, we don't need to teach partners new behaviors, but rather need to help them apply what they know to their intimate relationships.

Not-so-Healthy Variations

Understanding the healthy standard, we can now look at the common less-healthy variations that you are likely to see in crisis situations, namely the martyr, victim and persecutor (or bully) roles. We'll take them one by one.

The Anatomy of Martyrs

Martyrs were often the only or oldest child in the family, or grew up in a chaotic emotional household, such as what you might see when there are alcoholic, abusive or mentally unstable parents. He usually did not have many buffers between him and his parents, and learned early on that he could avoid conflict and the anger of others by being good: "If I can stay on my toes, follow the rules, and just do what my parents (and teacher) want me to do all the time, I won't get in any hot water." Out of necessity this type of person learns to be very sensitive to others because they need to stay alert to the rules, and at an early age can read the nuances of emotions.

Such a person is essentially wired to be hyperalert and anxious, spending much of his energy surveying the environment, walking on eggshells, being ever-ready to do what his parents want. He adopts the psychological position of "I'm happy if you're happy, and I need to make sure you are happy." His head is filled with shoulds—the rules—and his stance is fortified by usually getting rewarded for being good. Underneath such behavior, however, lies magical thinking: If he just does what others want him to do, they will somehow give him what he needs, even if he doesn't express to them what those needs are.

All this enables the child to survive his childhood. But unfortunately, what works for the child doesn't necessarily work so well for the adult. Now his world is bigger. Rather than just having two or three important people to pay attention to, the martyr now has many more—his boss, the president of the local Rotary Club, the committee chair at church. He feels pulled in a lot of directions and is stretched thin as he scrambles to accommodate what he thinks others want from him. Because he has a difficult time saying no and is always doing his best to avoid conflict and confrontation, he is always stressed and at risk of burnout.

He also has a hard time knowing what he wants. By spending so much of his energy as a child looking outward and doing what others wanted, he never had the opportunity to sit back and discover what he wanted for himself. Unlike following rules, which is a heady, cognitive process, wanting, in contrast, is a gut feeling, and he is often not aware of what he is feeling. If you ask him in a session, "But what do you want?" he'll often hesitate. He gets stuck because he can't sort out the shoulds from wants, because he forever worries about making the wrong decision and upsetting those around him, or setting off an ever-present critical voice in his head.

Because he is wired to be sensitive to those around him, the martyr is always comparing himself to others, and can periodically feel resentful towards those who don't seem to be as conscientious as he is, who are not doing what he thinks they should be doing. He also can feel resentful towards others who fail to provide him with the rewards, appreciation and meeting of his needs that he feels he deserves and expects for all his hard work and accommodation. But all this expectation is never brought up and resentment gets stuffed down until he gets fed up. Eventually and periodically he will blow up, usually about something small—dishes in the sink, clothes left on the floor—or will act out—have an affair, get drunk, buy a hundred pairs of shoes. At those moments he feels that he deserves to do whatever he does—the blowing up, the acting out. But the subsequent drama that ensues also feels like his worst nightmare coming true; he was, after all, being good to avoid all this confrontation. Once the dust settles, his critical voice flares up, leaving him feeling guilty and shaken, and resolving never to do that again. He returns to shoving his resentment back down, only to have it build up again, setting off another round of explosions or acting out.

Unlike the adult who has a good sense of who has and what is the problem, martyrs do not. Instead, they tend to be over-responsible; their "I'm-happy-if-you're-happy" stance causes them to view "your problem as my problem." If his partner is having a difficult time, for example, his instincts are to do something to help her feel better. Partly he does this because he is sensitive and cares, but partly because he is anxious and helping the other person feel better reduces his anxiety. For the partner over time, this over-responsibility and need to step in and take over can begin to feel like control, a certain rigidity. The partner feels like she is being treated more like a child or teen than an equal.

Over time the martyr may decide the over-responsibility and the getting-too-little-back is too much. He is burned out and decides to leave or puts pressure on the victim to grow up, take more responsibility and appreciate him more, creating a crisis in the relationship.

The Anatomy of Victims

In contrast to martyrs, victims were often the baby in the family, and while the term connotes having abusive parents or severe trauma, it can also reflect, at best, those who had helicopter or intrusive parents who were always micromanaging, being over-protective, bailing them out. The end result is that, like martyrs, victims, too, grew up feeling anxious. But while the anxiety of martyrs came from being hyperalert and ever-accommodating, the anxiety of victims derived from their inability to build a firm foundation of self-confidence: Because others were always taking control, telling them what to do, bailing them out, they never had the esteem- and confidence-building experiences of solving problems on their own; their world was and remained frightening and at times overwhelming. Now as adults those same overwhelming feelings can take hold; they easily feel that problems, which they struggle to manage, are always falling on their heads. Not surprisingly, victims often hook into and pair with martyrs who are sensitive and willing to step up and take over to help them feel better. A perfect match: over-responsible martyr meets under-responsible victim.

But just as the martyrs can feel resentful for not getting back from others what they feel they deserve, victims can periodically build resentment over the martyrs' control, micromanagement and implied or direct criticism. Like martyrs, victims, too, periodically blow up about something small or act out, and feel that they deserve to do so. And they then, like martyrs, often feel anxious and guilty. They make up and sweep problems under the rug rather than solving them before falling back into their victim stance.

Like martyrs, victims too may get tired over time of being in their one-down position. Through work or parenthood they may gain self-confidence and either leave the relationship or demand that the martyr-partner back off on control, increasing the martyr's anxiety and creating a crisis.

The Anatomy of Bullies

As the name implies, bullies are domineering; they control others through intimidation and/or violence. Though some of them are sociopathic and able to appear charming and manipulative in their professional roles, or entitled and demanding of what they want now, a good number of them are anxious and hypervigilant. Rather than resorting to the walking on eggshells of martyrs, or the mental flight or freeze of victims, these individuals, through parental modeling and identification with an aggressor, learned to cope by becoming angry and belligerent.

In intimate relationships bullies can be emotionally and/or physically abusive and, like others with anger issues, tend to blame the victim for their anger, rather than taking responsibility for it. Their partners, not surprisingly, fit the victim personality where their self-esteem and sense of power is low, and if their own parents were abusive, are wired to have a higher tolerance for such abuse than others, all helping to keep the victim engaged in the relationship.

But what seals this dynamic and leaves the victim feeling psychologically trapped in the bullying relationship is intermittent reinforcement: While the bully is often aggressive, she is not always so. Other times, for no apparent reason, she is kind, and her more-gentle control is welcomed and appreciated by the victim, especially when he is feeling overwhelmed. But this unpredictability keeps the partner always off-balance—just when he is ready to leave, she suddenly changes modes, giving the victim a false hope that things will be better—and encourages magical thinking: If he just can figure it out, the right combination of dos and don'ts that will avoid triggering the bully's aggressive behavior, they will be able to be a happy couple. But such magical thinking is like trying to solve a Rubik's Cube blindfolded; the victim can never figure it out because there is no set pattern or path to decode. Hopefully, the victim eventually gains the courage to leave.

Leaving, of course, breaks the relationship pattern, creating anxiety for the bully. Her first reaction is likely to become more aggressive and try to intimidate the partner into coming back. If that doesn't work, she may "get nice" and swear to change, go to therapy, control her temper. And if that doesn't work, she may fall apart, even threaten suicide, as a way of pulling the victim back in.

Adult vs. the Others

With these martyr, victim and bully roles in mind, we can now go back to our adult and see where the gaps lie between healthy and unhealthy. We're back to the question of "What can't each of these individuals do that our model adult can do?" The answers are easy to see.

The challenges for martyrs are several: They need to stop being over-responsible; rather than trying to control and fix the other, they need to learn to tolerate their partner's and their own anxiety; they need to speak up when something bothers them, rather than sweeping it under the rug and blowing up later; they need to learn to say no, and tolerate confrontation and the possible disapproval and anger of others; they need to learn to "trust their gut" and focus on what they want rather than constantly worrying about what they should do. In broad terms, they need to stop being good and walking on eggshells, and be more adult by tolerating other's emotions, setting clearer boundaries, being assertive.

Applying this to intimate relationships translates into helping such individuals recognize what is and is not their problem; they need to support their partners based on what their partners say they need, rather than trying to relieve their anxiety by dictating what they think their partners should do; they need to do the reality check, and realize what they can reasonably do and control and what they can't; they need to focus on themselves rather than constantly monitoring the other. By developing these clear boundaries, resentments are less likely to build, and the victim-partner is less likely to feel treated like at child.

For victims, the challenges are equally as clear: They need to step up and be more responsible, rather than collapsing and allowing the martyr to take over. While they may need emotional support, their self-confidence will increase by stepping outside of their comfort zones, taking acceptable risks, and having success handling problems on their own, often by learning to break problems down into smaller manageable steps, so as not to be overwhelmed. And finally, like martyrs, victims need to step up and be assertive, the key element in moving towards an adult stance and healthier pattern.

For bullies the most obvious need is for them to rein in and take responsibility for their anger—regulating their emotions and not blaming others for their reactions—all keys to breaking the crisis and abusive cycle. Self-regulation, however, does not mean bullies need to simply learn to bite their tongues. Instead, it's about their learning to use their anger as information, telling them, and hopefully others, what they need, in an assertive, rather than angry, blaming and controlling way. Finally, because those prone to anger have limited emotional range, they need to increase their emotional range and learn to discern softer emotions—worry, hurt, fear—that usually lie beneath, as well as recognize the often-underlying anxiety and hypervigilance. Expressing these, rather than their default anger, goes a long way in helping partners and family members feel less frightened, and potentially see bullies in a new and more positive light.

Just as brief treatment doesn't require you to think in terms of personality overhaul, assessments do not require your unearthing the nuances of each client's personality. You want and need to make your focus and goals smaller. You're looking for self-responsibility, self-regulation, clearly defined problems, and proactive and rational ways of solving them.

Like your doctor, you can compare what clients present against healthy norms. What, you ask yourself, is the gap between this model of an adult—a reasonable, responsible and assertive individual—and what the clients in the room present? What roles do they take, how do their emotions interfere with their abilities to share intimate thoughts, manage confrontation and solve problems independently?

We can reduce these questions and dynamics into an even simpler form that applies to so many couples: One partner needs to step up and the other needs to step down. The one who tends to be more withdrawn, who emotionally or verbally shuts down or gives in—the turtle—needs to step up and stick his head out, speak up, be assertive, take the initiative, say what he wants. The other who is more in charge, more initiating, more vocal, more responsible and more aggressive needs to step down verbally and behaviorally in order to create space and make it safer for the other to step up. Each needs to go against his grain and instincts in order to transform the relationship dynamic.

This is certainly a challenge, but one that you can succinctly lay out and support the individuals through in the session process. The larger challenge comes in those gray zones—when the turtle needs to step up, even though it doesn't feel completely safe, or when the more controlling partner feels the pull to step in because the other seems unable to move. This is where you become the fulcrum, where you use your active focus and support to move the couple through these difficult points.

Our Model for Families: Ideal Family Structure

The adult gives us a healthy model for adult behavior and a means of assessing the dysfunction of individuals in couple relationships and predicting the negative patterns into which they can fall. The equivalent for families is Minuchin's structural family model (1974). It's best to present these diagrammatically:

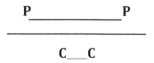

Here we have parents, represented by P, with the children as C. There is a hierarchy in that the parents are on top, having more power and control, with the children on the bottom, having less, and a solid line between them indicates that there is a clear boundary between the adult

20   *Core Concepts*

and child worlds. The solid line between the parents indicates that they have a solid adult relationship, with each being able to self-regulate and define clear lines of responsibility. Even though their styles may be different, they agree to expectations, consequences, and so on, in managing the children. If this is a single parent rather than a two-parent family, a hierarchy is still in place. Finally, the solid lines connecting the children mean that, even with age differences and some amount of sibling rivalry, they can get along and can support each other.

Some families that you see may actually fit this healthy model, but come in because they lack some practical skills and knowledge on parenting—they don't know how to best respond to an oppositional child—or are struggling with stressors—grandpa died, mom lost her job. But for a majority of families, the real source of their struggles lies in having a faulty and unhealthy structure. Here are a few of the common less-healthy variations:

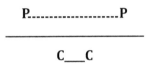

Here the dotted lines between the parents indicate that they are not working together as a team, are on different pages regarding parenting and, in extreme cases, are polarized, in that one parent who is strict causes the other parent to compensate by being overly lenient. What happens in these situations is that the children are constantly testing because expectations aren't clear, or they have learned to play one parent against the other to get their way. As we did before, we need only to compare and contrast what we see against our healthy model.

What needs to be fixed? It's easy to see: The dotted lines need to be replaced by solid ones; the parents need to work together as a team.

```
    P  |  P___C
   _____
          C
```

Here we have parents who are not just on different pages but are disengaged from each other. The solid vertical line between them essentially represents the emotional wall between them. What we also see is the migration of one of the children up, connecting with one of the parents.

Here a child has moved up the hierarchy and is becoming a surrogate partner. Here we could imagine one parent using a teen as a confidant and treating him more as adult; the break in the hierarchy causes the teen to often feel overly responsible for the parent and/or entitled. This, of course, only increases the disconnection between the parents, and this other parent may have his or her own form of solace, a line connecting them to someone else in an affair or a strong connection with an addiction—for example, alcoholism or workaholism.

Again, what's the gap between what we see and our healthy model; what needs to be fixed? The wall between the partners needs to come down, and the child needs to be bumped back down to the child group.

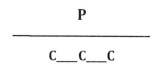

What we see quickly here is that one parent is alone and in charge, and the other parent is joined below with the children. This one-down parent is treated like one of the children by the one in charge, the children treat the disempowered parent as a peer, and sometimes the disempowered parent, acting as ringleader for the children, will lead periodic attacks against the other parent. While the controlling parent has power, what the diagram clearly shows is that she is isolated and alone.

What needs to be fixed? The other parent needs to move up and regain power; the parents need to work together as a team and have a strong adult relationship.

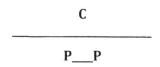

This last diagram is in some ways the worst-case scenario. Here we have not a parent on top, but a child or, most often, a teen. The teen, rather than the parents, is emotionally and/or physically running the family. Sometimes this occurs because the teen is filling in for incapacitated parents—there may be severe illness or addiction that keeps the parents from fulfilling their roles, but more often it is that the child is acting out, in charge, setting the emotional climate. The parents feel helpless; the teen feels entitled to do whatever she wants.

What needs to be fixed? The child needs to be bumped down. If the child is filling in for the parents because they are unable to care for themselves or the family, the parents need outside adult support or treatment in order to fulfill their roles as caretakers and reduce the pressure and responsibilities on the child; if the parents are unable or unwilling to do so, the child needs to be removed and placed in alternative care. If the child is acting out, entitled and intimidating the parents, often the courts need to get involved to support the parents in placing limits on the child.

By having a healthy standard in mind and knowing what variations to be aware of, you now have a quick means of assessing families. Like the physician, you match in that first session what the family presents against where they should be. You take into consideration cultural and ethnic differences—a more paternalistic or child-centered structure, for example, based on the parent's values—but you are always curious about how their structure may fuel the presenting problems. Here are questions you can ask and observations you can make to help you see where the gaps lie:

> *Even though their styles may be different, do both as parents agree on rules and expectations for the children? Are there areas they disagree about? Do they have an effective means for resolving them? Do they describe themselves as polarized?*
>
> *In their overall couple relationship, does each partner feel supported by the other? Do they do things as a couple? Do the parents say they have no time for each other, are child- or work-centered, or seem disengaged from each in the room?*
>
> *How do the children get along with each other? While you expect some sibling rivalry, do they basically care for each other?*
>
> *Do one parent and the children gang up against the other parent?*
>
> *Is there one child who is driving the session process, and the parents seem unable to contain him?*

As with couples you need not think in terms of individual personality transformations, but rather where do the parents get stuck, fail to set hierarchy and work together as a parenting team? They may be polarized and be on different pages about how the children are and need to be managed. There may be a power differential, with one parent running the family and the other sidelined because of her own personal issues or because the other is just too aggressive and controlling.

This is also where the couple dynamics fold into the family dynamics: The inability of the parents to communicate effectively prevents them from problem-solving; the anger of one overrides any opportunity for assertiveness of the other; the dominance of one child overwhelms the parents and leaves them unable to take control. The starting point is usually with the parents and uncovering the obstacles to teamwork. Again, usually one needs to step up, one needs to step down.

So here you have two models that you can use as a foundation for brief couple and family work that provide a good starting point for assessment. By noting the deviations from the standards, you have a foundation for treatment planning.

The Relationship Rollercoaster

While the adult behavior and family structure models provide a foundational base for assessment, the relationship rollercoaster provides a developmental one for couples and families alike. When we look at census data regarding the average length of marriage before couples divorce, it centers around seven to eight years (U.S. Census, 2011), and this has been true for at least the past two censuses. The question is why.

Research tells us that normal adult development is characterized by six to eight years of stability, then two to three years of instability (Sheehy, 2006), and the divorce statistics tell us that couple relationships are caught up in some way in this dynamic. The psychology is as follows (Taibbi, 2017): When two people meet and fall in love, it's usually due to the right mix of common and complementary interests and qualities. Steve and Megan, for example, may share the same sense of humor, and both are politically liberal, but Steve is outgoing while Megan is shy. On the conscious level, they both instinctively weigh out the pros and cons of their respective similarities and differences—Steve sees Megan's quietness as intriguing and comforting, Megan admires Steve's ability to reach out to strangers and somewhat enjoys him dragging her out to parties that she would never go to alone. There's a physical chemistry between them, but also a psychological one shaped by their childhood experiences and other dating relationships.

But their chemistry is also shaped by the present. At the particular moment they meet they each have something at the top of their list of needs. Megan may have recently ended a relationship with a controlling abusive boyfriend, or she may have finally begun to emotionally separate from her depressed, withdrawn father; what she appreciates the most is Steve's gentle humor and support. Similarly, Steve may have just bounced out of a relationship with an exciting but impulsive woman, making Megan a welcomed contrast, or his mother may have recently died, and Megan's quietness reminds him of her and allows him to open up and grieve. While they may or may not be fully of aware of these needs at the time, and may not be able to fully articulate what they feel, if you later ask them what most attracted them to each other, these are the elements they will usually claim.

And so they get married. They unconsciously make a contract with each other saying in effect that I will give you *this* (my outgoingness, my energy and humor) if you give me *that* (your quiet support). In the first year of marriage, they work out routines and rules about how they will live together, how they will handle differences and conflicts, who will be in charge of what. Sorting this all out and the jockeying around power can be stressful and difficult—battles over toothpaste tubes left uncapped, garbage not taken out, who is in charge of the laundry and who decides when, how and who will do it. But if they can work through all these, after about six months or a year, they settle into routines and roles. They work together to carry out their vision of their relationship: They work their two jobs and save up money to buy a house. They have a child or two. Megan decides to stay home or work part time while Steve commutes to the city and tries to climb the career ladder. Everything is fine.

But then things begin to change. By year five, six or seven there is a shift. Perhaps the couple finds themselves moving into parallel lives. Steve is working until 8:00 most nights, while Megan spends Saturdays going shopping or visiting her mother. The time they spend together often seems boring or too routine. What was most attractive now turns into an annoyance: Steve's outgoingness now seems to Megan a distraction, his humor now seems to slide into a cruel sarcasm, while Megan's quietness now seems to Steve like indecision, a passivity that is driving him crazy.

There is tension—they argue over the kids, or money, or in-laws. Or—here is where the characteristics of roles take hold—Steve accommodates and accommodates and his emotional flare-ups are big, but his shell-shock causes arguments to fall into limp "I'm sorrys" and problems go unsolved. Or each "tries" and gives in for a time, only to collapse in frustration when the other doesn't seem to be doing their share of the trying. Things are not working as well as they used to. Both sense a growing gap—between the routines and rules and even the vision that they hammered out at year one—and who they are now as individuals.

What has happened is that the relationship contract has run out because the relationship has been successful. They each gave the other what they needed at the start and filled those emotional holes. Steve has recovered from his ex-girlfriend, no longer misses his mother or needs one; Megan, thanks to Steve, is no longer so timid or fearful and shaped by old boyfriends and her father. They both have changed; something else has now risen to the top of their needs list which they may or may not be able to fully articulate. Each feels cramped within the box of the life they have created and are living.

One way to visualize this process is to imagine the start of the relationship to be like moving into a large empty house. The couple is free to decorate it and use it as they like, and this is what they do in that first year. But over the years the rooms get filled with psychological junk—unvoiced resentments, arguments that are never resolved, situations and events that were hurtful but never really healed. As a room gets filled, the couple unwittingly chooses to simply close the door to the room rather than clearing it out. They do this over and over through the years until the couple one day finds themselves living in the entranceway near the front door, talking only about the kids or the weather, wishing there was more.

This is the point where we see the divorce rates spike. Because the house that is their relationship has grown too cramped, it's easy for some couples to think that moving out and starting over in a new house/relationship would solve the problem. If this option is too frightening, they may instead decide to distract themselves from their feelings and the emotions, with the couple relationship moving to a back burner. Steve may take a promotion that takes him out of town three days a week; Megan may find herself in an affair with the neighbor across the street; both may decide that it is time to get another dog or buy that cottage on the lake and spend the weekends teaching the kids to water ski. Or they may distract by focusing on a more "comfortable" problem—they become child-centered and both worry about Tommy's school performance, or offer that Megan's newly divorced sister and her kids can come live with them.

And this distraction works, at least for a while. But then the kids get older—Tommy goes off to college, Megan's sister moves out. The couple faces the changes and challenges of the empty nest, staring at each other from across the room with no one to distract them, and panic sets in. Again, the notion of divorce looms. Steve faces a mid-life crisis and decides he really hasn't been happy for a long time. He resents the pressure that he has been feeling from Megan to succeed. He wants to quit his job and sail solo around the world and stop being the martyr. And Megan decides it is time to stop being one-down, get back into her career, get that degree or go after that high-powered job in Chicago. They battle over resentments and competing visions, or don't, and instead move further apart into their own parallel lives. Or they may distract themselves once again—pulling in grandchildren or foster children, or getting more dogs, to fill the space between them.

Or they come in for therapy. They tell you they are talking about divorce or are feeling like the relationship is stale and empty. They individually realize that large chunks of themselves have been pushed to the back corners of their lives. Their early dreams have withered and they are seeking to reconnect with them once again. You want to help them to discover and say what they each want, unloose their imaginations to re-envision their present and future. But most of all, you want to encourage them to go back down the hall and up the stairs. In order to revitalize and open their relationship they need to clean out the rooms that were closed off so many years ago.

So how does this help you when meeting a couple or family? When you ask them how long they have been together, you are alert to these timetables. When they talk about being together for seven or eight years, or 15 or 20 and the children are leaving home, your next question is: What has changed for them individually during that time? How are they different now than when they first met? What is it that they most need now that they didn't need before?

You then can talk about the relationship rollercoaster, normalizing their feelings and concerns, and how there is this gap between the life they have each constructed and what they each as individuals most need and are not able to fit into the routines and rules that they have created. This requires your leadership and support to help the couple be honest, to understand the processes that limit them and the patterns that constrain them. It requires that both partners be empowered—once again, the stepping up and stepping down, the moving away from martyr, victim and bully roles to the adult. If they can bring the contract up to date, and learn the skills that allow them to stay closer to their lives and handle problems as they arise in an adult way, rather than continuing to fill the rooms and close the doors, they can be successful over the long haul.

The rollercoaster of relationships and the need to update the relationship contract map for us the larger developmental terrain of couple and family life. When we move in closer, however, and look at the everyday stuckpoints that make it difficult to solve problems, it is usually a mix of three areas: communication, emotional wounds and differing visions. Let's start with communication.

Communication Skills

One way of describing communication in couples and families is to compare it to driving a car. There are two parts to driving a car. The first is knowing where you want to go. This means that before you start a conversational car, you want to be clear what the point of the conversation is—what problem to solve, what it is that you want the other to most understand. This helps you be proactive rather than reactive, thoughtful rather than defensive and emotional.

The second part is keeping the car on the road. This is where most couples and families can get into trouble. Rather than focusing on the issue—solving the problem that is the conversational address—it has all now turned to Christmas 2011 again, somebody's brother, that time you went on that business trip and did . . .—once again, the stacking of evidence that is part of the fueling of anger, the setting in of tunnel vision, the pushing to make your point and win. Once this happens the conversational car is going off the road and ideally someone needs to try to keep the car from going off into a ditch: "I don't think we need to talk about Christmas right now, right now I want to talk about . . ." If that doesn't work—if both partners are emotional and the communication car is stuck in a ditch—then the car and conversation have to stop rather than continuing to spin wheels.

All this is about skills, and we can look at them as individual skills and couple skills. The individual skills are implied in our view of the adult, but let's break them down more clearly.

Ability to Use Emotions as Information

This is both a concept and skill. While some clients are already able to do this well, others struggle. Some are able to feel their emotions, but get easily flooded by them, either spewing them out through content or shutting down. At the other end of the spectrum are those who live only from the neck up; they think, but have trouble feeling. Finally, there are those who can feel but can't identify; they always say they are upset and don't know what they are feeling except bad. Or, as we noted with bullies, they may be restricted to only one or two strong emotions, like anger or hurt, and have little awareness of or ability to identify the subtler ones.

Identifying and monitoring one's emotions are obviously essential elements of emotional self-regulation; those who struggle with anger management issues, for example, often go from 0 to 60 in nanoseconds, with little awareness of the buildup of anger within them. But identifying emotions is also essential to relationships, because it creates the language of intimacy; helping the other know how you feel in a wide variety of emotional colors allows him to better understand what makes you "tick."

While emotions need to be regulated, identified and expressed in a responsible way, there is more to emotions than just managing them. They are an important source of information about what individuals need. Those prone to anger, for example, are often told in anger management classes that they need to track their triggers and emotional levels so they can rein in and prevent explosions, but often what doesn't get talked about is using their anger to help them know what they need. Similarly, those who react with hurt and withdrawal, or those who try to suppress their emotions through rationalization, need to learn how to translate this hurt and these emotional reactions into assertive communication so the larger problem and underlying cause can be addressed.

You can facilitate this skill-building by walking clients through the process in the session: "Sue, you seem to be getting upset. See if you can take a couple of deep breaths. Okay, good. Can you tell Tim what you're feeling or needing from him right now?" Or "Tim, you said you were angry that Sue criticized the way you were handling your daughter's whining. How can she help you when you seem frustrated, in a way that feels supportive for you rather than scolding?" Map these out in the session and then give the homework of practicing these skills at home.

Ability to Be Aware of Who Has the Problem

As mentioned in our discussion of the adult, if I feel or see a problem, it's mine; if you are upset or have a problem, it's yours, but tell me how I can help you with it. This taking responsibility for oneself sidesteps the victim's under-responsibility of "I feel bad and expect you do something to help me feel better," the martyr's over-responsibility that "As soon as I can get you to change, I'll feel less anxious," or the bully's lack of responsibility, "I'm only angry because you made me mad." Repeatedly in the session process with couples and families, you will undoubtedly be helping clients clearly define who has and what is the problem at that moment, both to define the point of the conversation and to help clients learn to take responsibility for their own issues rather than displacing them.

This clarification of responsibility does not mean that there should be an egocentric quality to intimate relationships—I take care of me and you take care of you. Actually, it is the opposite. Once the boundaries are clear, it is possible for each to be more compassionate towards the other. Sue can see Tim's frustration as a problem he is struggling with, rather than one she is responsible for, and one she can or cannot try to help with, instead of getting upset herself and swooping in and sounding critical. And if Sue does swoop in, Tim can step back and understand that Sue is feeling anxious rather than assuming once again that she is being critical and controlling. This adult stance bypasses the assumption of malicious intent.

You can help the individuals learn to adapt this perspective by encouraging them to practice these problem-defining skills in other, less emotionally entangled, relationships. Suggest they try to mentally draw lines of responsibility when dealing with a work supervisor or an upset friend. Apply it to children. When Tim's daughter begins to melt down in Walmart because she wants candy, help Tim see that it is not about candy and it is not about him. Rather, it is his daughter's frustration or tiredness, her emotional problem, and he doesn't need to fix it by buying her candy, or feel resentful because she is not behaving as he thinks she should. Instead, he needs to remain calm and clear, acknowledging her frustration, but not give in to her demands until she is able to calm herself down. With these successes under their belt, clients can then begin to apply these skills to their own couple dynamics.

Be Honest

Being aware of emotions and labeling, using emotions as information, and realizing who has the problem, all lay the foundation not only for self-responsibility but also for honesty and genuineness. By self-focusing, recognizing and labeling your emotions, and defining and taking responsibility for your problems, you are being transparent: What you show is who you are. Without such honesty relationships become distorted—you don't speak up because you are afraid, or you assume others should know how you feel. Rather than being clear and direct, you resort to manipulation. Words can never be trusted or taken at face value.

But such honesty requires a willingness to take risks—to examine your own sincerity, to look deeper into yourself in order to help others fully understand what is going on inside. Once again, in sessions you can take the lead. Encourage risk-taking in the session by asking clients to clarify fuzzy language, by commenting on non-verbal cues so they can be brought into the conversation, and by asking the hard questions—Are you saying you are feeling____, that you are wanting ____, that you are really thinking___? Model risk-taking and clarity yourself—"I'm hesitant to say this, but I'm thinking . . . ." Resist settling into your own personal comfort zone, and instead be curious and press on while maintaining the client's trust. Stay in the moment and track closely the session process so that the client learns to do the same.

By doing this adult self-focus, by taking responsibility for their own emotions and using them for problem-solving, by being honest, couples and families are best able to communicate and create a foundation for intimacy. This is the individual side of the communication equation. But there is the other side, namely the couple and family communication skills. Here are the ones you want to focus upon.

Awareness of Process

We mentioned this in the first chapter as one of the essential ingredients of brief therapy. It is vital for couples/parents to be able to distinguish between content and process, and be aware of when the process is deteriorating. You help them do this by pointing out the dysfunctional patterns and the escalation of emotions that you see in the room: "Hold on, let's stop for a minute. You both seem to be getting angry. John, I notice that every time you say to Ruth that she was wrong, the more you, Ruth, get angry and bring up details about the affair, which in turns makes you, John, angrier and more critical of Ruth. Can you see how you are bouncing off each other and escalating the argument?"

This interrupting and pointing out of the patterns is something that you will need to do over and over so that the couple develops that "third ear," and can recognize for themselves when the content is no longer carrying the message, but is merely serving as fuel for rising emotions. Help them become more sensitive by stopping them and asking if they can tell that the conversation is going off course or that neither one is listening well. They need your help to realize that the problem in the room is the escalating emotion, not the other's seeming inability to understand, and to recognize that they are getting angry, and have ways of calming down and cooling off before they can effectively tackle the content of the problem. Over time their increased awareness of the process will enable them to self-correct.

No Name-Calling, Defensiveness or Dredging up of the Past

Because emotions are important information, your goal is not to help couples and families to be unemotional, but rather to learn to keep the emotions in bounds. Rather than "fighting dirty," they need to, as Gottman and Silver (2015) put it, "fight clean." To do that they need to know what is out-of-bounds. Name-calling clearly falls in the dirty category and invariably undermines the process. Defensiveness—that firing back with counterattacks ("But at least *I* didn't . . .") or weak excuses ("But you *knew* I was so stressed out about . . .") to retaliate or save face—shuts down active listening. Dredging up the past ("And what about that argument you started last Christmas . . .") and especially old wounds ("At least *I* didn't have an affair!") drags the conversation off course and just provides more ammunition in an escalating emotional battle.

The couple or family learns to become sensitive to these tactics by your pointing them out—"Jake, you're sounding defensive again. Molly, we're not talking about the affair right now; instead, can you say how you are feeling about what Tom said?"—and putting a halt to the interaction, if necessary, so that everyone can cool down. By doing this in the session and helping them map out a plan for better managing this at home, you help them avoid adding new emotional injuries to old ones.

Active Listening

One antidote to fighting dirty is active listening—the reflecting back what you believe the other is saying and feeling—which can both help keep a conversation on track and be an effective means of reducing the emotional temperature when it begins to rise. It is a basic clinical skill, and you'll be modeling this for clients. But some clinicians believe that it's valuable to teach this more formally and structure the conversation to hone these skills. This is where the clinician asks the partners to make "I" statements rather than "you" statements, explaining that "you" statements reflexively cause the other to feel blamed and defensive.

Harville Hendrix (2007) asks partners to say what they thought they heard the other say and how they think they felt, and getting the green light that they are correct by the other partner before replying: "It sounds like you are saying that you are want me to help the kids with their homework after dinner and that you feel irritated that I seem to leave it to you—is that correct?" John Gottman (2015) will try to slow the process down by asking the partners to take turns taking notes—literally writing down what they think the other is saying before replying. Michael Nichols (2009) suggests that listeners elaborate on what the other said to show they are really interested, rather than quickly summarizing in order to switch to what the listener wants to say.

While some clients feel that the more structured approach gives them something solid to hold onto, other clients, and therapists, dislike this because it feels artificial, and it becomes easy for some clients to miss the point. Rather than slowing down and listening, they wind up arguing with each other over who is or isn't following the rules. Your own style and clinical strengths can dictate how structured you feel it is important for communication in the session to be. What is important is keeping in mind the goal, namely helping the couple or family become more aware of the process and change it so that it doesn't deteriorate.

Willingness to Return and Repair

Every couple will miscommunicate from time to time; that's to be expected. What prevents the miscommunication from undermining the relationship is the couple's willingness to come back together (return) and discuss (and repair) both the miscommunication ("Sorry I got so angry...") and the problem ("Let's try again. What do you think we should do about helping Joey with math?") when both partners have cooled down.

It's always surprising how many couples don't do this. Usually, they never saw this modeled in their own families of origin, or, because their argument felt so emotionally devastating, they fear that bringing up the topic again will only set off another war. So they try to sweep the argument and problem under the rug, go through the motions of making up ("Are you okay?—I'm fine"), and both silently agree to "forget about it." Usually the problem comes up again (sometimes as part of another fight), and sets off another war, only further confirming their fears and the need to avoid the topic. If they manage to really lock it away and not go there, we are back to the house metaphor, where the rooms get filled and closed off, leading to the weather and kids' soccer as the only safe topics of conversation.

The ability to circle back around and re-discuss a problem is essential to avoiding a land-mined relationship. You can help couples do this by your doing this within the session process—stop the action, help each partner calm himself down and begin the conversation again with active listening skills. If they again get heated, stop them once again.

You want to encourage them to move forward towards their conversational destination—solving the problem—rather than getting emotional and side-tracked. In the early stages of treatment when they may be gun-shy about re-discussing issues at home, you can ask them to stop arguments at home if they become too emotional and bring them into the next session to discuss. Once they have the experience of taking the acceptable risk, applying their new skills and seeing that the discussion doesn't inevitably turn into a World War III, their fear will be reduced, their courage will go up and they can begin to do this themselves at home.

The key here, again, is helping the individuals move towards the adult and take responsibility for their own emotions. They need to be able to calm themselves down, and be able to wait until they are emotionally calm before taking up the conversation again. Invariably the partners will differ on how long this takes for them to calm down (five minutes vs. four hours), and how well they can tolerate the unresolved tension, but it's important that neither one pressures the other to return and resolve before he or she is ready.

Ability to Problem-Solve

Some couples have no difficulty circling back to problems, but lack the problem-solving skills needed to resolve them. They may have difficulty breaking the problem down into manageable chunks, articulating what it is that they want or translating changes into specific behaviors. They may not know how to compromise.

Your job is to lead them through this process. You want to help them stay present and focused on the bottom line. If the discussion is about "helping around the house," or "making the children be more responsible for managing their homework," encourage them to clearly define what helping and responsibility behaviorally mean, and how, when and by whom this is to come about. Move them towards compromise by suggesting various options—"How about you both try taking turns making dinner during the week?"—or agreement to trade-offs—"If you do _____, I'd be willing to do _____." Make clear to them that you are not trying to solve the problem for them, but instead are trying to show them how the problem-solving process works. Finally, encourage them to try out the new agreed-upon behaviors at home and help them fine-tune them as needed.

Obviously, you want to point it out to couples when they are engaging in a power struggle—trying to get their own way rather than solving the problem—but stay alert to the lack of power as well—for example, Tim passively agreeing with Sue in order to stop the conversation and reduce the tension. Good problem-solving and effective compromise only comes when partners have equal footing—Tim needs to approach confrontation and step up. If they don't, you need to support the one-down partner. Encourage him to speak up—"Tim, it seems like you are going along with what Sue wants, but is this really what you want?"—and with your support help him articulate what he truly feels.

Finally, in a variation of passive compromising are those couples who are essentially both sensitive, "nice," and accommodating, who fall into the "pre-compromise." Sue is thinking about where she wants to go for a vacation and thinks that she would really like to go to the beach. But then, in her own mind, she says to herself, "Tim hates the beach, doesn't like the sand, the sun. Okay, skip the beach. We can go to the mountains. It's okay for me and Tim would like it better." Meanwhile, Tim is thinking the same—what does he want to do on vacation? He really would like to go to New York City and see some Broadway shows. But then he says to himself, "Sue hates the city, the noise, the traffic. Going to the mountains is okay, she would probably like that." So they sit down to discuss where to go on vacation. "I was thinking the mountains," says Sue. "Me too," says Tim.

So off to the mountains they go. While they're there, each is checking in with the other—"Are you having a good time?" (because they are essentially doing this for the other guy). "Sure," they each say. Is it okay—yeah, it's okay. But . . . after years of doing this, one or both of them start to feel that they are having a watered-down life—, okay, but not what they really want. The way out of this is for both to start the discussion from a clear, strong position and then talk about compromise: Sue and Tim do one week at the beach and one in New York; or Sue does a few days at the beach with her sister, Tim goes to New York with his college buddy, and then Sue and Tim do go to the mountains together for a few days.

You want to be alert to such patterns and couples where their accommodating styles handicap their ability to be honest. When you detect it, educate them about this process and support them in being bolder. Only when both sides are clear and on an open and equal footing does compromise becomes a more viable, honest and ultimately successful option.

Provide Positive Feedback

Through his research Gottman found that couples and families need a 4:1 ratio of positive to negative comments for anyone to actually hear the positive. Anything less and the partner is going to complain that the other is always critical or unsupportive. For couples and families in crisis, negativity is saturating the emotional climate in the home and the ratio needs to be even higher and deliberate. Where couples and families get stuck is believing that they need to feel positive to be positive or that, because of all the negativity, the other person doesn't deserve it

("She doesn't do anything for me to compliment her for"), or they may make slight attempts and when the other doesn't notice and compliment in return, they stop making the effort.

Ramping up the positive is clearly one of the cases of "faking it till you make it." Looking for and proactively making positive comments ("Thanks for making coffee" or "I appreciate you not getting upset about my coming home a bit late") even if you don't feel like or the other person may not reciprocate is again part of being adult—not seeing the other's actions as malicious or manipulative. It is also an essential part of good communication (letting the other person know what you appreciate and works well, rather than just complaining about what is wrong), as well as skill-building and mind rewiring (training to be mindful and attend to the positive), and changes the overall emotional climate in the relationship. While couples may complain that, like the active-listening responses, these suggestions feel awkward and artificial, you want to underscore the importance and purpose of proactively providing this feedback, and reassure them that it will become more natural with time.

You can bring this into the session by modeling making positive comments yourself, but also look for times when compliments are offered but not acknowledged or minimized by the other—"Don't make a big deal about it, it was nothing." Individuals who grew up in critical homes have a difficult time not only making positive comments but accepting them as well. You can help them by gently (you don't want to recreate the criticism that they are sensitive to) pointing out their minimizing response and encouraging them to allow themselves to take it in. Similarly, you can ask each partner what types of things they would most like noticed or be appreciated for—my cooking that I'm proud of, the way I'm supportive of your daughter—to offset the particular lack of appreciation each may feel.

Though you want to give them homework about being more verbally positive, you want to watch out for couples who use homework assignments as additional fuel for unresolved anger ("I complimented Joan 12 times last week and she only complimented me once!"). If this happens, point out the competition, and encourage the individuals to once again be responsible for themselves and focus on their role in changing the relationship.

Part of your assessment in the first session is looking for the couple's and family's ability to implement these communication skills in the session and in their overall relationships. As you observe the process, note what is missing and where they seem to struggle, and specifically ask about their ability to revisit issues, problem-solve problems, etc. Again, by noting what they seem unable to do, you know what to help them to do.

Emotional Wounds

Communication is the first place that most couples and families get stuck solving their own problems; emotional wounds are the second. Hendrix has described the need to help couples be aware of and heal these wounds originating in childhood, in order to create intimacy, and his approach is largely historical—helping couples unravel the sources in the past. The view of childhood wounds in our brief approach is a bit different, and our approach to addressing them bypasses the past and instead focuses on present behaviors—explicitly helping individuals respond differently to each other in order to stop rewounding and promote healing.

But first, let's discuss the wounding process.

Everyone in childhood learns to be sensitive to certain parental reactions, not necessarily to anyone's fault. Your dad seemed critical to you and so you became sensitive to criticism. Your mom was depressed or preoccupied and you became sensitive to withdrawal and abandonment. You felt like you were always striving to please your parents, but they rarely seemed to appreciate your efforts, and so you became sensitive to not being appreciated. Usually your sensitivities are one or two of a small handful—anger, criticism, control and micromanagement, lack of appreciation, not being heard, abandonment. When these arise, you no longer feel safe.

As a child you basically only have one of three ways of coping with these wounds when they are triggered—you get "good" and follow the rules, try to make your parents happy, and avoid conflict; you get angry; or you withdraw. If you have siblings, you are usually bouncing off of them—my brother is the angry one, my sister the good one, so I'm the one who withdraws. Whatever you learned to do works, in that it helps you cope with your wounds.

The problem comes when, as an adult, others, particularly those close to you, inadvertently trigger these old wounds—your friend doesn't respond to your text quickly and you feel neglected; your supervisor doesn't seem to notice your working overtime and you feel unappreciated; your partner complains about how the apartment looks and you feel criticized. When these situations arise, and they will, your childhood wounds are triggered and your 10-year-old self and coping style kicks in—you withdraw, get angry or get good.

What now often happens with couples is that your 10-year-old reaction triggers your partner's wound. You feel criticized, you withdraw; your withdrawal now triggers your partner's feelings of abandonment and she gets angry, causing you to feel more criticized and withdrawn, and her angrier. A negative loop is created with both partners feeling rewounded. Over and over this happens, the patterns becoming more entrenched, and problem-solving becoming undermined.

What keeps this going are two dynamics: One is that because these reactions are part of your past and your view of life, and because your brain is wired to be sensitive to and respond to these emotions in a certain way, when they arise you both hate the feeling and have a high tolerance for it. Someone else with different wiring and different sensitivities would draw a line: You can't do this or I'm gone.

The other is magical thinking. With the triggering of the wound and reverting to a little-kid state of mind comes magical thinking: If I can figure out how to just do the right things, how to say things in just the right ways and solve the puzzle that is this problem, my partner will stop treating me this way. (This is the same type of thinking that we discussed earlier that victims can easily fall into in abusive relationships.) Unfortunately, this easily becomes a psychological Groundhog Day. You try and try, long past when others would put up with it, to find the right combination of actions and reactions that will make *it*—the criticism, control, neglect, anger—stop. You can't figure it out because you're operating out of a child state of mind with childhood reactions.

At some point, after years of rewounding, many couples and parents get fed up. Essentially one or both decide that they are tired of feeling this way, of being treated the way that they been treated for most of their lives. The couple argues more or disconnects more, goes into crisis, decides to divorce. Five years later they remarry and are likely to start the process all over again. This being-fed-up point is often the point that brings couples and families in crisis into therapy.

The primary issue—namely, each partner's emotional wound—lies not with the other but within the self. The solution you came up with at age 10 no longer fits the bigger adult world. It's like old software in a new computer. To upgrade it you need to expand your ways of coping and move from the child mindset to adult thinking and behavior. You can do it now, you can do it later or you can do it never, but in order to better run your life, to avoid the stuckpoints in relationships that these old wounds create, you need to stop falling into old default modes.

That said, the challenge and the opportunity for any couple is to help each other heal, rather than constantly rewounding each other. In our brief therapy approach we are not going to tackle this by unraveling childhood histories in order to reach the sources. Instead, we are going to focus on the present and on behavior. The solution is in three parts.

The first is helping each partner identify and understand what the other's wound is—the criticism, the not being appreciated—and make a commitment to be sensitive to not trigger it in clear concrete ways. If my partner is sensitive to criticism, I need to be careful how I say what I feel when I am irritated; if my partner is sensitive to being unappreciated, I need to make an effort to increase my compliments. This is not about giving in to what the other person wants or an opportunity to complain about all the injustices of the past, nor is it a falling into an argument over whose reality is right—"But I do compliment you; no, you don't . . ." or "You are just too sensitive!" The focus is taking at face value each partner's perception, and moving forward to reshape the patterns.

This taps into the second element—actually saying to your partner what you could not say to your parents. As a child you could not tell your father that he needed to be less critical or tell your mother that you needed to be appreciated more and have more attention. But now, as an adult, you can: "It's not about you, but about me; I'm sensitive to criticism so I need you to be careful how you sound (in these ways) when you are upset." Saying this to the triggering partner brings the past into the present, creates a corrective emotional experience and helps the healing process.

Finally, the most important and most difficult step: In order to become more flexible, each partner needs to do the opposite of what he was wired to do.

Here we see an overlap with our other concepts—the breaking out of martyr, victim and bully roles and into adult behavior, the stepping up and the stepping down. If your childhood coping style was to withdraw, you need to now step up and speak up. If you tend to get angry, you need to calm yourself down, then use your anger as information about what you need and talk about that. If you tend to be good, you need to calm your anxiety stirred by the emotions of those around you by not focusing on and fixing them, but instead by figuring out what you want; then, rather than walking on eggshells to avoid confrontation, take the risk of saying what you want. It doesn't matter what the topic is or situation is, it's about breaking out of old patterns and going against your grain.

Your job is to walk the couple or parents through this process. How? You start by quickly assessing the emotional wounds of each of the partners. You listen to their complaints or you ask directly what bothers each most about the other. Here Tim says that he feels that Sue is always being critical. What does Tim do when Sue does this? He gets good and walks on eggshells. What is Sue sensitive to? That Tim never seems to step up, that he is not reliable, that she has to be always responsible. What does she do when Tim doesn't step up? She becomes frustrated and demanding, which Tim hears as criticism, igniting the negative loop.

You make sure the process is balanced, with both defining their wounds. You now underscore these sensitivities, cut them off from arguing over each other's realities and educate them about emotional wounds. You help them see it is about them and their past and not the other guy. You make sure that they are in lockstep with you and agreeing that this makes sense. You now lay out for them the way out—through moving against their grains and doing the opposite, saying to their partner what they couldn't say to their parents, being sensitive to each other so as to not trigger the wounds and help heal—and you provide concrete behavioral steps for doing so.

So when Tim feels criticized by Sue for not paying a bill on time, his challenge is to realize that old buttons are getting pushed—that he is over-reacting, feeling like a 10-year-old—and that he needs to regulate his response by saying to himself: "I'm getting triggered; this is old stuff from the past. I'm an adult; I can handle this in an adult way." He then takes a couple of deep breaths and says to Sue how he feels and what he needs—that he is sorry that he paid the bill late, and in the future, he will put a Post-it note reminder on his calendar. And she, being committed to helping him heal, works hard to not get angry and slip into her wound of not being able to rely on people. Instead, she actively listens and says to herself, like Tim, "This is old stuff, and I appreciate his being considerate, and I can offer to find good ways to support him."

Will this automatically change how they feel? No, not for the few dozens of times they do this; emotions always lag behind behaviors. But if they stick to it, eventually the emotions will catch up. They will, as a couple, as parents, learn not to be locked into magical thinking, but instead begin to rewire their brains so they are less sensitive to these old wounds. This will help them not get stuck in moving forward in solving problems as a couple, as parents. This will help them be adult.

Differing Visions

Tim and Sue may learn to effectively communicate and stop rewounding each other, but there is still one other roadblock that may snarl them, namely differing visions. Here we are talking about each partner's view of everyday life, as well as that of the future. This is about priorities in a variety of shapes and sizes—about the balance between family or couple time and individual time; how much is work or children the center of daily life; how much attention is given to extended family; how important are healthy behaviors and diet; what do we do for recreation, etc.

All these become wrapped into an image and expectation. Tim's idea of a good week is coming home at 6:00, having dinner as a family, helping the kids with homework, and then he and Sue sitting on the couch watching their favorite television shows. On weekends he's fine with chores around the house, taking the kids to their soccer games and having his parents over on Sunday afternoon.

Sue, on the other hand, is fine with working late if she needs to and grabbing whatever to eat when she gets home. She likes to unwind not by watching television but by going on Facebook, and actually likes to occasionally go out with friends after work. On weekends she prefers to sleep in, would like to hire a cleaning person to take care of the house, resents going to all those soccer games and would like to go camping on weekends rather than have Tim's parents over.

Some of this may reflect own personalities but, even more likely, changes over time in the relationship rollercoaster. Tim was actually more of a workaholic early in the relationship, but when the kids came, he decided to decelerate his career, just as Sue decided to accelerate her own. Or as the children leave home and mid-life issues arise, Tim may want to finally move to a big city where there is more culture, while Sue may want to move closer to her family instead of Tim's, or translate her passion for the outdoors into raising chickens and goats out in the country.

Such differing visions can obviously make for difficult conversations. When communication skills are poor, when emotional wounds in each partner are being constantly triggered, all this becomes much worse. You need to clean up the communication and often isolate the wounds in the session before any adult conversations can take place. Even still, without the power struggling or the emotional over-reaction, you are trying to help the partners navigate difficult waters. They are sitting together on your couch possibly looking for a supporter to break the deadlock, or an arbitrator, but you resist taking on those roles. Instead, your job is to provide a safe place for a deeper conversation. You ask the hard questions—why now, what makes these elements so important, what is the other not understanding about you, where are you both willing to compromise, is there anything in what you each envision or desire that is more important than each other and the relationship? You stir the mental pot and see what settles. It's the best you can do.

By keeping these three obstacles in mind as you see the couple or family, you have, like in the adult and family models, a starting point for assessment, a point of focus in the initial sessions and a starting point for treatment. By pointing out in the session process how these elements come into play, clients can begin to move away from content and into interactional patterns that are derailing them.

Learning Problems vs. Problems About Learning

We've been toggling in these last sections between issues of skill—such as communication skills—and issues of emotions—such as emotional wounds. Another way of delineating these two and using these as clinical filters in your assessment is what Ekstein and Wallerstein (1958) described as learning problems vs. problems about learning. Basically, they said you have two types of problems in the world: those tied to what you don't know—these are learning problems, problems of skill and information—and those problems where you know but your emotions override what you know—problems about learning.

So, if I am a new dad and have never diapered a baby, I may be a bit perplexed about how to actually do this. Someone shows me one or two times, I'm good to go. Similarly, if my job installs a new software program, I am initially clueless about how to use it, but after taking a couple of classes and working through it for a couple of weeks, I have it down. These are skill issues, what I don't know, learning problems.

On the other hand, basically I feel I am a good parent, but when my 14-year-old daughter gives me that "look" and puts her hands on her hips and rolls her eyes, I feel like I want to strangle her. This is about me and my emotional reactions overriding what I know—problems about learning.

Sorting through which is which can help you with assessment. Are these parents struggling over bedtimes with their 6-year-old son because they don't know how to set up bedtime routines—parenting skills—or because their son throws a tantrum and they emotionally melt down as well? Is this couple struggling with money because they don't know how to set up a budget or use a checkbook, or because they use shopping as an emotional release?

You don't need to have the answer to these questions, but instead, ask the question: Essentially where do you get stuck? If it is an issue of skill—the parents don't know how to set up bedtime routines, or the couple doesn't know how to work a checkbook, your next tasks are clear—to show them how to do it. Similarly, if the parents report that they do become emotionally unraveled when the son tantrums at bedtime, though they manage his tantrums well at other times, then it is matter of shifting through the triggers for their reactions.

Thinking in terms of learning problems vs. problems about learning, skills vs. emotions, can be a quick mental shorthand for assessing the source of presenting problems.

The Big Six

Finally, by way of summary in a chapter of concepts, here is a list of the Big Six—the skills you can always build upon and return to if at any point you get stuck and are unsure how to move forward.

Focus on How, Not What

How you do anything is how you do everything, say the Buddhists, and as we have been saying all along, you want to focus on and always return to the *how*—the process—rather than getting lost in the *what*—the content. This is where you go when you or the clients are flooded with too much content: not what they are talking about but how they are talking.

Problems as Bad Solutions

Whatever appears to you or others as a problem that someone is having, the next question you want to ask yourself is: How is this a bad solution to another underlying problem? Ellen comes in complaining that her husband Sam is alcoholic because he drinks a pint of bourbon every night. Sam probably doesn't think he is alcoholic. For him the bourbon is a solution to something else—his poor relationship with Ellen, his worry about his job or money, his depression. Likewise, "anger issues," eating disorders, running away, stealing and emotionally shutting down can all be seen as solutions to underlying problems. So when someone labels a problem, you want to automatically become curious about how is this a bad solution to another problem.

As with learning problems vs. problems about learning, you don't need to know the answer, you just need to ask the question. By doing so you unravel underlying individual and relationship dynamics, and reframe the conversation—"Sam, Ellen is worried about you and doesn't understand why you drink so much at night; can you tell her why?"—and then see what Sam says next. The goal here is changing the conversation and providing a new problem to replace the old stuck one, as well as offering Ellen a new perspective on her concerns. This doesn't mean that you and Sam may need to address his drinking at some point soon, but at first steps it's about finding the problem under the problem.

Change Emotions Through Behavior

Alan is laid off from his job and is understandably depressed. He complains that he has no energy and spends his days on the couch watching endless old episodes of *Seinfeld*. If only he could feel better, he says, he could start looking for a job.

In our brief therapy approach, he needs to reverse the equation. As mentioned in the first chapter, rather than waiting to feel better in order to act, he needs to act in order to feel better. As long as Alan sits on the couch rather than looking for a job he's going to stay depressed, simply because his life is depressing. While he may certainly benefit from some medication, he also needs encouragement and support to simply get moving. His wife needs to help get him up and out of bed, make him a good breakfast and go with him down to the unemployment office. Or you need to come by on Tuesday morning and pick him up.

The point here is that emotions, thoughts and behaviors are all interconnected, but the one that we have the most control over is our behaviors. By choosing to act in spite of how we feel (although it feels difficult), our emotions and thoughts will come to change as well. This is the reason that you want clients to define problems in concrete behavioral terms—what can your partner *do* to help you? This is why behavioral homework assignments are assigned as a way of behaviorally changing patterns. The message to couples and families is: Don't wait to feel like it; do and you will feel like it.

Doing Different Rather Than Doing Right

Just doing gets complicated for martyrs and perfectionists because the doing needs to be done *right*. Both clinicians and clients are susceptible to this way of thinking. It's easy for less-experienced clinicians to feel that they need to have all their clinical ducks in a row before they can act—they need to do a thorough assessment, need to feel certain that their treatment plan will be successful, need to remove emotional obstacles—before beginning treatment. Similarly, many clients—those who are driven on strong "shoulds" rather than wants, who avoid confrontation, who have those critical voices—deliberate excessively, mentally mapping out all potential consequences before acting for fear of making a mistake.

There is the well-known expression, "Ready, aim, fire." This is where such less-experienced therapists and clients can get stuck, making sure that their aim is steady and true before pulling the trigger. A more pragmatic and perhaps more realistic approach is, "Ready, fire, aim." You take action, see what happens, then adjust. You make an interpretation ("It sounds like this reminds you of your mother") and you see what happens next—the client nods her head or tears up, or shakes her head, saying, "What are you talking about?" If she nods her head, you're good to go; if the latter, there is a new problem in the room. Your interpretation didn't work. This doesn't mean you made a mistake and shouldn't have said what you did; rather, it means that you need to fix the new problem.

This "try it and see" approach is actually the nature of therapy and especially brief therapy. Change is about, well, change, and it is the notion of change itself that stifles clients. You want to move clients out of their comfort zone; they need to only do it different rather than obsessing about doing it right. This is the message they most need to hear—ready, fire, aim and we'll fine-tune later—and that you most want to model.

Empathize With Emotions, Not Irresponsible Behaviors

The message here is that you certainly want to empathize with clients' emotions within a session—their depression, their anger, their anxiety—but not to let them eschew accountability for their actions. Couples and families easily do this, falling back into using their emotional state as a pass for their behaviors: If you hadn't brought up my mother, I wouldn't have gotten so hurt and stomped out; if you had only listened to me and not given me that "attitude," I wouldn't have gotten so angry and grounded you for a month.

This is both blaming the other for one's emotions and not taking responsibility for one's actions. This is counter to the adult, where you take responsibility both for emotions and actions. Those prone to anger and violence, and those with addictions and the behaviors they generate, as well as those who rationalize acting out—affairs, shopping therapy—can easily fall into this way of thinking. Your job, through your leadership and response, is to acknowledge that their emotions are genuine and not to be minimized or dismissed, but . . . that they need to take adult responsibility for their actions.

Be Honest

Honesty was listed in communication skills for couples and families because it is key to both problem-solving and intimacy. We're including it in the Big Six because this is another default for you when you are not sure what to do. Honesty here refers to talking not only about the process in the room but also about the elephants there—acknowledging what others are afraid to acknowledge. This means asking the hard questions—whether a father is burned out with dealing with his son's drug addiction, or whether a mother would prefer that her son lived with his father; asking the couple that have on-and-off separations why they have never taken the final step towards divorce; asking a mother if she in some way feels responsible for her daughter's suicide attempt, or the daughter whether she has ever thought of suicide. By moving towards these difficult topics and emotions, you are deepening the conversation as well as letting the couple or family know that you can handle such tough discussions.

But honesty can also come from your side. Here is where you speak up and voice your concern and frustration when the family fails to do their homework again or cancels yet another appointment; or where you challenge the father who continually pulls back and abdicates to his wife, rather than your colluding with the rest of the family and allowing her to set the agenda and tone. All this requires that you be bold and avoid the walking on eggshells, the doing it *right*. You once again model risk-taking so the couple or family can do the same.

The theme running through each of these six points is clear—process trumps content, action trumps emotions, some action trumps right action, risk-taking and interaction trump hesitation and caution. Think of these six as ballast to keep you centered and focused in the session; return to them when you begin to feel adrift.

As we said at the start of this chapter, these concepts can hopefully provide both a foundation and a set of frames upon which you can build and view your assessment and initial treatment plan. Some may resonate with you, your style or your clinical orientation more than others; some will stand out to you more clearly with certain problems and certain couples and families. The theme once again running through them all is identifying stuckpoints: what can't the couple or family do, where and how does emotional regulation and problem-solving break down? We'll look more fully at integrating them into the opening sessions in Chapter 6. In the next two chapters, we'll provide one more tool set—treatment maps for common couple and family problems.

References

Bowen, M. (1993). *Family therapy in clinical practice.* New York: Jason Aronson.

Ekstein, R. & Wallerstein, R. (1958). *The teaching and learning of psychotherapy.* New York: Basic Books.

Gilbert, M. & Gilbert, R. (1992). *Extraordinary relationships: A new way of thinking about human interactions.* New York: Wiley.

Gottman, J. & Silver, N. (2015). *The seven principles for making marriage work: A practical guide from the country's foremost relationship expert.* New York: Harmony.

Hendrix, H. (2007). *Getting the love you want: A guide for couples.* New York: Holt.

Minuchin, S. (1974). *Families and family therapy.* Cambridge, MA: Harvard University Press.

Nichols, M. (2009). *The lost art of listening* (2nd ed.). New York: Guilford.

Sheehy, G. (2006). *Passages: Predictable crises of adult life.* New York: Ballantine Books.

Taibbi, R. (2014). *Boot camp therapy: Brief, action-oriented clinical approaches to anxiety, anger, & depression.* New York: Norton.

Taibbi, R. (2017). *Doing couple therapy: Craft and creativity in work with intimate partners* (2nd ed.). New York: Guilford.

U.S. Census Bureau (2011). *Number, timing, and duration of marriages and divorces: 2009 US census.* Retrieved from https://www.census.gov/prod/2011pubs/p70-125.pdf

3 Treatment Maps for Common Couple Problems

In the last chapter we discussed an assortment of frames, especially our models for adult and ideal family structures, that you could use both as assessment tools and rough outlines for treatment. In this chapter we fine-tune these outlines with treatment maps for specific couple problems.

As we mentioned in the last chapter, it is having such maps mentally at her disposal that enables your physician to quickly step forward with a treatment plan—what medications to prescribe, further tests to perform, when and what specialists to refer you to. Similarly, your treatment maps allow you to do the same when meeting couples and families. They save you time by sidestepping the need to dig deep into the couple's or family's history and reinvent the clinical wheel with each client, which is essential when working with crises.

In this chapter we'll present a clinical overview, goals, challenges and a treatment process for common presenting problems of couples in crisis, so you can hit the ground running. But first, let's discuss an important broader treatment map, a common one that runs through much of couple and family work, namely that of combining such work with individual treatment.

Individual vs. Couple/Family Focus: Guidelines

When first meeting a couple or family in crisis, you are always starting from the clients' own expectations to gain a clear sense of what they are or are not willing to do, in order to formulate appropriate goals and treatment plan. But another important aspect of your initial assessment is that of identifying individual issues that are part and parcel of the couple and family dynamics, and deciding how much these issues may undermine the stabilizing and repairing of the relationship. We talked, for example, in the last chapter about the way those prone to anger, bullies, tend to blame others for their anger, with blame replacing responsibility. If you meet an angry partner who is able to see his role in arguments and acknowledges that his own reactions are under his control, then you may decide to work with the couple on changing the process and pattern; if he still struggles with self-regulation, you may refer to an outside therapist to help him learn the skills he needs to be successful.

On the other hand, if the same partner cannot take responsibility for his emotions, and continues to blame, you do want to refer such an individual out for a couple of reasons: One is that by directly addressing the issue, you can easily replicate the problem in the room by essentially minimizing the individual's behavior. The second and related issue is the need to underscore by the referral that yes, you believe that they do in fact have a problem that they need to acknowledge rather than continuing to blame the victim. Your strong stance is a strategic move necessary to break the dysfunctional patterns and abusive cycle.

But while anger management issues are often obvious and are part of the initial presentation, other issues are not—you become aware of the impact of Ed's drinking only several sessions into treatment, or that Cathy shows the signs of a potentially dangerous eating disorder, or that Lucille shows borderline tendencies. Mapping out in advance your own policies regarding with whom, when and how you are willing to work with particular problems, as well as how to integrate individual treatment with couple and family work, increases your own effectiveness, avoids your getting lost in content, and saves time.

Here are some guidelines to help you shape your own thinking.

When in Doubt, Refer Out

If you suspect that Ed may have a problem with alcohol, but aren't sure about whether or not he needs treatment first before he can focus on his relationship, it's time to refer him to a specialist for an evaluation. This is what your physician would do if she were unsure about her diagnosis about your skin rash. This is good clinical practice.

But it is an ethical issue as well. If someone presents with a possible addictive disorder, eating disorder, bipolar disorder or anything else that you are not solidly familiar with, you need to refer the client out to have a specialist make the clear and proper diagnosis. Even if you strongly suspect that Sam, for example, has a sexual addiction or is struggling with bipolar disorder, resist the urge to wing it and make a snap judgment in the initial couple of sessions. In the age of ready access and permanent medical records, you don't want to make the mistake of writing down a serious diagnosis that can haunt the person forever. Be ethical and responsible and refer to someone who does that work.

Sidestep the Role of Judge

There's also a practical element here. Some couples may honestly come to you to provide professional guidance on a particular issue. Sam is worried about his mood swings, Camille knows that her marijuana use is derailing everyday family life, and the couple is looking to you for help with diagnosis and next steps. If you are competent in these areas, by all means march ahead and provide the service the couple is looking for.

For couples and families in crisis, however, you are more likely to see the courtroom presentation that we have been discussing—arguing over who has and what are the problems, and looking to you to pass judgment. Even if you are experienced in substance abuse treatment, declaring that Camille is addicted in the first session, when both partners are pushing you to take sides, risks unbalancing the system; rather than stabilizing the relationship, you are unbalancing it further. Instead, it's better to take a neutral stance and refer the potentially addicted partner out for a more formal evaluation. Based on the results you then can design a treatment plan that seems fair and balanced.

Bring in Experts for Coordination

Certain problems clearly benefit from medication or require medical coordination and/or individual therapy, such as anger management or addictions, which we mentioned. But there are others, such as attention-deficit/hyperactivity disorder (AD/HD); eating disorders such as anorexia and bulimia; clients struggling with post-traumatic stress; bipolar disorder; severe anxiety disorders such as ongoing panic attacks or obsessive-compulsive disorder (OCD); and major depression. Having other professionals on board can not only provide additional medical and emotional support, it can help you decide on clinical priorities. Ellen's psychiatrist may feel that Ellen needs to get her OCD under control with medication and individual therapy before utilizing couple therapy; Sandra's physician may recommend that Sandra go into residential treatment to medically stabilize her and begin treatment for her anorexia; Ben's individual therapist may say that Ben's AD/HD medication seems to be helping, that she will work with him on organization and procrastination, but sees no reason that Ben can't also focus on his marital problems at the same time.

What's important is that you and the other professional are clear about your own goals and roles so that the couple does not become confused, or split and play one professional against the other. Get a release of information form signed quickly so you and the professional can stay in lockstep throughout.

Handling Those Gray Zones

Aston complains in the couple session that Lucy is a clean freak and is driving him crazy. Lucy may declare that no, she is not, and Aston is just a slob, or yes, she realizes that she has OCD tendencies but has a difficult time reining them in, especially when stressed. Warren has always had a chronic "why bother, don't care" attitude that, until recently, Sylvia was able to work around in dealing with the children, but you immediately wonder if Warren has untreated depression. These are situations where an individual disorder, like lower level anxiety and depression, is clearly in play, but unlike consistent bully behavior or out-of-control addictions, its impact on the system and success of treatment is less clear.

So you start by seeing what behavioral changes Lucy can work on that are particularly bothersome to Aston, while you also focus on behavioral changes Aston can make to reduce stress in the home. You suggest to Warren that he seems to have symptoms of depression and that medication may be helpful to discuss with his doctor, but he quickly dismisses the idea or says he will think about. You decide to march ahead with the couple's presenting issues and focus on getting them to work better as a team regarding the children. With both Lucy and Warren you are looking to see how much they can and cannot follow through with the proposed treatment plan. If they are struggling, you can then decide to raise the topic of medication or individual therapy.

Moving From Couple to Individual Treatment

Such a pragmatic, try-and-see approach usually works well. The clinical fork in the road arises if and when Lucy or Warren agree and ask if you would be willing to help them with their individual issues. What happens with a shift to individual work is a major unbalancing of the system. Even if you believe that Lucy, for example, would benefit with individual work, you undermine a balanced focus with the couple. To do both the individual and couple work at best leaves Ashton feeling that you now know Lucy better than he and that you may be biased. It is more likely that he interprets the individual work as confirmation that his theory that Lucy is the one with the problem is, in fact, correct.

Unless you clinically believe that Lucy's issues are truly the source of the relationship problem and couple therapy is not needed, which is not likely, it's better to refer Lucy out to someone else and coordinate services, or decide to see Lucy and refer the couple to a new therapist. By your decision and your actions to maintain balance, you avoid sending the message to Ashton that he was right after all and has only a supportive role to play in changing the couple dynamics.

Moving From Individual to Couple or Family

Finally, we need to discuss working from the other side of the fence, namely shifting the focus from an individual to that of the couple or family. Here Sylvia contacts you for an individual appointment to talk about her frustration with Warren over parenting, or her ongoing worry about his depression, or her being fed up and needing help deciding whether she wants to stay in the relationship at all. At the end of the third session she says that she and Warren talked and she persuaded him to come in with her next time. Is this okay, she asks?

Sure, you say, but . . . . The "sure" is that seeing the couple together makes sense. The "but" is that the system is starting off unbalanced. Warren can rightfully imagine that Sylvia has spent her time with you filling your head with her side of the story and that you are probably solidly in her corner. You need to balance the system and help Warren feel that he is not in a one-down position. If you don't want to spend a majority of the first couple session building rapport with Warren, a better option would be to ask him to come in first by himself just to meet you and give you a chance to know him; if that is logistically difficult, do it over the phone. Take the time to understand his view of the relationship and, in so doing, build rapport.

If Warren declines your invitation, say he's fine waiting until they come in together, and go ahead and explain your concerns—that you could imagine that it may feel awkward to him since you have seen Sylvia several times. If he reassures you that it's not a problem, have them come in as a couple and judge the need to spend time balancing the system in the session.

What if Sylvia says she would like to have Warren come in, not to begin work on the relationship, but instead, just to use the session to express her desire to separate? Although the session is unbalanced, your role here is more about supporting Sylvia and facilitating a dialogue between the couple, rather than starting couple therapy, and no separate session with Warren is needed. If Sylvia changes her mind, and the couple decides that they do indeed want to start couple therapy, you can then build in a separate session with Warren to balance it out.

Finally, suppose we have the scenario where Sylvia has actually been coming in for months individually and then announces that she would like to start couples therapy. In these cases there is a lot of catching up for Warren to do. Here you can make an attempt to see Warren separately for perhaps several sessions with the clear goals of helping him feel comfortable and gathering whatever background information you need. Or you may sidestep this and simply say to Sylvia that you think it is best that she and Warren start out on an equal footing with someone new together. She can then decide whether or not she wants to continue in individual therapy with you as well.

These are my guidelines; take the time to develop your own based upon your own expertise and comfort zones. Create ones coherent with your clinical model so you don't have to sort through these decisions with each new client.

Let's now turn to treatment maps for specific presenting problems.

Affairs

Karen was looking up the contact information for one of their friends on her husband Simon's phone when she accidentally stumbled on a trail of flirtatious messages that Simon had been exchanging with an employee who headed up one of the out-of-state field offices of his company. She confronted him and Simon immediately admitted to engaging in these ongoing "conversations" for the past several months. He says that he realizes it was "stupid," it didn't mean anything, he didn't know why he did it and, seeing how upset Karen was, he stopped them immediately. But now, several weeks later, Karen remains understandably hurt and so they come together for couple therapy. In the initial session Simon again apologizes for hurting Karen, says again it was stupid and vows to never do it again. He hopes that he and Karen could just put this behind them and move forward.

Affairs come in various shapes and forms—from Bill Clinton's famous line that he didn't really have sex with Monica Lewinsky because there was no intercourse involved, to those partners who feel betrayed when they find their partners sharing intimate details about themselves and their marital relationship that are not shared with the partner—and what constitutes an affair is obviously in the eye of the beholder. That said, when we look at statistics and various studies, the number of men having affairs has held relatively steady in the 22–33% range, while the number of women engaging in affairs has increased 40% in the past eight years to the 14–19% range ("Cheating Wives," 2013). Affairs no longer fit a particular stereotype and are one of the most common sources of crisis bringing couples to you.

Like Karen and Simon, many couples come in because an affair has recently been discovered. The couple may or may not have separated, and the offending partner may or may not have ended the outside relationship. While any physical contact is usually the biggest emotional trigger, at a deeper level, all affairs are actually about a loss of trust and grief. The trust, or lack of it, is obvious: "You lied to me or withheld this from me; I feel betrayed, a fool; now that this line has been crossed, how can I ever believe that this will never happen again?" Here is where the wounded partner demands the short leash—show me your cell phone anytime I ask, give me your password to your email, be home right after work—and generally the offending partner complies. Like Simon, he feels repentant, he is sorry and he wants to move beyond this crisis state and get the relationship back on track. So he does penance and makes his cell phone available—an understandable request, in his mind, that he hopes will calm the domestic waters. But if this continues for months, he likely starts to resent the short leash; he feels he'll never get out of the doghouse; he starts to yank and protest.

The sense of grief is more subtle and multilayered. The wounded partner's image of the relationship has changed: "Though I realized that things have been difficult lately, I never thought that our relationship was this bad or would ever come to this; I am struggling to wrap my head around seeing our relationship in this new light." But there is another layer—the loss partner's image of the other: "In spite of any problems we have had, I never thought you would be the kind of person to do something like this." With this powerful sense of loss the wounded partner now begins to move through stages of grief.

What you see in the initial session are both these dynamics at work. The loss of trust often translates into what feels like micromanagement: Have you really erased her from Facebook? Why didn't you call me like you said you would when you were running late? What were you doing on the computer so late last night? Those tied to grief result in a constant questioning by the wounded partner of past events and the seemingly endless rehashing by the other of what exactly happened: So did you take her with you on your business trip? Is that why you decided you needed to stay an extra day? Did you ever have sex in our house, in her house? When you said you were working late last month were you really working late? Can you prove it?

As with the short leash, the offending partner, like Simon, is willing to answer questions and rehash details at first, but even by the time they come into your office, he may be complaining about why they have to keep going over and over the same ground for hours at a time. What's happening here is that the wounded partner is ruminating—a normal part of grief—and mentally trying to connect the dots in order to eventually develop a coherent story and explanation about what happened.

You have a couple of challenges in these cases. One is to maintain balance—by staying aware of the triangle in the room, tracking the process and making sure that the offending partner isn't feeling ganged up on or left out of the conversation—but all this balancing becomes even more important when dealing with affairs. Both partners are hyperalert to any possible bias on your part. If you are a female therapist, Simon may worry that you will all too quickly take Karen's side; if you are a male therapist, Karen may similarly worry that the "boys" will join together, and that you will be too easy on Simon.

Their concerns are likely to be fueled even more by their tendency to think in terms of content and their inclination to play courtroom and view you as the judge: Do you agree with her, thinks Karen, that this was really an affair as she does, even though there was no physical contact? Do you understand that this is an affair because it was intimate communication and this relationship was emotionally replacing our relationship as a priority? Similarly, Simon is wondering if you agree with him that Karen is over-reacting a bit, that her demands and endless questions are becoming too unreasonable? Even if they don't openly ask, they are each making their case and waiting to see what you think.

So you remain sensitive to balance. You don't, for example, want to risk replicating the problem in the room by spending most of the opening session grilling Simon with detailed questions about the affair. If you do, he leaves the session feeling that you are in her corner. You also don't want replicate the problem by seeming to dismiss Karen's concerns, leaving her feeling that her reactions are not justified or important. Instead, your way out of this courtroom scenario is to clarify your role and the process. You want to be sympathetic to Karen yet make clear in word and deed that your concern is not making judgments about bad behavior.

So how do you manage these issues? Here are the specific topics you want to focus on in the opening sessions.

Determine What Each Partner Wants From Therapy

Though you might be right to believe that because Karen and Simon are sitting on your couch, they want to repair the wound and the relationship, you don't want to make that assumption. Simon instead comes in saying that he hasn't stopped his correspondence at all, and that he is, in fact, ambivalent about staying in the marriage. He is waiting to see whether the relationship can change through therapy, and essentially trying to keep his options open.

Or Simon may not be ambivalent at all. He already has found an apartment and will be moving out this weekend. "Why are you here?" you then ask. He wants to use the session to help Karen understand how he feels, he says. What he is doing is essentially using this initial session as a choreographed drop-off—a safe place to end the relationship, and leaving you, the therapist, to emotionally mop up and support the other partner while he moves ahead. Couple therapy is not the expectation.

It's helpful to decide in advance your own policy regarding working with partners who are still engaged in some form of an outside relationship. Some therapists take a hard line—if both partners are interested in using therapy not as a drop-off, but as a way of exploring what may be possible in the couple relationship, the therapist is only willing to work with them if the offending partner agrees to get off the fence, end the affair and make a commitment, even if it is for a matter of months, in order to throw themselves full force into repairing the relationship. Several opening sessions may, in fact, focus on whether or the not the couple can make such a commitment, or the therapist may recommend that one or both partners seek individual therapy to resolve any ambivalence before moving forward with couple work.

Other clinicians are willing to bypass this issue and go with what the couple is willing to do. If the wounded partner is genuinely willing to temporarily tolerate this situation, the focus will be on using therapy to in fact help the couple sort out whether and how the relationship can be saved. What's important is your knowing your own values and clinical priorities in advance. If you are uncertain about your own stance and way of working, you risk replicating the couple's process by your feeling uncomfortable, on the spot, and ambivalent and indecisive. Crisis work requires clear leadership.

In other cases the affair is less the point of the crisis but more the source of crisis, because it is the last straw. What Simon has done now is old news. He's done this before, or he had a sexual affair several years ago, or he has occupied his free time with sexual chat-rooms or heavy use of porn. There may be non-affair issues—complaints about endless incidents of lying or mishandling of money, or violent arguments. The initial session is likely to be filled with charges and counter-charges about past injustices, arguing over whose reality is right, who is to blame. Here their playing of courtroom is less about the current injustice and more about looking to you to tell them whether they should or should not get a divorce. Again, you respond by focusing on concrete goals: What is it that each partner is looking for most in order to feel that things are getting better? Are they each committed to try and make such changes? Sometimes you get little or no response. The session turns out to be one where it is a safe place to say clearly and aloud that one or both of them is done.

If the couple has separated, you want to know what each sees as his goals for the separation and how this fits into their expectations for therapy. The wounded partner may be simply enraged and can't stand having the other in the house. The offending partner may view a separation as a way of "getting some space" and "clearing his head" so he can decide what he wants to do and what he truly feels. Their stated goals in coming may actually be less about the affair and more about negotiating rules of engagement—that is, clear, agreed-to guidelines around types of interaction, relationships with children, money arrangements, the possible timeframe for how long the separation may last before a more final decision is reached.

Or they may not know: One partner has moved out and now they are in a nebulous no-man's land. Raise the issue of rules of engagement and see if this is something they want help defining. Doing so creates clear expectations that reduce misunderstandings and miscommunication, alleviates the anxiety of the left-behind partner and provides a clear structure for you to operate within.

Regardless of the presenting variations, the point here is that you want to clearly define in the first session what each wants most by coming to see you, and then you decide whether you can or cannot provide what they are seeking. What you won't clearly know, of course, are those hidden agendas—about the partner who says he has ended the affair but actually hasn't, or who has essentially made up her mind to end the relationship and is going through the motions of therapy to say that she has "tried therapy" rather than just walking out. These you try to discern through the therapy process—by being honest and asking hard questions, monitoring whether or not they do the homework you assign, and monitoring whether they both consistently show up for and actively participate in the session.

Define the Affair as a Bad Solution

Even if Simon says that "It was just a stupid," you say that you're wondering about why the affair happened at all, that for most couples there are likely other dynamics afoot in the relationship or within the offending partner. You are reframing the affair as a bad solution to other underlying problems. While you understand how traumatic these events can be, you want to help them, you say, to get beyond the facts of what has happened, and instead look at what may need to change in the way they communicate, express their feelings and solve problems. For some couples this is a hard sell, especially if their only goal in coming was to have a professional pass judgment and arbitrate who was wrong and who is over-reacting. But unless you are able to define and reshape their expectations, they are likely to both be disappointed and not return. (We'll talk more about handling this process in Chapters 5 and 6.)

Educate Around Grief and Trust

If they do follow your lead to shift focus towards their relationship dynamics, you still can't assume you have a green light to march ahead. You still need to provide a safe environment for processing the range of emotions that come with Karen's grief process—allowing Karen, for example, to express her anger and sadness or to directly ask Simon those questions about the affair that most haunt her.

This, too, is part of redefining and broadening the issue as well as beginning treatment. Just as your physician lays out for you the cause and course of your condition, you do the same. You talk about trust and grief as a way of helping both partners understand the reason for the obsessing, the wanting of the short leash, the constant questioning as a way of making sense of what has happened. It also increases their confidence in you—that you are taking leadership and are able to explain to them and normalize what they are experiencing.

Connect and Balance

You balance the relationship and minimize the triangle by connecting with the goals and needs of each partner; you connect with each partner by balancing the process. What this means is that while you quickly want to empathize with and support Karen, you just as quickly want to help Simon define what he wants changed in the relationship. This is what not only broadens the context but also keeps him from seeing therapy as mere penance that he needs to endure.

One good way to do this is to have, early on, an individual session with each partner. You can define this as your opportunity to "get to know the individuals apart from the relationship." Some clinicians do this before the first couple session. My preference is to do this in the second or third session after I've been able to gather impressions to bounce off of in the individual session about coping styles and reactions to the other's comments. It also gives you an opportunity to individually reinforce your relationship with each partner if you were concerned about it after the first session.

In these individual sessions you can drill down and ask the hard questions to come up with your own clear and concrete goals for each individual. Your goal with Karen, for example, might be to help her more fully assess her grief and depression, or better understand what she wants to be most different in her relationship with Simon on an everyday basis. With Simon your focus may be to assess how strong is his commitment to the relationship, or to help him move beyond his mea culpa stance by asking what he needs most that he is not getting, or find out what he feels that Karen doesn't understand most about him. Depending on your clinical model, you may ask about their childhood models, or assess the gap between their overall behavior and the adult.

You can also ask in this individual session if there is something that the client feels you should know that he didn't feel comfortable saying in the first session. It is here, in the intimacy of the one-on-one, that deeper concerns can often be revealed—that Karen has never felt sexually satisfied with Simon, or that Simon hates his job, would love to start his own business, has kids to put through college and is afraid to share his feelings for fear of upsetting Karen. You then can question if there is link between these problems and the affair, and see if she and he are willing, with your support, to put these issues on the table.

Finally, you can also assess more fully in these individual sessions if there is a need for a referral for individual treatment—that Karen does have severe problems with, say, anger management or depression, or that Simon has a possible pornography or substance addiction requiring a recommendation for individual therapy or medication.

You want to leave these individual sessions with the client feeling more connected and engaged, and you understanding better each person's level of commitment and primary needs, both from therapy and from the relationship.

Begin to Deconstruct the Relationship

While focusing on grief and trust is part of the therapeutic process, you need to be careful to not get bogged down and have this take up most of the first session, and you certainly do not want to focus on this session after session. Your challenge is to facilitate the repairing of the trust and grief issues while, without seeming to minimize Karen's emotions, helping the couple do exactly that.

The way around trust issues and the endless questions about the details of the affair is to focus sessions on deconstructing the relationship problems. What is useful to say to couples is that regardless of whatever choice they make about the future of their relationship, your hope is that they don't walk out of the relationship or current crisis with too simple an explanation. If Simon and Karen's takeaway from this incident is that Simon just did something stupid, or if their explanation for divorce is that Simon was cheating on Karen, they have little to take with them into their next relationships. Simon will, at best, blow it off as a crazy time in his life; Karen will leave believing that men cheat, and will be hypervigilant about her next partner, either being constantly suspicious or finding someone extremely passive.

What they both need to gain is a more complex understanding of the dynamics of their relationship. Karen and Simon both need to understand what makes Simon tick. It is not about whether or not he had sex at his office and where, or even why he couldn't draw lines and say no. He needs to unravel why he was tempted in the first place; why now, not last year; or why he couldn't talk to Karen about how he felt their relationship was struggling. This is about emotional wounds and his 10-year-old brain being triggered, but is also about how his emotional needs over-rode his rational mind and values. Similarly, Karen needs to understand her role in the incident—that Simon felt like he couldn't talk to her because she was easily critical and he has always been sensitive to criticism, or that her depression caused her to emotionally pull away in spite of how hard she was trying not to, leaving Simon feeling lonely.

What you are encouraging and helping the couple to do is define and understand the problems under the problems. By helping them draw out the nuances of their own psychologies, as well as those of the relationship, you help them create a more complex picture to learn from and build upon. This is what will help Simon move beyond "it was just stupid" to a deeper understanding of his own needs and limits. This is what will help Karen come to resolve her grief and build trust through understanding rather than control. You can begin these conversations in your opening sessions, but you want to encourage them to not be afraid to reflect and talk outside the sessions on their own.

Help the Couple Move Forward

Because many individuals get stuck in resolving problems, and because they believe they need to feel better to do something different, the couple stunned by an affair thinks that they have to fully quell the repercussions of the affair before they can move forward in their relationship. This is where Simon is partly correct. Even though Karen may feel depressed, having a date night with Simon—going to a movie or show, traveling to someplace new, something they can share as an experience—is a good idea. If the couple is committed to working on the relationship, part of the work is their creating new memories in spite of how they feel. If they don't, their lives are only shaped by the past. They need new experiences to pull them forward.

The tricky issues, of course, in moving forward are about affection and sex. The first time Karen has sex with Simon, she is going to be wondering whether he is thinking of the other woman, and for offenders who have had physical relationships with others, the emotional impact is increased a thousand-fold. What you do is acknowledge such feelings to normalize them. What's needed, you can say, is desensitization around physical contact, meaning that the partners need to start slow. Suggest that they try giving each other hugs whether they feel like it or not, just to help them re-acclimate to body contact. From there they can move forward at their own pace.

The message you are sending out is that we will work together to heal the wound, fix the underlying problems and, at the same time, help you move forward. By moving forward in the present, you can begin to heal the past.

With this map mentally in place, you can plan your initial sessions and avoid getting overwhelmed by emotion and content. You can combine these with our ideal models—where does the couple get stuck in solving their own problems, what keeps them from being a differentiated adult, what roles are they each prone to fall into—together with your own clinical model to set a course for treatment.

Once you set the course, the following sessions fall into line. You'll be focusing on: (1) Monitoring the grief process—checking in with Karen, seeing how she is feeling, whether her obsessions have decreased; (2) Deconstructing the relationship—shifting the focus from detailed questions about the affair to the emotional and cognitive process that allowed it all to happen; (3) Focusing on the underlying issues and the individual goals of each partner—this means helping Simon step out of that mea culpa role and instead talk about his job frustration, helping Karen talk about her sexual dissatisfaction, and helping both of them improve their communication and risk-taking. Your goal is to move among these in any given sessions, looking for stuckpoints, fine-tuning the overall plan, not getting lost yourself in the content.

Domestic Violence

The term domestic violence generally stirs images of some abusive brute who literally beats down anyone in his path—women and children alike.

Couples where such out-and-out victimization and brutality occurs are, unfortunately, not likely to show up in your office unless under court order, and in those cases the focus is on treatment of the abuser. What you are more likely to see in couples in crisis is one of two interrelated presentations: One is where the last argument, though not much different than others, becomes for one or both the partners the last straw; an emotional bottom line is reached, where one or both partners are ready for change. In the other scenario, the most recent argument reached a new and frightening level. Here is where Ashley threw a dish at Mark, which missed him but almost hit their 3-year-old daughter, or where Jamal actually slapped Tonya rather than just yelling at her, or neighbors called the police. Now the couple is shaken.

Here are your primary interrelated goals, in order of priority.

Determine What Each Partner Wants From Therapy

Just as we could have a mix of expectations from partners dealing with affairs, couples dealing with domestic violence are no different. Those couples who are on the verge of divorce may look to you to be the judge and decide who is really to blame for the arguments and chaos of the past years, or tell them whether or not you believe the relationship is hopeless or salvageable. Other couples, less certain, voice wanting to use therapy as a last attempt to see if the relationship can be turned around (no pressure!). Still others come with mixed agendas: One partner is leaning in and is clearly wanting to repair the relationship and stop the violence; the other, as with affairs, has made up her mind, though she may be willing to go through the motions to say she tried; she then drops out or drops off, leaving the relationship and leaving you to now support the abandoned partner.

Obviously, much of this may not be clearly voiced up front and true motivations may be hidden until later in the process. But in the first session you want to get a clear sense of expectations that everyone can agree on. If, for example, they agree that this is their last chance, you want to know what they most want to focus on and how long they are willing to "give it shot." If you sense ambivalence in one partner about moving forward, you may want to address it openly: "Jill, Ed has said that he really wants to see if you both can communicate without fighting, but you seem warier. What are you thinking about all this?" If they are looking to you to be the judge, explain to them how you envision your role and educate them about what therapy can and cannot do. If they are willing to commit to coming in the short term (ten sessions, for example), are willing to do the homework you assign them to help them break old patterns and build new communication skills during the week, and are willing to work on the issues that most trouble each of them, you reassure them that therapy can in fact make their relationship better.

For those couples coming in on the heels of an explosive episode, they are essentially feeling shell-shocked. If one partner feels particularly wounded, he, like the wounded partner in the affair, is likely experiencing a sense of loss. Mark and Tonya are struggling to reconcile their partner's recent behavior—the throwing of the dish, the slap—with their previous image of them. Their sense of trust is shattered, and Ashley and Jamal are apologetic.

But once things seem to improve, where Ashley and Jamal make an effort to be kind and considerate for the next several weeks, Mark's and Tonya's grief and loss of trust begin to subside, and their motivation for real change and for therapy can begin to wane; the danger is that the couple all too quickly begins to settle back into their baseline patterns. They are replicating in therapy what they do at home, namely emotionally kissing and making up, rather than looking at the underlying dynamics or building the skills they need to prevent such situations from arising again.

Your challenge is to try and prevent them from cutting and running. While you acknowledge Ashley's and Jamal's efforts to change the emotional climate, you also use your leadership and authority to encourage them to move beyond patching things up and learn the lessons their fighting is trying to teach them; you do your best to make it safe and welcoming for them to stay. You do this and they may or may not stay, at least not at this go-round. They may drop out and may come back when it all happens again. Again, this is a dynamic common with those in crises in general. You do the best you can do.

Determine How Balanced the Couple Is

In our example above, the assumption is that the couple is relatively balanced in terms of power: Mark and Tonya are both able to push back against Ashley and Jamal. If, however, it is one-sided—Mark and Tonya are clearly being victimized, and Jamal and Ashley are constantly blaming their partners for their anger—then you need to make your case for individual therapy.

You can cover this ground in the first session by asking about how bad other arguments have been, by tracking the sequence of events in the precipitating incident and other incidents and by observing the process in the session. If Tonya quickly shuts down when Jamal becomes annoyed, or if Mark seem tentative and walking on eggshells in the session and minimizes past events, you can assume that there is not enough safety in the room to both allow the abused partner to speak and to avoid retaliation for doing so back at home.

In these cases you need to separate the couple and meet individually with each partner so you can more fully judge whether couple therapy is appropriate and safe at the present moment. What you don't want to do, once again, is replicate the problem by allowing Ashley or Jamal to blame the other for their anger, dismiss it as a one-time event (unless it clearly was) and make it worse by not stepping in and clearly challenging or stopping such a one-sided perspective.

If you decided that the relationship is clearly unbalanced, you need to recommend individual therapy rather than couple therapy. You need to take a gentle yet firm stand that each needs to focus on themselves, that you feel that there is important individual work that both needs to do, rather than focusing on the relationship at this point in time. The goal of individual therapy is for the aggressive partner to learn to self-regulate and take responsibility. The goal for the abused partner is to help them stop the abusive cycle from their side—by being assertive, by deciding on their own bottom lines rather than magically thinking that they can just "do things right" and end the violence, and by increasing their own self-esteem.

The bully will likely drop out at this point. Your focus then turns to the abused and ways of helping him to break the cycle, sorting out with him behavioral and logistical options, including leaving the relationship.

Help the Partners Learn to Self-Regulate Their Emotions

If the relationship is relatively balanced—and for most couples coming in crisis, it is—you want to help each partner rein in his own emotions when arguments begin to escalate and, as we discussed in the last chapter, learn to keep the car on the communication road. This is probably the most important goal with violent couples, the key to changing the climate of the relationship. While most couples will be on their best behavior, especially in the first session, many violent couples will quickly replicate the problem in the room by escalating as they begin to tell their stories. Again, this can be overwhelming for less-experienced clinicians and it is easy to lose control of the session.

Your antidote to such situations is to anticipate such scenarios and have a plan in place. Usually your first line of defense is to use your leadership. Step up and control the process—have them each take turns speaking, set down firm rules about interrupting and have each person talk to you in a monologue fashion rather than reacting to the jabs of the partner.

And if, after several attempts, your efforts are ineffective, separate the couple—send one to the waiting room and help the other calm himself by your active listening, while keeping a close watch on the clock so you can be certain you have enough time to meet with the other partner before the end of the session. Your goal, while it can feel emotionally difficult, is actually simple—to have them, with your leadership, be able to self-regulate in the session and have more or less sane conversations. In extreme cases, it may take several sessions before the couple (or a family) will be able to remain calm in each other's presence.

As with affairs you can use education to place their behaviors in a larger context, as well as prescribe concrete behaviors to help them de-escalate at home. Here is an example of a short educational speech that you can give towards the end of the first session:

"You both are understandably shaken by what happened last week. It sounds like we need to help you develop some communication skills to help you better communicate and solve problems. It also sounds like there are several problems that keep coming up that we need to find ways to resolve, and that is something we can do here, as well as something you can work on at home. What I'm most concerned about right now, however, is the way your discussions so quickly go out of control. It's okay to disagree, to get angry, but it's important that you each are able to rein yourself in in spite of what the other guy may do or say. I know this is difficult, but this is something that I can help you do.

What makes this hard to do is that when you get angry, the amygdala here (point to your temple), the emotional part of your brain, fires up and sends chemicals to your frontal lobes, the rational part of your brain, and it effectively shuts them down. When that happens, the topic you were talking about is no longer on the table. The problem is now the emotion in the room, and it's like an emotional fire. And when you're angry (or tired or stressed about other things), you get tunnel vision, making it hard for you to process what the other guy is saying; you can't rationally solve the problem because your rational brain is offline. What you tend to instinctively do when this happens is try and get the other guy to understand what you're saying, to make your case, to get the last word. You start heaping on evidence to make your case—you start talking about Christmas 2013 again, you pull out a text message to prove what you said. Anything you say at this point is like throwing gasoline on a fire—it just makes it worse. The other person is apt to misinterpret even the most innocuous statement, and get even more ramped up. Instead of heaping on facts, you need to put out the fire.

You have two lines of defense here. The first is that you be quiet. As soon as you can tell that the other guy is getting upset, you just listen; you say you know he is upset, but do not argue back. This *does not* mean that you are giving in to whatever he or she is saying; you're only putting out the fire. Once things have calmed down you can go back and talk about your own point of view.

Now if you stop arguing back, it's likely that your partner will ramp up even more—call you a name, say something nasty about your mother. It isn't about your mother; the reason the other person ramps up is because you've broken the pattern by not continuing to argue. When you break patterns the other person gets anxious and instinctively try to drag you back in. Don't take the bait. Do your best to remain calm. If you do, your partner will gradually, with your active listening, begin to settle down.

If listening, however, is too hard because your partner really knows how to push your buttons and you are getting too upset, then you need to call a halt. What this means is that as soon as either one of you can tell that you are getting upset and can't rein it in, you need to stop and call a time-out. Here we need to decide on a non-verbal signal that you can use to let the other guy know that you need to take a break. The reason you want a non-verbal signal is that if you just say that you don't want to talk anymore, the other person feels like you are being parental and feels cut off, and gets even more upset. What might be a good signal that you could both use? (Let them decide on a signal.)

Once you call a time-out, set a timer for, say, 45 minutes. The reason for a timer is to let the other person know that you are stopping to calm down and that you are coming back; if you just walk away, the other person gets anxious because he feels he doesn't get a chance to say his piece, and the problem will drag on rather than getting settled. Your next step is to do what you need to do to not re-engage—lock yourself in the bathroom, sit in the car, drive away if you need to—don't get sucked back in.

After the 45 minutes, come back and see where you both are in terms of anger. If either one of you is still upset, reset the timer, or decide to wait till the next day and sleep on the couch if necessary. Don't try and talk until you both are totally calm. If you still can't have a calm conversation after a couple of attempts, hold off trying to talk about it, and instead bring the topic into our next session. Does this make sense? Any questions?

You may want to write down a list of the steps to give to the couple, and encourage them to stick them on their refrigerator. In the heat of an argument they can easily forget the steps and revert to their familiar patterns. The purpose of this de-escalation plan is to emphasize the need for self-regulation and personal responsibility, as well as provide them with a clear behavioral alternative. Again, through your leadership you are trying to move them away from content and blaming of the other to process and self-awareness and individual change.

Teach Communication Skills

The de-escalation plan is to help the couple stop the violence patterns; they now need to be able to replace those patterns with healthier communication skills. Here you talk about using emotions as information, not fighting dirty, returning and repairing and problem-solving—all the basic communication skills we mentioned in the last chapter. You will do this in the session by shaping the process—stopping the dirty fighting and the go-nowhere arguments over whose reality is right—and guiding the couple towards clear solutions. Once they have experience doing this in the session, you can ask them to try and do the same at home, see where they have trouble and use sessions to fine-tune their process.

Help the Couple Stop Rewounding

Understanding each other's childhood wounds and the negative loops of mutual rewounding that we discussed in the last chapter is important because they are often the source of strong emotions and the unsafe feelings that fuel the arguments. You can ask about these directly—"What is it that your partner does that you are most sensitive to?" You can also observe, as the couple escalates, the flaring of emotional triggers; look for the gap between how each reacts and what you would expect from adult behavior. So you ask Ashley what particularly hurt her feelings that caused her to throw the dish at Mark, or ask Jamal what caused him to get so angry that he slapped Tonya.

It's not about pinning blame but helping each identify his and the partner's wounds. You then can use education to explain the process, and provide concrete homework around self-regulation—defining and asking the other for what each needs—and mapping out with each ways of stepping up and doing the opposite of their learned coping styles. Because these reactions and behaviors are so ingrained, you will need to constantly check in around these relationship potholes, and in the session slow or stop the action, label the igniting of wounds and the negative looping process, and encourage each to respond in a more adult way.

Address and Resolve Conflictual Issues

The goals we discussed so far have been on process—helping the couple be aware of and stop the dysfunctional emotional cycles and substitute healthy communication skills. This is what will ideally keep them out of crises and enable them to solve problems as they arise in the future. But obviously, content—the sorting through and solving of recurring and stubborn issues—is also important. Couples are needing the safety that you and your office can provide in order to successfully tackle specific problems; they also are appreciative of your insights as both an outsider and professional.

While we'll discuss some of the more complex and thorny presenting issues below, there are often a host of everyday, more simple, issues that couples struggle with which create the ongoing tension that periodically explodes: the division of household chores, individual vs. couple time, managing the logistics of getting the kids in bed on time at night or out the door in the morning. Your job in these discussions is not to arbitrate or provide "right" answers, but to point out when partners are falling into martyr, victim or bully roles, offer "out-of-the-box" ideas to stimulate their thinking, and to provide education around the art of compromise or the behavior of young children, in order to help them move forward and do it different, rather than arguing about how to do it right.

As with the map for affairs, this treatment map around violence hopefully offers you a clear outline of dos and don'ts, based on the key of a brief approach, on which to build. These are difficult couples to work with and what you obviously don't want to do is essentially what the couple does—that is, get lost in content, and believe that through "better content"—the sounder solution, the more effective approach to a problem, showing the other how he is wrong—that the issue and the emotions it generates will be put to rest. Instead you need to stay in charge and focus on controlling the process so they can learn with your leadership and support to do the same.

Addictions

William discovers a stash of empty wine bottles that Anne has hidden in the shed and is angry and fed up. Carly uses her husband Mike's computer because hers is down, and finds a long history of porn sites that he apparently visits several times a day. Teresa sees that her husband, Carlos, has been smoking a lot more marijuana in the past months since his dad died, and is worried.

Like in domestic violence, those couples who come in around addictions come with varying triggers and expectations. Some are like William, who has been tolerating an ongoing problem and now wants it all to stop. Others are like Carly, who is shocked by the unexpected and unexplainable. Still others are like Teresa, who is not so much fed up as concerned about a new level of behavior. Let's talk about the approach to each of these couples:

William and Anne

Our starting point once again is determining what each partner wants, and why now. William may say that finding the stash is the last straw, that he is tired of Anne's drinking behavior and wants her to stop. Or he may begin by making a case for why he believes Anne is alcoholic and wants you to agree. Anne may counter that actually those bottles have been accumulated over years, not weeks or months; that she doesn't drink as much as he thinks; or that while she may drink more than he does, she is fully in control of her drinking, while he often is not. What the couple is doing here is likely replicating the conversations they've had many times at home; they are playing courtroom in the session and looking to you to arbitrate who and what is the problem.

As you do with the other presenting problems, sidestep the judge role and instead change the conversation by making it deeper, less aggressive and less angry. Why now, you ask William, is this particularly bothering you, since you say that this has been going on for some time? What worries him most about Anne's behavior; what he is afraid will happen if it continues? Ask Anne if she is worried at times about her drinking, and if not, why not? How does she respond to his worry? By asking these questions, by shifting the tone of the conversation by focusing on worry and concern rather than anger and defensiveness, Anne can hopefully better understand William's deeper motivations and William can hopefully better understand what is driving Anne.

Explore the infrastructure. As with other presenting problems, you express your curiosity about why things have reached this point; why have William and Anne not been able to discuss and hopefully resolve these issues on their own? Here is where you dig down into emotional wounds, the relationship triangle, the playing out of roles, the imbalance of power. This is where you and they look at where communication breaks down, where visions and priorities differ.

You say you are curious about the secrecy—in this case Anne's hidden stash of bottles. Secrecy often threads through addiction. Part of this can be tied to the shame that comes with such behaviors, but it can also be an additional indication of an imbalance of power—where Anne fears getting caught and William's scolding. So you ask Anne: Why the secrecy? What were you afraid of? How much is hiding and anxiety a larger part of your relationship?

You ask these hard questions to get them on the table, change the dialogue, move them out of their polarized positions by broadening the scope of issue. You now need to see what they are each willing to do. If Anne says she is worried at times about her drinking, ask if she is willing to see someone for an evaluation and suspend therapy until she does. If she says she is willing to try and reduce her intake, but believes that the real underlying problem driving her drinking is the loneliness she feels with William, is this something that William is willing to work on changing?

What you are doing here is negotiating a starting point and initial focus for treatment of the partner with the possible addiction, as well as for the relationship. Decide for yourself whether you are comfortable trying a few weeks of couple therapy to see if in fact Anne can cut back, as William makes an effort to engage with Anne more. If you are not, say so and why. Being clear about your own bottom lines and priorities will help the couple to do the same.

Carly and Mike

The approach we just outlined for William and Anne can certainly be applied to Carly and Mike. Just as you may want to rule out alcohol addiction for Anne, you may want to rule out pornography addiction for Mike. Decide in advance, according to your own guidelines and comfort, at what point you want to press for an outside evaluation. Just as shame and denial may cause Anne to minimize her own behavior, Mike's awkwardness and shame in openly discussing the topic may cause him to minimize his behavior—it's just something that guys do. You need to be careful that your own feelings of awkwardness don't push you to collude with Mike. Step up and ask the hard questions, perhaps in a separate individual session.

But Carly and Mike also have much in common with Karen and Simon and his affair. What drove the couple to come in is Carly's own sense of shock. Much like Karen, who felt emotionally rattled after discovering Simon's trail of sextexting and possible affair, Carly too is likely to be rattled by her discovery of Mike's pornography trail. As with affairs there's an uncovering of a secret life separate from the relationship. Like Karen, Carly is likely filled with a sense of, perhaps, anger, but certainly one of loss—about her image of the relationship and her image of Mike. Like Simon, we could imagine Mike responding much like Simon did: It was nothing, Mike says, and she needs to not let it bother her; or that, fine, he'll stop, and let's move on.

As with affairs, you want to provide Carly with a safe place to express her feelings, but also to create a conversation that helps her make sense of Mike's behaviors. And so you deepen the conversation, explore how Mike thinks about porn, and why porn at all rather than something else as an outlet, a way of coping. You want to deconstruct the behavior and explore how it may be a bad solution to an individual or larger relationship problem. You want to look at the larger infrastructure, the possible playing out of roles, the ways the couple has or doesn't have of initiating honest conversations and solving problems. You want to assess Mike and his behavior, but also help the couple place it a larger context.

Again, these discussions can feel awkward and raise your own anxiety. Having a treatment map already in place can help you override your caution, as can good supervision and support.

Teresa and Carlos

In this scenario there is not sudden discovery or anger, no secrecy. What you're presented with instead is Teresa's clear worry. Does Carlos have an addiction to marijuana that may require treatment? These questions need to be raised and explored at some point, but for now you start with Teresa's concern. You too wonder about the way Carlos has coped with his father's death. It is not uncommon for many men—who tend to internalize their emotions and who, in times of family trauma, step up and take charge—to push their grief to the side. It goes underground, often resulting in greater substance use, or in other cases irritability, explosions of anger or hypervigilance. Your clinical concern is finding out both how he views the marijuana use that is troubling Teresa and whether he agrees with Teresa that it is tied to his recent loss. You ask the questions.

Carlos may acknowledge the loss but minimize its impact, saying that he doesn't think about his father much. He may acknowledge that he has been smoking a bit more, but he is willing to cut back. Or he may say that he misses his father deeply and is not sure what to do about it, but he clearly has no interest in using therapy to help him deal with it. We're back to doing what you can do. Here you help Teresa articulate her worry, as you did with William. You talk about grief and loss, how it often goes underground for many men, how the grief process itself gets truncated or gets turned into hypervigilance or anger, and see if any of this resonates with him. You broaden the theme and assess the couple's communication and ability to problem-solve. You educate him about the therapy process, how it need not be long term, how it may help. You are looking for a problem that can motivate him, to discern what he is willing and not willing to do and whether his caring for his spouse is enough to encourage him to address her concerns and not minimize them.

And this is the theme running through these cases, that of sorting out who has and what is the problem or problems, and then determining the priority, with consultation with the evaluator or supervisor, of individual vs. couple work. Your job in the opening session or sessions is having these conversations, seeing if the couple can reach consensus about next steps and helping them not battle over whose reality is correct.

Sexual Issues

Do couples come to therapy in crisis over sexual issues? Not usually. If they do, the profile is often similar to what you might see with addictions—a concern on how to help the other and resolve a frustrating problem, or the reaching of a bottom line over an ongoing problem. Harry, for example, has been struggling with performance issues and erectile dysfunction due to anxiety for the last several weeks or months. While Harry is more likely to come to therapy by himself, he may come with his partner, Sue, because she, like Teresa, is being supportive and wants to know what to do to help. It's not getting better and they are looking to you to provide some professional guidance.

Or Chao and Kia have been having low-grade but persistent arguments for the past few months over Chao's feeling frustrated because they haven't been having sex as often as he would like. Like William and Anne, they both reached their wits' end, which resulted last weekend in their worst argument ever: Kia screamed that Chao needed to leave her alone and stop talking about this or she was going to leave. Both come in a bit shaken, looking to you to play judge or help them mediate the problem.

Sexual issues are often a distillation of other dynamics in the relationship. They are complicated in that they are complex—the combining of the physical and emotional, vulnerability and intimacy, communication and emotional wounds; and also power. Sex, along with money and kids, is one of the big three power issues in a relationship, where it is not just about how we solve the problem but a tension about whose way is going to win out. We could imagine Chao and Kia easily falling into such a struggle, where her giving in to Chao's pressure feels to her like a defeat.

Once again, your goal in a brief therapy framework is to help put out the emotional fire, uncover the problems under the problems, move the couple towards problem-solving. Here are some of the goals that are most helpful to focus upon.

Open Communication

As we mentioned when discussing Mike, any open talking about sex easily creates a sense of emotional vulnerability. For even the healthiest of couples, having detailed conversations about what each likes and doesn't like, how and why things turn out differently than they hoped, or how they feel when engaging in sex creates enormous anxiety. For partners who have negative or traumatic associations with sex, this all is made more difficult.

Your challenge is to create safety by building rapport and showing sensitivity. Often it helps to state the obvious, that you realize that this is an awkward conversation to have with a stranger, and then be supportive and attentive. But they are looking to you to help them out, to move the conversation forward, and here you gently open the communication by asking detailed, hard questions in order to deepen the conversation: asking Harry detailed questions about his erectile dysfunction, Kia about her feelings about their sexual relationship and Chao about the why and how of his frustration. As you drill down, you want to keep the conversation balanced.

You also want to be sensitive to gender. Even if you assume that they decided it was okay to see you as a male or female clinician, you also need to keep in mind that Kia may have a difficult time opening up to you if you are a male, just as Harry may have a difficult time if you are female. You need to present yourself as warm and non-judgmental, the "ideal partner," in order to prevent triggering further anxiety or old wounds. Offer to have an individual brief conversation with each if that may be an easier starting point. Usually this combination of sensitivity and flexibility is enough to help the partner relax.

Uncover the Problem Under the Problem

Performance issues like Harry's sudden erectile dysfunction can easily be triggered by a spike of anxiety and stress, or they may be situational, such as feeling performance pressure with a new sexual partner, or they may have physiological causes, such as drinking too much alcohol. Like other anxiety issues, the problem persists because the worry about it happening again itself creates anxiety, creating its own self-fulfilling prophecy.

The downward spiral is set in motion. The underlying issue and goal here is breaking the negative cycle of anxiety.

For Kia and Chao you are interested in unraveling their underlying dynamics. If less sex than Chao would like is the bad solution, what is the underlying problem? Do they have differing libidos? Has this been a more sudden problem or one that has steadily increased over time? What are their own theories about why they are struggling now? Is there a power struggle going on, creating tension and avoidance? Are there other problems in the relationship that are or are not being addressed, making it difficult for Kia to feel close to Chao? Is there something that Chao is doing during sex that turns Kia off or makes her feel uncomfortable? You raise such questions in order to help them and you uncover the possible source.

Here, for example, you may hear that Kia actually has a history of sexual abuse that she has never talked with Chao about and never been treated for, but which has been triggered in some way. You open the conversation enough so that Chao can better understand how Kia feels and what she is sensitive to and can place the problem in a different perspective. You also explore whether she might benefit and be open to individual therapy.

Or no, it is not about past abuse, but instead it is that their sexual drives are in fact different. Once the oxytocin rise of the early months of the relationship began to naturally fall, they each went back to their physiological baselines. You explore with them if they are willing to consult a medical specialist.

Or no, you discover that it is not about abuse or libidos but it is in fact a power struggle—that Chao feels that Kia is always withholding, that Kia often feels emotionally pressured or even bullied by Chao and is fed up and digging in. The conversation now shifts towards these larger issues: the probable trigging of emotional wounds, the playing out of roles, the teaching and creation of good communication, and the moving towards problem-solving.

Teach Skills

Depending on your practice, you likely do not need to be a specialist in sexual therapy, but you do need to have a baseline of skills to help the couple resolve common problems such as Harry's erectile dysfunction. There is plenty of good information available, such as McCarthy's *Sex Made Simple* (2015), that provides you with behavioral protocols that you can offer. Your goal becomes one of coaching and providing encouragement; sessions are used to fine-tune stuckpoints, as well as to provide accountability for doing homework assignments.

Once again, your biggest challenge is often overcoming your own anxiety in dealing with these issues. Your antidotes to this anxiety are having concrete information and protocols at the ready, as well as your own willingness to move forward in spite of the way you feel. Use supervision or colleagues as support, and if you feel over your head, be willing to refer out.

Money Issues

Couples coming in around money issues often begin by expressing their frustration with their partners. The complementarity of relationships means that the money-saver often joins with the spendthrift; the partner who wants to pay off the credit card as soon as it arrives in the mailbox is married to one who is fine carrying a $5,000 balance. By the time they see you such couples are often polarized. Each is entrenched in his own position, arguments abound and each is hoping you will get the other to change.

If you quickly discern that the struggle comes from a difference of philosophy, usually arising from reactions or modeling of parents, your goal is that of deepening the conversation—talking about worry rather than frustration, and helping the spendthrift, for example, explain why he doesn't worry about the balance, or why he is unwilling to adjust his behavior simply because it bothers the other who he cares about. You ask how these conversations go, and where and how they get stuck in solving their own problems, and often you find that this is the tip of the iceberg of their difficulty in solving problems overall. You sidestep the arbitrator role, broaden the context and redefine the therapy focus on helping them better navigate the process of problem-solving and reaching compromises.

But other times it is clear that this is about power and not philosophy; there is an imbalance in the system. Henry's sudden and independent splurge on a larger television is less about what was on sale or better picture quality and more about acting out his frustration over his wife's micromanagement. The relationship triangle is underway and either the martyr is fed up and moved to the persecutor role, or in this case, the Henry-the-victim is tired of being on the bottom and feeling that he deserves to do what he is doing. So you ask about emotional triggers: why now, why this, show them the triangle, see what connects. You are redefining the problem not as one of money or philosophy but as a relationship imbalance. The focus now is on moving out of roles and moving the couple and the system to the adult stance.

Finally, there are couples who struggle over money not because of power or philosophy, but because they really don't know how to budget or set financial priorities or even balance a checkbook. As a result they both wind up with high anxiety and lots of blaming and arguments about side topics that go nowhere. We're back to learning problems vs. problems about learning, and here it is learning problems and what-don't-you-know skills.

Your goal is to help them learn to communicate better, end the arguments and problem-solve, but you also want to help them learn the skills—about budgeting or checkbooks. You can usually help them do this within sessions. If you feel it is more complicated than you thought, or that it is better for them to be coached by and have accountability with a specialist, there are often consumer credit counseling services in most communities that you can refer them to.

Like sex, money issues can be multi-faceted. Your initial goal is to once again unbundle the emotional bundle.

Situational Crises

Clare's parents recently divorced and her mother has asked if she can come stay with her and her husband, Martin. George has always had a difficult relationship with his parents-in-law, but last Christmas he felt they spoiled his children, despite his protests, and he is now unwilling to see them this Christmas. Lynn has just lost her job that was supporting her and her husband, Ruel, while he was in school, and now Lynn is emotionally devastated and the couple is financially panicked and unsure whether Ruel should quit school or borrow money from family to help him finish. Oscar and Tina just found out that they are pregnant; Tina is wanting to have an abortion, but Oscar is opposed.

These are couples in situational crises. They present themselves in a state of shell-shock, unable to sort through their emotions, as well as communicate them, and/or are often arguing about what path to take, and are unable to find an agreeable solution. If they had been struggling in other ways and with other tensions before this crisis hit, if communication has always been poor, if multitudes of problems have been swept the rug, all this becomes worse.

They are coming in to find a way to sort this out. There may be time pressures—the mother will have to move in the next two weeks, the tuition for school is due, the pregnancy is moving towards the third month, Christmas is only two weeks away. The stress causes the communication to deteriorate; they may be polarized, each in his bunker; they are confusing means and ends; depression, anxiety and anger fill the space between them.

You are a voice of rationality and reason, the counter to their emotional turmoil. You provide the safe place for sane conversations. You help them untangle means from the end—that Christmas is not the end, but rather George's way of handling his philosophical differences and frustration with his in-laws, as well as his unresolved hurt feelings from last year. You help them untangle the emotions—Oscar's and Tina's emotions and values about abortion, Lynn's and Ruel's feelings about borrowing money from family or dropping out of school. You raise the practical concerns about Clare's mother moving in.

You are doing crisis interventions. While you ask where they are getting stuck in the process of deciding, while you label and assess the levels of depression, anxiety and anger, while you are curious about the backdrop of other relationship dynamics and unsolved problems, your focus in these pin-point situations is on helping find a path forward. You know and they know that if they can come to a solution to the problem right before them, their stress and anxiety will go down; the other issues can be addressed later.

Your challenge here is to not get overwhelmed yourself, or work harder than they do by feeling that you need to arbitrate or come up with possible solutions. If you find yourself getting caught up in seemingly endless "yes, buts," where your possible solutions are quickly shot down, it's time to point out the process, back off and deepen the conversation by asking hard questions. Help them shift through priorities and express their opinions and worries, but help them move forward, keeping their eyes on the end—the ultimate and primary they need to solve—rather than getting lost in the weeds of the means or the power struggle of whose way will win out.

While certainly each couple is unique, we've hopefully covered the most common issues you are likely to be presented with. The purpose of these treatment maps is to help you hit the ground running, not get lost in content or feel pulled to do excessive assessment, and provide a clear preliminary treatment path, one that results in changing the emotional climate of the session. In the next chapter we will look at treatment maps for common family issues.

References

Cheating wives on the rise. (2013, July 3). Retrieved from http://www.huffingtonpost.com/2013/07/02/cheating-wives_n_3536412.html

McCarthy, B. (2015). *Sex made simple: Clinical strategies for sexual issues in therapy*. Eau Claire, WI: Pesi Publishing.

4 Treatment Maps for Common Family Problems

As we did in the last chapter for couples, we'll turn now and do the same for families—present treatment maps for the most common problems you are likely to see with families in crisis. While there are a number of similarities between couple and family therapy—the need for leadership, the heavy focus of the family on content rather than process—there are some differences important to note.

The most obvious and frequent one is the inclusion of children and teens in the process. If they are participating in the sessions, they offer you new challenges in building rapport—accommodating an active 8-year-old, for example, or overcoming the huffy resistance of a 14-year-old. The children's participation also eliminates the dreaded triangle of couple therapy and your need to maintain balance. While it's important that you don't leave someone out or find yourself and the family ganging up on one family member, families, once they get started, naturally move into their own momentum. Your role in family therapy is less that of the point of a triangle and more like that of the traffic cop—guiding the process, stopping one to allow another to go ahead.

You're likely to notice that parents seeking help with their children are more motivated, less ambivalent and less leaning in/leaning out than their couple counterparts. While some parents present with skewed and unrealistic expectations that their role is to merely drop off their child for you to fix—much like leaving your car with a mechanic—expectations that you quickly need to correct, most parents are ready to engage. Even though they may disagree about what are the problems and how to manage them, at a base level most parents are sincerely worried and wanting their children to do well. This common goal is one you can use to rally parents towards showing up, doing homework and working together as a team.

Finally, the dynamics of families are different because the children, unless they are adults, lack the equal power status that is part and parcel of your concern when seeing couples. While a child may refuse to go to school, or a teen may run with a gang and break into houses, the bottom line is that the child can't win. There is community support to back up the parents and, if necessary, to push them to step up—all very different from the power stalemates that couples can fall into.

With these differences in mind, let's look briefly at the format options you have to choose from when working with families.

Whom to See: Format Options

Whom you choose to see when addressing family issues will depend upon your clinical models, as well as your own comfort zones. Here are the common options and guidelines for when to consider them.

Total Family

This can be considered the gold standard of family therapy—everybody in the room at the same time, including grandma and the family dog. The advantages of this approach are that you get to meet all the players, hear their views of the problems and build rapport with each, reducing your worry that the left-out grandma will in fact do her best to undermine treatment. Because we're looking at structure and interactional patterns as part of our assessment, it is all right here, unfolding in the room; you don't have to rely on hearsay. And because problems are process in action, you have the opportunity to see where a family gets stuck in solving their own problems, and can point out and stop the dysfunctional patterns as they emerge, and reshape them in the session.

The downside is that everyone in the room, including grandma and the family dog, can make this seem more like crowd control than therapy, and it can be overwhelming if you are a less-experienced clinician or new to family therapy. But because family therapy is more about a way of thinking about problems and family dynamics, and less about cramming as many folks as possible into a room, you can always start by breaking the family down into smaller more manageable units that fit your own comfort zone. If you don't want to take on the entire crowd, you can ask if older children can watch the younger in the waiting room while you talk to the parents, or have parents wait in waiting room while you see the children.

Parents Alone

Some clinicians start therapy by seeing the parents alone first. Why? Because it is not only more manageable but also gives you the opportunity to gather background information without needing to attend to the children. A better reason is that it helps you assess the parental and couple relationship, and see whether the parents are able to work together as a team, can communicate effectively and are in agreement about bottom lines, all fitting Minuchin's ideal structural model. Armed with this information you can then decide what and whom to include next, or whether to focus on repairing the parental relationship.

While meeting alone with the parents introduces the triangle problem that you need to be sensitive to, this is outweighed by the efficiency it provides for brief therapy, especially when the presenting problem is behavioral issues with young children. Suppose Sally and John contact you because they are concerned about their 4-year-old's night terrors. You could have all three of them come in for the first session, but this not only means that the child may distract you from your assessment of the parents, it also generally requires you to take time, usually with a play-therapy focus, to build rapport with the child—not an efficient first-line action. Instead, have Sally and John come in without their son; have them describe the problem and their attempted solutions, uncover where they get stuck and offer them clear and specific behavioral suggestions that they can try to implement at home.

Here you are essentially coaching the parents on how to be behavioral therapists for their child. Because young children are so sensitive to their parents and their actions, this is often a good first step. Have them try out your suggestions for a week or two and come back, then fine-tune the interventions. If things are still not better, you can then bring the child in and do individual work, or refer the child to someone who does it.

What this format allows you to do is both empower the parents to shape their child's behavior and help them learn, through your suggestions, important parenting skills. You can bypass having to spend time helping the child feel comfortable with a stranger and the therapy process.

Parents and Identified Child

This is a good format for troubled teens and parents. No play therapy is generally needed, and teens often appreciate the privacy of not having their siblings in the audience, particularly at the start. It also gives you a chance to more fully connect with the teen who may be reluctant and assumes that you are merely another adult who will not understand or will judge him.

If you want to include the school-age child in the initial session, decide in advance your own format preferences. Latency-age children can usually participate in the opening conversations, and spending some time as a family gives the child an opportunity to feel safer with you as he sees his parents relax in your presence. Depending on how open and productive the conversation is, how much the child is able to understand the parents' concerns, you can then decide whether to continue the family conversation through the rest of the session, or break off and spend some individual time with the child to build rapport and assess the child with or without a play-therapy focus.

Child or Teen Alone

Although most dedicated child therapists see individual work with a child as their primary format, this is generally not time-efficient for families in crisis, for all the reasons mentioned. Some clinicians, however, will mix and match; that is, see the parents to gather background, see the child individually for a couple of sessions to better assess the child and use this information to then make behavioral recommendations for the parents to implement at home. Your challenge is helping parents agree to give you the time you need to provide this feedback.

Teens, on the other hand, who are not being dragged in by parents but are open to therapy or are requesting help with individual problems, are obviously good candidates for making individual therapy the primary focus. As family or parenting issues arise—issues of sibling rivalry, for example, or conflicts between the teen and parents—you can invite family members in as needed. In preparation for these types of sessions, it is good to first map out with the teen the focus of the session and even choreograph the process: "So you want to talk with your dad about the argument you both had last weekend. What is it you most want to say to your dad and have him understand? How would you like me to help you with this in the session?" This type of planning not only makes the session more effective and efficient, your supporting role helps the teen be more assertive and less anxious.

Sibling Groups

Seeing siblings together without parents is often helpful and is an efficient use of time when one sibling is shy and difficult to engage, or when the sibling group is struggling with a common issue. An example would be a sibling group of children aged 10, 8 and 6 where all have been recently placed in foster care. Here you use the session to talk about their mutual transition to the foster home, as well as their own experiences regarding their natural parents. And if the 6-year-old happens to be quiet and reserved, having her siblings there with her can help her feel more relaxed and open; often her siblings' reactions will echo her own.

Sibling groups are also a logical choice for adult children. For example, two brothers and their sister come in to discuss their worry about a parent's health or increased drinking. You use the session to help them map out a next-step strategy or to choreograph with you how a session with the parent might unfold.

Again, which format you choose will be shaped by your own clinical model and comfort zone. As we discussed earlier, if at any point you feel over your head in dealing with a specific issue—a budding eating disorder in a teen, for example, or concerns about possible AD/HD in a young child—don't hesitate to get supervision or refer out for a consult or specialized treatment.

Parenting Guidelines

Let's cover one more topic before moving on to specific treatment maps; that is, general parenting guidelines. While this is not a text on parenting or in-depth family therapy, by keeping these concepts in mind and looking for their absence or presence as you talk with parents, you can quickly assess what changes to suggest to improve the overall infrastructure and functioning of the family system.

Rules

Rules are the beams that hold everyday family life together: you don't hit, you let us know when you are running late, you don't run out in the street but instead wait and look both ways. Families can get into trouble with rules in a few ways.

One is where there are too many rules, which dilutes the power of rules. When picking up socks is billed as just as important as crossing the street, the children feel micromanaged and struggle to remember all of them; nothing is really a priority and everything feels like a priority, making it difficult for them to follow through. On the other end are those families where there are no or too few rules. Here the children don't know what is important, because nothing is, and because the family system lacks enough structure, the children are likely to be anxious.

Then there are families where the parents are not in agreement; each parent has his own rules that often cancel out those of the other. The children become confused, or they split, playing one parent against another.

Finally, there are families that state rules, but the parents have no consequences in place for not following them. With no enforcement, the rule has no power. Functioning rules are those that are paired with clear, concrete and time-limited consequences—no "You are grounded for life," but instead, "Because you didn't call us to say that you were going to be late, you can't go out with your friends next weekend." Natural or logical consequences are generally better than punitive ones, especially with teens.

As part of your assessment you want to find out where the parents stand regarding rules. If they are too short on rules, help them develop them; if there are too many, help them prioritize and pare them down; if they are lacking consequences, help them define them and pair them with rules. Generally, good rules are those connected with safety, health and courtesy.

Routines

Children love routines. This is often why some children do well in school, which runs on routines, but are hellions at home. Like rules, routines provide structure and help reduce anxiety, and without them children are often constantly testing limits. Help parents map out morning, after-school, dinner, post-dinner and bedtime routines with forced choices as input from the children: "Do want to take a bath before or after you brush your teeth?"

Positive Feedback

Just as partners need that 4:1 ratio of positive to negative comments, so too do children.

Only by knowing what they are doing well can children know what to do well. In the absence of positive feedback, children will go for the negative feedback because no feedback is, for them, the worst of all. In such environments children act out as a way of getting attention, quickly creating negative interactional spirals, and negatively affecting their self-esteem.

The key to positive feedback that has the greatest impact on children is feedback that is specific, pre-emptive and delivered with high energy. Rather than calmly throwing out "Good job" when the child holds up the picture he drew, it's better for the parent, as the child is drawing, to say, "I really like the way you drew that brown cow, David," and say it with a lot of emotion.

Risks

One of the ways children (and adults) increase their self-esteem is by taking on challenges, doing things outside their comfort zone and finding that they survive. Some parents are over-protective and don't give their children opportunities to have these experiences, or provide the experiences, but instead focus on the child's results rather than emphasizing the child stepping up and meeting the challenge. You can encourage parents of children with low self-esteem to create opportunities and model appropriate risk-taking sans high expectations about outcome.

Trust

Feeling safe and trusting go hand-in-hand. Children whose parents are always emotionally over-reacting, are not following through on what they say, and are not supportive and positive not only learn to be distrustful of their parents but also take that into their mindscape and become distrustful of the larger world. The antidotes are clear: emotional regulation, reliability, and positive and supportive parenting.

Warnings and Transitions

Children get rattled by sudden changes. Parents need to avoid being abrupt and shouting, "Go to bed now!" and instead do the prep: "You need to shut the TV off when the show is over and go upstairs and take a bath." Better yet, set a timer that the children can see: "When the timer goes off, you need to shut off the TV and get ready for bed."

Some parents are reactive and impulsive, causing anxiety in their children with their sudden outbursts; the agitated children then push back, creating a negative cycle. Help parents get in the habit of smoothing transitions.

Talk and Problem-Solve

Important for couples, important for children. Parents and children need to solve problems and, like adults, do so when everyone is calm. If a teen blows up, the parent's goal is to help put out the emotional fire, not focus on the content of the problem. But later, when things have calmed down, there is the need to circle back and come up with a solution: "So let's talk about what time you need to be home from your date . . ." Help the parents come up with concrete, age-appropriate options and solutions.

Adjust Parenting to Fit the Age and Personality of the Child

Being age-appropriate is always important. Kids are not cookie-cutter and neither should parenting be. Good, sensitive parenting is adaptive to the needs of each child, encouraging each child's unique talents and strengths and adjusting their parenting styles as children naturally grow and change.

But some parents struggle with adapting to their changing children. They fail to consider the different ages of the children when setting up routines and expectations; they are the same drill sergeants of their 15-year-old as they were when she was 8. Often this is a skill issue, a learning problem, rather than a problem about learning, and the parents need help learning what is developmentally appropriate, how to move toward less control and more guidance as children become teens, and how and when to pick their battles.

Do Floor-Time

Stanley Greenspan, the well-known researcher on autism, was a strong advocate of this for all children because it makes for good child mental health. The idea here is to dedicate time for one-to-one parent–child interaction with each child in the family. The time doesn't need to be extensive, but it does need to be consistent—it is not taken away as punishment. The other rule is that the child gets to decide what he and the parent are to do during that time.

The notion behind this that guaranteeing a child quality time with the parent reduces the danger of the child substituting negative attention, and the child, for a change, is in charge of the process, rather than having it always shaped for him. This shift often frees the child to be more emotionally open with the parent.

Again, keep these principles as a guide for assessing skills and helping parents break dysfunctional patterns.

Polarized Parents

Let's shift now to our treatment maps. One of the most common problems, and one where a parents-alone format needs to be used, is with parents who are not on the same page. Eric and Beth come in because they disagree about chores that the children need to do or about bedtimes or whether their 14-year-old teen should be allowed to date a 17-year-old from her school. This will very much seem like couple therapy and essentially it is. The parents will likely play courtroom, with each stacking up evidence and looking to you to decide who is right. As with other scenarios like this you want to sidestep taking on that role and, as in couple therapy, focus on helping them reach a unified agreement.

As we mentioned earlier, parents who are not on the same page create confusion, anxiety and, often, acting-out behaviors in their children. Consistency and structure are lost as each parent undermines the other. The children learn how to slip through the cracks, and often develop a one-sided view of each of the parents—dad is always tough and unapproachable, mom is easy and supportive—and are having to live in a home of conflict.

Your approach with such parents is to be honest and clear: that you believe that the main problem is not what is the appropriate bedtime for the children, but the fact that they are not on the same page and are counter-balancing each other. You appeal to their joint interest in caring for their children, and you help them understand the impact this polarization can have. You want to resist the temptation to arbitrate or make their decision for them, and instead focus on facilitating the decision-making process between them.

Their struggles with parenting are often the tip of the iceberg and the dysfunctional patterns are likely systemic. The couple is often unable to resolve a multitude of problems in their own relationship, which are swept under the rug, and they may use parenting issues as the forum for playing out the imbalance and resentment in the relationship. You help them learn good communication skills, you look for and educate them about emotional wounds, you show them the relationship triangle or Minuchin's ideal family structure. Your goal needs to become theirs, namely creating balance and teamwork. Having this consensus is the starting point for any other parenting issues.

Families in Transition

Here we are talking about families who are trying to adapt to a change in the family structure. This may be the introduction of a stepparent, or the shift from a two-parent family to a single-parent household, such as through divorce, death or a parent out of the home due to military service. These can present as crisis situations because of the high level of anxiety brought about by the breakdown of the previous structure.

Here you may meet Paula, who feels overwhelmed not only by increased responsibility and workload but also by the behavior of her oldest teenage son, Brad. While Brad initially stepped up and helped Paula manage the younger children, he is now becoming defiant with her—ignoring her requests, arguing back. You quickly discover that Brad's father, who recently went to prison, was the disciplinarian in the family, enforcing his own set of rules, while Paula was both a buffer and nurturer. With the hole in the family system that the father's absence created, Brad stepped up to fill that role. Essentially Brad identified with the aggressor and now is feeling entitled and replicating the father's role with his mother.

The challenge for any new single parent is one of providing continuity, maintaining as much of the same rules and routines as much as possible. But this can be difficult for a parent such as Paula, where she and her husband were polarized before he left the home.

Paula's challenge is to step up so that Brad can step down. But Paula may lack to the skills to do this, and Brad's behavior may trigger her emotional wounds. If Paula, for example, grew up in an abusive household and learned to cope by withdrawing or accommodating, it is easy for her to fall into that coping style when Brad challenges her. Each time she backs down, Brad is likely to feel more and more entitled and grow more and more defiant.

While you need to help the entire family at some point openly deal with their grief over the loss of the father, your more immediate goal is to help Paula not collapse under Brad's defiance. Here you may need to bring in community support, such as putting Brad on probation if he is truant from school, assaultive or staying out late. Or you may want to refer the family for home-based services in order to provide Paula with support and direction at those times when Brad acts up and out.

What you don't want to do, and need to be particularly careful about, is fall into the role of replacing the father yourself in the family system—that is, using sessions to directly rein in Brad yourself. While this may possibly work in calming the waters in the short term, it doesn't help Paula learn the skills and have the success that she needs over the longer term to manage the children and heal her emotional wound. What she needs from you is a clear behavioral approach with specific prescriptions of what to do, with the emotional support to carry them out.

For families moving in the opposite direction—growing rather than shrinking—the goal of retaining the rules and routines of the past also applies. Here you meet Henry, a new stepparent, and Terry, the former single mom. Henry comes on board as the stepdad and is aggravated by Terry's seeming laid-back attitude towards the children. He feels that they are "walking all over her," that the children are cuddled and not responsible, and sets out to "straighten them out." What likely happens next is that either Terry and Henry fall into polarized roles, with Terry undermining what Henry is trying to do, or Terry accommodates, but the oldest child who acted as the junior parent for many years rebels and battles Henry. Why? Because the child has been dethroned, and quickly takes the position that "you're not my father." The couple comes in in crisis with Henry either wanting Terry (or you) to straighten up the rebellious child, or wants to find ways to get him out of the home; otherwise, he talks about leaving.

The rule of thumb is helping stepparents integrate into the family system is to instruct the stepparent to take on a nurturing role at the start, in order to build a solid relationship with the children before trying to implement any changes. If Henry feels that the children need more structure, you use sessions to help Henry and Terry get on the same page, and if changes are agreed to, focus on helping Terry implement the changes, with Henry's emotional support and sideline coaching, in small dosages. Terry needs to be the one to step up, and Henry needs to resist stepping in as the disciplinarian who appears, to the children, to be undermining Terry. As Henry becomes more settled in the family, particularly as he strengthens his relationship with the dethroned child, he can then gradually take on more and more of a disciplinarian role.

Finally, a different type of transition that you may see that throws the family and couple into crisis is one that is anticipated. Here Cheryl and her partner, Lucy, come in because they are planning on separating after being together for many years. They don't know what to say to the children and are worried about how to help them navigate what is to come.

Your role in these situations is that of a consultant. The children will be anxious if they don't know what is going to change in their everyday lives. Are they going to be able to see Lucy? Who is going to pick them from school, or what new school are they going to? What about their friends, the dog, etc.? Help the parents develop a speech that lets the children know what to expect and when. If possible, have them talk to the children together so that the information is consistent, or have them bring the children in so you can help facilitate the conversation. Let the parents know that they need to answer the children's questions, but they don't need to go into details about the couple relationship. For young children, whose sense of time is distorted, have them do this a few weeks in advance; for teens, more notice can be given. Encourage the parents to circle back and check in with each of the children as the process moves along, in order to answer questions and help calm their anxiety.

Talk to the parents about the importance of leadership and setting the tone—that the children will feel calmer if the parents seem to be the same. Encouraging them to keep the same routines and rules as much as possible is important, and give the children forced choices so they have some sense of control—how they might fix up their new room, or which night of the week they want to spend with Lucy. Finally, leave room in family sessions or coach the parents on how to help the children with grief and loss—gently asking them the hard questions about their worries and potential guilt, giving them room to express how they feel in order to help them navigate the terrain of change.

Helping parents with these transitions can be emotionally challenging for you as you watch children struggling and parents feeling overwhelmed. Get the support you need, but your goal is to treat the parents the way they need to treat the children.

Common Behavioral Problems in Young Children

Ramon and Maria are worried about their 5-year-old daughter. For the last several weeks she has had trouble going to sleep at night. They help her settle down in her bed, but she calls out within minutes of their leaving, saying that she is afraid of monsters, or that she wants a glass of water, or that she is simply fearful and wants one of them to lay down in bed with her or wants to come into their bed. The parents then come in and try and reassure her, sometimes laying down with her until she is able to fall asleep. However, instead of the problem getting better, it seems to be getting worse, with her calling out more and more. The parents come in ragged from lack of sleep and irritated.

The problem here is the child's anxiety. What is happening is that their daughter is training Ramon and Maria to reduce her anxiety. Each time they come in she feels better, but because anxiety tends to increase when its demands are fed, her tolerance for anxiety diminishes, resulting in her calling out more. In situations like these, the parents need to acknowledge and not dismiss the child's feeling, but they need to take control of the process, rather than allowing their daughter to do so.

What this translates into is Ramon and Maria settling their daughter down and saying that that they will check on her in five minutes. They need to then check on her in three minutes, before her anxiety ramps up. This proactive intervention—their taking the reins rather than the daughter driving the process—helps the daughter settle because it breaks the anxiety cycle; the daughter relaxes because she knows her parents are "on duty" and there to help her. A few nights of this approach and the daughter is likely to settle.

This shift to a proactive rather than reactive role is helpful in dealing with all forms of anxiety in young children, even with children who have slow-to-warm temperaments that cause them to be anxious and cautious.

If Billy is anxious about his first day on the soccer team, the parents need to talk with him ahead of time about his worries and reassure him that he will be fine, and stand on the sideline to encourage him to take the risk. What they don't want to do is fuel his anxiety by taking him home because he is upset, or pulling him off the team. The antidote to anxiety is approaching it rather than avoiding it. Children only build their self-confidence and learn to manage their anxiety through supported risk-taking and the approaching of their fears.

For other issues, such as inappropriate behavior and breaking rules—hitting a sibling, for example—help the parents understand that young children often engage in seemingly bad behavior either because they are struggling with underlying emotions or because they have learned to use negative behavior to get attention from the parents, or both. Help the parents develop a plan of rules, routines and consequences ahead of time, in your sessions if necessary, so they don't act reflexively, get angry and yell.

Such plans can be broken down into two parts: the first is to catch emotions and behaviors before they escalate. If the parent hears two siblings starting to fight over a toy, for example, or if a child is getting frustrated building something with his Legos, the parents need to listen and see if the children or child can self-regulate. If not—if the siblings are escalating and the child is becoming more frustrated, not less—they need to step in—to separate the children, to talk with the frustrated child—with the goal of breaking the negative pattern, and helping the children or child self-regulate. What is important is the parent remaining calm and taking decisive action. Once the child is calmed down, the parent then needs to talk with the child about his behavior and help him solve the problem, such as coming up with a way of sharing toys, or asking the child to ask for help with his Legos before he gets too upset.

You can role-play these situations with parents in the session, and again, you want to be certain that you have buy-in from both parents to your suggestions and that both are on the same page. Your goal here is not to arbitrate over which parent's approach is right, but to demonstrate leadership and help the parents learn the appropriate skills. Finally, if any problem behaviors carry over to school, encourage the parents to coordinate with the teacher so the approaches are consistent.

Intense and Persistent Sibling Rivalry

When parents come in describing ongoing, intense sibling rivalry in the home—the children are always fighting, the acting out is violent—you can certainly begin by encouraging them to use the same approach that we just described. But when sibling rivalry is so intense and persistent, it goes beyond more simple behavior management; the key to quelling such behaviors is uncovering the likely ongoing source.

Sometimes the children are merely copying what they see the parents do—that is, arguing among themselves the same way the parents do. Other times the parents may not be arguing, but instead there is ongoing and undiscussed tension in the family that is making the children anxious, resulting in their acting out. Underlying both these sources are marital issues that need to be solidly and directly addressed. Still other times the children have learned that sibling rivalry is a good way to get the parents' attention, albeit negatively. In these cases, the problem is a lack of positive attention, an ongoing critical environment.

Finally, such sibling rivalry can result from there being too little attention to go around—the children are competing over the small amount of emotional resources in the family. The parents are not engaged and there is little or no consistent structure. They are emotionally absent parents, and are often preoccupied with their own issues such as addictions, depression, incapacitating anxiety, post-traumatic stress.

So you ask about each of these possibilities and identify triggers for the children's acting out and coach parents on appropriate skills. While you can have total family sessions to help set structure and rules of engagement among the children and encourage the parents to set structure and give positive feedback, your focus is likely to be on the parents' underlying issues. These become the focus of treatment.

Teen Oppositional Behavior

Parents come in complaining about their adolescent's attitude—she is always talking back, seeming to pick fights, flares up over "nothing"; the parents and teen have fallen into arguments that have been escalating—if they say black, she is likely, nine times out of ten, to say white . . . and roll her eyes.

Your first-line antidote to this is education: letting the parents know that a certain amount of pushing back is normal teen behavior, part of the individuation process, and that teens who are solidly compliant or withdrawn may be actually struggling. This can be a hard sell for parents who grew up in abusive or terribly restrictive families, who now see such behavior as unacceptable and feel that their only recourse is to mimic what their parents did. You want to empathize with their frustration, assess whether the teen is able to behave appropriately outside of the home and judge whether the parents are able, in fact, to circle back and have calm problem-solving conversations.

If not, you need to encourage them to do so. You also want to assess whether there is enough positive feedback offered to balance out the negative, whether the parents are on the same page and not undermining each other, whether there are age-appropriate limits and rules in place. If consequences are not consistent or clear, or the teen is playing one parent against the other and, in effect, has no consequences, the teen becomes entitled; we're back to Minuchin's dysfunctional structure, where the child is on top and the parents are the victims.

The biggest concern that you are apt to see for families in crisis is where battles with the teen do in fact consistently escalate, with both the teen and parents losing their tempers, getting tunnel vision and engaging in a power struggle. Here the protocol is the same as that with violent couples. You need to let them know that the teen is struggling emotionally and picking a fight as a way of coping. The parents' goal is to put out the emotional fire by remaining calm. Let them know the teen will likely now escalate to draw the parents back into the familiar pattern; they need to hold steady, allow the teen to come down and then circle back and problem-solve.

What makes this more difficult for parents than for couples is that they feel that by listening and letting the teen vent, they are in fact giving in to the teen, that the teen is winning because she has the last word. Here they need to be reassured that the teen cannot win, that she is not an adult and that there are consequences for bad behavior. The goal is helping the parents break the cycle by stepping up and changing their own behavior. If the teen comes into sessions, you can use sessions to help the family learn to self-regulate in the room, as well as help them solve the underlying problems triggering the power struggles.

Teens Who Are Acting Out

Here we are talking about teens who are falling into addictions, cutting behaviors, aggressive or anti-social behaviors, eating disorders, suicidal talk and/or gestures. Obviously, the behaviors themselves are not appropriate for brief treatment, and the issues, while having a family component, need individual attention. What you are likely to see in the first session is one of several possible presentations.

#1: The parents or parent comes in alone. They talk about their concerns and needing help understanding what clinically is the problem, how to talk about or manage it in the home, or what might be appropriate next steps: "My daughter is cutting herself. How do I get her to stop? What should I say when I notice cut marks on her arm? What does this mean, how can we help her?"

The problem is not yet helping the teen but helping the parent. You ask questions that give you a sense of the broader context: How long has this been going on, how has the parent dealt with it, what is her theory about why this is happening? You provide information about the diagnosis: Teens who cut tend to be like this. You talk about ways people cope with emotions, the internalizers vs. the externalizers. You talk about treatment options, about ways for the parent to respond at home, about how to talk to the teen about coming with her into a therapy session.

#2: The parents come in together but are arguing over whether or not the teen's problem is a problem, or how to deal with it. Unlike other courtroom dynamics, here you step up and educate the parents, letting them know what does and does not help. You don't need to help them sort out whose reality is right, but instead use your leadership to help them move towards helping their teen.

#3: The parents and teen come in together. This can go one of several ways. The best way is that the parents calmly express their concerns— "We're worried about your cutting and we don't know how to help you"—and the teen acknowledges the cutting and that she herself is worried about it and sees it as a problem she wants to fix. Here you talk about next steps of getting the teen into individual therapy.

#4. The parents and teen come in together, and the parents calmly talk express their concerns, but the teen denies it is a problem or doesn't want to talk about it. At home the parents and teen may argue over whose reality is right. Here you ask the parents to leave, build some rapport with the teen and look for the problem under the problem. Your challenge, as we'll discuss more fully in Chapter 6, is to be the ideal parent, get under the teen's defenses, find out the source of the self-injury behavior and see what the teen is willing to do next.

#5: The parents and teen come in and the parents gang up and rail at the teen. Often this replicates what has happened many times at home, or, in the safety of your office, what the parents have been hoping to do for a long time. Your first line of defense is to manage the process; try and have the parents settle and be less aggressive, and then draw the teen out.

What you are looking for in those opening moments is whether the teen can, in fact, push back. Teens who externalize generally do—they will emotionally ramp up and argue back. Now your challenge is to monitor and control the process: "Hold on, let her talk," or "Wait a minute, what you are most worried about?" If, however, the teen collapses under the parent assault and falls into a non-verbal slump, you need to stop the action. To continue only replicates the problem, the process that the teen probably experiences or fears most of the time. You lose rapport with the teen because she sees you as just another adult who is insensitive to her needs.

Ask the teen if it is okay to talk to her alone. She likely will grunt yes. Ask the parents to leave. Spend the time showing her that you are not like her parents: "Is this what they do a lot?" you ask. Build rapport by simply getting the teen to talk—ask about school, friends—then circle back to the parents' "worry." See what she sees as the problem. Express your own concern about the cutting behavior. Your goal is to establish a problem that the teen is willing to work on as the start of therapy.

As with other disorders, you need to decide in advance your own skill and comfort zone in dealing with the presenting and underlying problem. When in doubt refer out. Ask if the teen is willing to talk with someone about her problem and the underlying issues. If you are comfortable moving to individual therapy, offer that.

The goal in a crisis situation like this is to help the teen and family agree on next steps. You can start where the motivation is—that the teen is willing to possibly work on her cutting behavior, but what she wants is getting her parents overall to be less critical and micromanaging. Fine, go with it for now. Problems are all connected; your goal is to open the door to treatment, whatever form it may initially take.

Adult Children and Parent Issues

James and Marion, who are both nearing 60 years old, come in flapping an email. While they just returned from what they thought was a wonderful Christmas with their son, Howard, and his family, they now have received this email. Seemingly out of the blue, Howard writes about the way his parents have undermined his parenting of his children, yet again, and he is fed up. The email closes with words to the effect of: "I never want to talk to you again."

This is the cutoff that sends parents reeling. They have trouble connecting the dots. They come to you asking what they should do. Cutoffs like these are not unusual for adult children in their late twenties and thirties. What developmentally is often going on is that adult children are individuating. They are at a stage in their lives when they want to be their own persons, are sensitive to micromanaging, and usually are reflecting on past childhood injustices. They want to be seen as the adults that they are.

The aging parents are in a bind. If they do what Howard is asking, the danger is that cutoff will solidify; the longer they go without contact, the harder it is to re-engage. If they work hard to initiate contact, Howard feels that his parents are yet again dismissing his feelings and trying to be intrusive and controlling. You want to help them develop a middle ground.

The middle ground in these situations is to encourage the parents to not become defensive and to write a letter or email that acknowledges Howard's feelings and apologizes for the injustices that he feels he has incurred; that is the best they can do. Next, they need to try and keep the door open—sending cards for the children's birthdays, sending a one-line email saying that they are hoping he is doing okay. The idea here is that if Howard defrosts from his hard-line position, the awkwardness created by the past distance doesn't override the desire to connect.

Howard may, of course, merely throw the cards out and delete the emails; that's fine. If he reasserts himself and firmly sets up the boundary, the parents need to back off. Your focus then becomes one of helping them deal with their loss, deconstruct the source of the cutoff and encourage them to wait for an opening to re-engage.

But sometimes it is not the parents who come in, but the adult children. Now it is Howard who comes, saying that his parents are driving him crazy with their micromanagement and treating him like he is still a child. Or a group of siblings come in because they are worried about their mother's increasing struggle with memory, or are worried about their father's increased drinking and don't know how to approach him about it. Here your role is one of a consultant: helping Howard decide what he might want to say to his parents in a way they can hear it, to help them understand how he feels; or helping the siblings brainstorm options, helping them reach a consensus among them about courses of action and coaching them on how to communicate with their parent effectively.

Because you are doing brief therapy and because they are looking for specific help, your focus is generally not on possible deeper issues—whether or why Howard, for example, may always have a difficult time with individuals who seem controlling or do not recognize his own capabilities. You're free to raise these issues as part of your assessment and let him know what your kind of therapy can focus on, but unless he shows an interest in pursuing it, stay focused on the presenting problem; you don't want to replicate the problem by questioning his goals and needs. Finally, with both Howard and the sibling group, let them know that they are welcome to come in with their parents, offering them a safe place to have these important discussions. Coach them on how to present the invitation to their parents. Knowing that there is someone in the room who can monitor the process and help everyone feel heard goes a long way in helping them reduce their anxiety.

Situational Crises

Just as couples may come in because they are overwhelmed by life events and need support and guidance, so too may parents and families: a teen just got arrested for selling drugs and the parents are in shock; Grandma suddenly died and the youngest child is regressing and shows signs of separation anxiety; Dad was just diagnosed with Stage Four cancer and the mother is overwhelmed and the children haven't been told. Your focus here is to help the family put out the emotional fire, reduce the anxiety, help them break down the problem into smaller more manageable pieces and develop a preliminary course of action that they both can agree on. Education can be a powerful tool—you're once again like the family physician helping the parents or family put things in perspective, normalizing the symptoms that are overwhelming them. Allow them to talk about their shock and loss, but help steer them away from blame or self-criticism that can paralyze them. Offer behavioral strategies for dealing with the regression and separation anxiety. Help the parents develop a script for talking to the children or invite them to bring them. Yes, you will undoubtedly see the emotional wounds, the differing visions and the breakdowns in communication that may have been part and parcel of their relationships come to the fore under the stress, but your initial focus is, for now, on decision-making and action. Other issues can be addressed later once the crisis has subsided.

As with our couple treatment maps, hopefully these maps will help reduce your own anxiety and maximize the focus of those opening situations with families. Again, when in doubt, get supervision or consultation from a colleague or refer out. In the next chapter, we will shift gears and drill down into the goals of the all-important first session.

5 First Session Goals

Imagine yourself driving to your first therapy session. You may not be in crisis, but you are eager to talk to someone, to get started. You're also understandably a bit anxious about talking to a stranger, and are wondering what he or she will be like. What is it you most would like to get out of this session by the time it is over an hour later?

Probably a few things: You'd like to feel that the therapist really heard you, that she understood your story and how you were feeling and that a connection was in fact made. That she seemed competent, and that sense of competency helped you relax and lean into the relationship, knowing there is someone there to help you sort out your thoughts and feelings and guide you through the process. You probably want to have some new or better sense of what is really the problem and some idea of how to fix it. Finally, and probably most importantly, you just want to feel better when you walk out—because all these other expectations were met. You now feel less alone with your struggles, that there is path out of them, that you're glad you made this decision and took this step.

For couples and families in crisis, they, like you, want to feel better when they walk out than when they walked in by having these same needs and expectations met. This is what this chapter is about: mapping out the goals and structure, both theirs and your own, of that all-important first session. Just as having treatment maps at the ready helps you hit the ground running and effectively use the session time and process, so too does knowing ahead of time what it is you most need to do and not do in the first session.

So what is it that you need to do? How do we translate the client's needs into your own clinical tasks? Here is list of what needs to get accomplished by the end of the first session:

- Build rapport
- Define problems and expectations
- Assess
- Change the emotional climate
- Link problems and offer a preliminary treatment plan
- Define next steps

We'll take this one by one, discussing the content and means of accomplishing each of these goals.

Building Rapport

Building rapport is the most elemental of clinical tasks and the core of any clinical approach. Rapport is basically helping the couple or family members feel safe. It is the sense of comfort and connection that you are most hoping to find as you drive to your therapy appointment. Let's look at specific ways of creating this:

Listening

In a 1997 landmark and well-cited study, Levinson, Roter, Mullooly, Dull and Frankel (1997) brought together two sets of doctors—those who had never been sued for malpractice and those who had been sued two or more times. While the basic information that each set of doctors gave to the patients in the study was the same, what was different in the styles of the two groups was that the non-sued doctors took time to explain to the process, were funny and helped the patients laugh, and listened a mere three minutes longer to their patients. As a result the patients of these doctors essentially felt heard and liked their doctors more. What this study underscores is just how powerful an antidote active listening and positively engaging with clients are to the anxiety that clients so often feel. For clients in crisis who are likely even more anxious than the typical client, this is even more important and powerful. Listening helps clients settle and creates that sense of caring and safety, something they often don't find in their own close relationships.

Mirror and Match

John sits with his legs crossed; you sit with your legs crossed. Ann leans forward; you lean forward. Mirroring someone's body position subconsciously builds a sense of connection and trust. So too does using the language of each client's perceptual system. John may be a visualizer—he thinks in terms of images. You can tell by the fact that his eyes move up when he is thinking and he uses visual language when he talks—I *see* what you mean, the way it *looks* to me. You talk back to him in the same language: "What do you *see* going on here, John?"

Ann, on the other hand, thinks in terms of feelings and sensations. Her eyes look down when you ask her a question and she uses kinesthetic language: "I *feel* that John doesn't understand me; I can't *grasp* what he is saying." You again use her language when talking with her.

Finally, there are those who think in terms of words rather than images or sensations. Here Tom looks straight ahead when thinking and uses auditory language: "What it *sounds* like you're saying is . . .", or "What I *hear* you saying is . . . ." Again, talk in Tom's perceptual system.

You also, especially at the beginning of the session, want to match the individual's energy level. If John is animated or talks loudly, you want to do the same, while with Ann who is quiet and cautious, you gear it down and match her tone. This mirroring and matching is subtle but, like active listening, is powerful in building rapport.

Highlight Similarities

Good salespeople know that customers are likely to trust them if the customers sense that they have something in common. Here is where you mention to a car salesperson that you need more space, not only for your kids but also for all their school and sports stuff, and she, too, starts to talk about loading up strollers and soccer bags into her own SUV. Or the customer mentions needing to drive to Kansas to see relatives for Thanksgiving, and the salesperson mentions having a brother who lives just outside of Kansas City. Rapport is built when there are similarities between two people.

Many of us do this naturally in our personal relationships when talking with someone we've just met, but such self-disclosure in therapy has often been considered inappropriate by those in psychodynamic circles. In our brief framework, where we need to connect and build trust with clients quickly, self-disclosure as a way of building similarities goes a long way. This doesn't mean that you need to ramble on about yourself, but intentionally mentioning that you had the same problem with your kids and bedtimes when they were young, or making a quick reference that you too were in the Army helps overcome the strangeness of meeting a stranger; it helps clients feel that you can understand what they have experienced, and this in turn helps them relax.

As with other aspects of developing your own clinical style, proactively decide where you stand on this issue of self-disclosure, and define your own clinical boundaries in advance, rather than reactively responding to your own countertransference with any given couple or family.

Demonstrate Leadership and Expertise

Demonstrating leadership, as we discussed earlier, comes from taking an active role in shaping the process of the session. Alongside listening, this is probably the most important approach to building safety and rapport. By stepping up and demonstrating leadership, you counter the high emotion and, often, chaos that couples and families in crisis are experiencing. By actively managing the process, you create safety by not allowing the problem to be replicated in the room.

Here you make sure that everyone has the opportunity to tell their story and define what they see as problems. You prevent interruptions, but also make sure that one person doesn't dominate the session in either emotion or time. You take an active role in shaping the conversation by asking leading and hard questions rather than falling into the "and how does that make you feel" type of response. The impression you want to create is one of being sensitive, in charge, without being micromanaging and controlling.

If leadership is letting clients know what you are able to step up and be in charge, expertise is stepping up and letting clients know what you are knowledgeable and experienced. Just as you are likely to feel reassured knowing you're talking to the attending physician in the emergency room rather than the intern who looks like your younger brother, so too do clients. Let them know about your experience, and if you do happen to look like a younger brother, offset this impression by freely sharing information that helps them understand your clinical perspective and knowledge base.

While more of the heavy lifting of building rapport will come in the opening minutes of the first session as you help the couple or family "settle" and feel comfortable with you and the environment, it is also likely that you will be weaving these rapport-building techniques throughout the session, especially when you encounter caution and resistance—whether it be the "leaning out" partner, the slow-to-warm shy child or the don't want-to-be-here teen. Your goal is to build that connection before the session ends in order to ensure that all the clients agree with your treatment plan and see you as the right person to deliver it.

Define Problems and Expectations

As we discussed in Chapter 1, it is important to track the process and stay in lockstep with the couple or family throughout sessions. Because this first session sets the foundation for all that is to follow, it is especially important that you and the clients be on the same page about problems and expectations.

Problems are obviously about what each individual wants to get fixed and are generally imbedded within the story you hear after you ask "How can I help?" or "What brings you here?" Linda talks about uncovering Brad's sextexting and that she wants it to stop, but also that she doesn't know what to do about the anger and hurt that she feels. Brad wishes Linda would not "blow things out of proportion" and would stop interrogating him about details, but also says that he wishes that she would be more affectionate. Similarly, Davon wants Alicia to back him up when he disciplines the children, while Alicia wants Davon to stop being so tough on the kids and spend more time with the family rather than watching sports all weekend. The number of problems can quickly multiply; add more folks to the mix—the live-in grandmother, the defiant 14-year-old—and it can be easy for you to feel overwhelmed.

You need to sort and sift and make sure that everyone is heard, that what each want changed is noted. And because we are doing brief therapy, you want these problems and goals stated in concrete behavioral terms so the partner or family member knows exactly what the other is looking for. What does Linda need from Brad to know that he has stopped sextexting, or what is she looking for to feel that she can begin to trust him? What does Brad mean by Linda not "blowing things out of proportion," or wanting her to do differently to feel that she is truly more affectionate?

What you will often see and hear at this point is defensiveness and arguing over whose reality is right—Linda denying that she is not affectionate, Davon pointing out the chapter and verse of times that he has spent with the family that seem to go unnoticed. This is where the courtroom behavior settles in as they each make their case to you to arbitrate and rule. You emphasize that each person at this point doesn't need to agree with the other's perception, but also that it is not your role to arbitrate. Instead, you say, you want to help them understand exactly what each needs most; arguing over realities is counterproductive.

Your stance here is that of reshaping expectations as they are unfolding, but there are other ways you can uncover their expectations more directly. One way is to ask about previous therapy experiences: Have Brad and Linda been in couple therapy before? If yes, you ask about their experience: "Why didn't you go back to see that person again?" They respond by saying what while the previous therapist was "nice," she didn't do much during the session except ask them how they were feeling. They felt like they were having the same arguments in the office that they were having at home, so they saw no point in continuing.

Their response tells you two things: that they are looking for someone who is more active and able to change the process, and that they are not ones to openly speak up when they are not getting want they need; instead, they fade away. You can talk at this point about your own style and how it is different, and tell them that you will be asking if what you are doing is helpful and that you'd like them to speak up.

You can also directly ask them what they are hoping to get out of coming to see you. Here they may say that they need to have a safe place to talk things out, or need help learning how to communicate better, or that they really don't know, having not done this before. Here again you speak up and let them know how you think about therapy, what you focus on and what you can help them do.

For couples and families in crisis, their expectation is that you will somehow put out the fire of the crisis; we're back to your doctor and your skin rash. While they likely would each like to know who you think is right or wrong and are sensitive to whose side you may seem to take, all this will be cancelled out if they feel better by the time they leave—because you have helped them feel safe and heard and you have offered them a path forward. As the session progresses, look for opportunities to clarify your approach—by saying, for example, that you are less interested in the content details but more interested in helping them together come up with a plan to resolve a problem, that you want to help them see where their communication breaks down, that you hope to help them uncover the problem under the problem. Such defining and clarifying helps ensure that your style and their needs match.

Assess

Okay, you're up. While the first two goals were about the clients and laying down a foundation, here it is about you and what you need to know to frame out your initial treatment plan. Following your own clinical orientation or treatment maps, you may ask questions to understand where and how the couple or family gets stuck in solving their own problems, and to track down emotional wounds and differing visions. Just as your doctor asks about whether or not your rash is itchy or whether you have been out in the woods lately, you might ask Linda, after you note that the couple has been married eight years, how she feels she has changed over the course of the relationship, matching her answer to your own relationship-rollercoaster framework. Similarly, if Brad says that he tends to avoid conflict, you may ask more about other elements of the martyr role—following shoulds rather than wants, periodically feeling resentful because he doesn't feel like Linda appreciates all his hard work or doesn't step up and help—that are possibly fueling his risk for having the affair. You may explore with Davon how he envisions his role as a father, or with Alicia what it means to her that Davon is watching sports on the weekend.

With each answer you are looking to discover whether they are struggling with a learning problem or a problem about learning. Davon, perhaps, simply doesn't have a variety of parenting skills in his parenting tool set—a learning problem—and so could benefit from your suggestions. Or he actually does, but with his anger comes tunnel vision, which makes it difficult for him to use them—a problem about learning. Their answers also help you see where and how the couple or family falls away from the adult stance, and helps you confirm or adjust your initial hypothesis, giving you a more solid footing before moving on to presenting your plan. But the questions do more than give you new content; they also change the process and, potentially, the climate. With each question, you are poking a hole in the bubble that is their stories. Your questions raise new perspectives and deepen the conversation in the room, changing each client's narrative and assumptions.

As you assess, keep in mind each person's presenting problem so your questions maintain a linkage needed to keep the client in lockstep with you. If you decide to explore with Davon, for example, his own father's style of parenting or drill down into Brad and Linda's sex life, explain your rationale for moving into this territory: "The reason I'm asking about your dad, Davon, is that often our parenting styles are either copying or reacting against what our own parents did, and that your vision may be different from Alicia's." Or "I realize that my asking about your sex life probably feels a bit awkward and I appreciate your being open. Often it is these same feelings of awkwardness that keep couples from understanding what they each need and want." By helping them understand how you are thinking and where you are going, by connecting it back to their concerns, you reduce their anxiety and encourage them to be more open.

As we'll discuss further in the next chapter, your assessment in this first session needs to be contained. Some pieces of the clinical puzzle may have to explored in future sessions. For this first session your goal is to gather enough of the information you need to confirm your initial hypothesis and diagnosis.

Change the Emotional Climate

Deepening the conversation through your assessment questions is one way of helping to change the emotional climate in the room, which is so essential to creating a successful first session. Without such a shift, clients are likely to not only feel frustrated but also question the usefulness of therapy, and will likely not return. As with rapport, you are looking for opportunities to create this change throughout the session. Here are several additional techniques you can use.

Focus on Soft Emotions

As mentioned earlier, most couples and families in crisis come in angry or frustrated. One of the simplest and most effective ways of changing the climate is to focus on softer emotions like worry, fear and sadness. You can do this in two ways. One is to simply change the language that a client is using. When Davon says he is angry at Alicia for not supporting him in his discipline of the children, ask in a quiet tone what he is most worried about. If he denies that he is worried and says he is just angry, rephrase the question: "What are you worried will happen with your children if they don't receive the structure and follow the standards that you are trying to create?" or "What are you worried will happen if Alicia continues to not support you?"

By asking the question in a calm, quiet way, you are going under Davon's defenses rather than assaulting them, and this is usually enough to shift the tone. What your question taps into is the fact that beneath anger and control is often anxiety; his emotions are reframed. And even if Davon holds fast to his position of anger, Alicia is also hearing what you are asking; she has the opportunity to make the connection that helps her possibly redefine her husband's anger and see what may actually be driving it. This in turn may change her emotional state.

You can also tap into softer emotions by picking up on non-verbal expressions. When you notice Linda getting teary in spite of her angry-sounding words, hold up your hand and stop her: "Hold on a minute, Linda. I notice that your eyes look teary—how are feeling right now?"—again, said in a quiet voice. Linda may then begin to cry.

What to expect next is that Brad may make some angry statement. Rather than being supportive, he may seem annoyed or complain about something that Linda has done in the past. Why may he do this? Because he is uncomfortable with her sadness; it is an emotional shift from their normal bantering; the old pattern is broken and he is now anxious. By getting angry, by bringing up the past, he is essentially trying to pick an argument to re-establish the old pattern. Your job is not to allow this happen. Hold up your hand, ask Brad to wait, help Linda not fall for the bait and shift back towards anger; instead, help her refocus back on her sadness.

Look for and Neutralize Transference Cues

Linda says that she always feels criticized by Brad. Brad says that Linda always shuts down when he wants to talk. Davon says his dad was never dependable. Alicia says that Davon easily talks about himself, but never really listens to her.

How do these comments help you? They tell you what not to do—don't be critical of Linda, shut down with Brad, be undependable with Davon, not listen closely to Alicia. Here we are talking about emotional wounds: what each is sensitive to. Many believe that therapy is, at some base level, about reparenting—being the ideal parent or the ideal partner to each client. Looking for transference cues is about that—proactively avoiding each client's emotional potholes and consciously offering what they each need most. By quickly realizing what you don't want to do, you can then know what to do. This neutralizes the stirring of negative transference reactions and helps you sidestep falling into the couple's or family's triggers, dysfunctional patterns and recreation of the problem. It is another element of building safety and trust.

So, just as you stay alert for clues to the couple's or family's expectations, you want to stay alert for such transference cues, such as Linda and Brad's comments. You can also ask about them directly: "Tell me, when you look over the range of your relationships, what it is that others do that most bothers you?". Linda mentions criticism, Brad shutting down and feeling closed off. You don't need to drill down into these as a psychodynamic therapist might, but now knowing what not to do, you can change the emotional climate by make a conscious effort to offer what each client needs—complimenting Linda and being more interactive and less passive with Brad.

In addition to changing the climate, and with it creating a positive impression of you and your type of therapy, your sensitive communication serves as good role-modeling for the other partner. Alongside the deepening of the conversation comes the opportunity to see how healthier conversations unfold; even over a short period of time, clients will absorb your approach and can begin to incorporate it into their own everyday communications.

Provide Education

Your doctor explains how your skin reacts to toxic substances, creating a rash; your mechanic explains that, no, you didn't connect the battery incorrectly or leave the car lights on too long, but the alternator is worn out, is not able to recharge the battery and needs to simply be replaced. You do the same when you talk about the relationship rollercoaster or the relationship triangle, explain to parents how their efforts to respond to their child's anxiety only seems to make it worse, or describe how dysfunctional patterns are easy to fall into and how they can be changed.

What information does is change, through your reframing, redefining and relabeling of the problem, the explanation and narrative that clients have understandably created in their minds. They connect the behavioral dots in a new way, as well as see you as someone with knowledge and leadership. By your psychological deconstruction of the dynamics they are describing, Brad and Linda understand how Linda's persistent questioning is tied to a larger sense of grief and loss of trust, and Alicia has a new way of looking at Davon's reactions to her non-support around parenting. The client's self-critical or blaming self-talk changes and with it their emotions, as they are able to connect the behavioral dots in a new way.

Link Problems and Offer a Preliminary Treatment Plan

Talking about education actually naturally brings us to our next goal: linking problems and offering a preliminary treatment plan. If we think of the first session as divided up into three sections, the first section consists of defining problems—this is what bothers me—and clarifying expectations—here is my approach, as well as building rapport and looking for transference cues. In the second, you uncover the information you need to understand the problems under the presenting problems, confirm your hypothesis and look for opportunities to change the emotional climate.

Now in this last section it's time to bring it all home, to link the first and second sections together and to offer a preliminary treatment plan: Given your problems, my approach and what I understand, here is what I think we need to do next.

This is the point that your physician turns the corner and says that that rash is probably contact dermatitis, explains why and pulls out her prescription pad, or the mechanic says that the problem is most likely the alternator and once it is replaced you won't have to worry about starting your car. This is what you do when you say to Linda and Brad that you think of affairs as being bad solutions to other problems that, as Linda has been struggling with, encompass grief and trust, and that her obsessing and questioning are common. You also underscore Brad's own discontent—the lack of affection and his tendency to fall into a martyr role and not speak up about his needs and resentments. You show them the relationship triangle, how the affair is about Brad moving into the persecutor role, and how the way out is by both of them taking concrete steps towards moving towards the adult position.

Here too you summarize Alicia's worry about the effects of Davon's disciplinary style on the children, and Davon's own frustration and feeling undermined by her, and how this inability to come up with an approach that suits both of them invariably leads to confusion for the children, and polarization and ongoing tension for them as parents. You draw a diagram of Minuchin's ideal family structure, emphasizing the need for them to have that solid line between, as well as below, them, in order to work as a team and establish a structure that helps their children feel safe rather than anxious.

You are bringing together your work in the first two sections, as well as linking together each client's view of the problems with the new framework you provide. Like your doctor, you address the symptoms and the worries and offer next steps. But first you need to see what they do next.

Countering Objections

Your doctor is ready to hand off the prescription but you pipe up and say you are worried about some of the side-effects that she mentioned. The mechanic is ready to roll your car into the shop, but you balk when he says it will cost $250 for parts and labor, and you say can't afford it. You suggest a medication consult for a client and he literally pulls back, saying that he doesn't do meds. Or you suggest that the parents bring in all the children next time, but they say they don't see the purpose in doing that and that it is way too much of a logistical hassle.

What you are always aiming for is agreement, the nodding of heads, the "that makes sense" from everyone, and if it is there, you, like the doctor and mechanic, move forward to the next steps. But sometimes you get push-back. As we'll discuss more fully in the next chapter, objections are most likely to come up when you have fallen out of lockstep somewhere along the way in the session, or failed to fully cover the other session goals. But independent of the cause, you need to know how to handle them. Here are some guidelines to help you navigate.

First Session Goals 101

Always Agree and Remain Calm

If you've ever watched a skilled interviewee—a seasoned politician or a CEO of a company, for example—you'll notice that their response to a question, even if it sounds critical or provocative, is likely to be positive. They say something like, "I'm glad you asked that," or "That's a good question," in a calm way, settling rather than escalating any tension. You want to do the same: "I'm glad you're letting me know how you feel."

Reduce Anxiety Through Consensus

Talking about consensus is pointing out how others have reacted or feel. Here your doctor says that yes, she realizes that the medication could have side-effects, but in all the years she has been prescribing it, she hasn't in fact had anyone complain of any adverse effects. Similarly, your mechanic may say that he could replace the alternator with a rebuilt one, but he has found that customers complain that they often fail within a year or two.

Your version may be to say to the client that while you understand he may not be comfortable taking medication, research shows that it reduces anxiety and depression, and taken even in the short term, it can break the cycle and help him put other behavioral tools in place. Similarly, you say to the parents that many families you've worked with find that having the children in the session helps to develop a plan that everyone can agree on, both saving time in therapy and creating positive results more quickly at home.

Uncover the Objection Under the Objection

What's the problem under the problem? Here you ask: "Just so I can better understand, tell me what concerns you most about medication?" or "What bothers you most about having all the children come to a session?" and you find out it is about becoming dependent on the medication or that the children will be too anxious meeting with a stranger and may embarrass the parents. Knowing the problem under the problem, you can then problem-solve: encouraging the client to raise his concerns specifically with the doctor, or coaching the parents on how to talk to the children in advance about what to expect and reassuring them that you are comfortable helping them maintain control.

Make It Easy for the Client to Circle Back

You want to counter their concerns, but don't want clients to feel pressured. If they do, you will, at best, get a passive compliance that will eventually collapse. Unless you feel that your suggestions are mandatory and are willing to go to the mat for your position—that you are not comfortable continuing therapy unless a client has an evaluation for addiction, for example—back off and leave the door open: "Okay, think about the medication; in the meantime, let's focus on some anxiety-reducing skills next time and see how they work" or "Okay, think about the idea of bringing in the children, and next time the three of us will meet again and we'll focus on coming up with a new bedtime routine."

Define Next Steps

Okay, they've agreed with your plan, or they had questions and objections, but you were able to address their concerns and reduce their anxiety through education, consensus and reassurance. It's time to wrap it up. Here your doctor says that she will give you a sample of the medication and call in the prescription, and asks that you give her a call if your rash isn't better in three days. The mechanic says that he can do the alternator Tuesday morning and can get you a loaner car to use. Here you may not only schedule the next appointment but also say what might be the focus in the next session.

But you also want to give homework. We mentioned assigning homework as a way of helping clients practice new skills outside the office and breaking dysfunctional patterns, such as those around domestic violence. Homework not only speeds up the treatment process; it also helps clients understand that therapy is not about playing out the "fight of the week," but actually intentionally changing what they do and applying skills in their everyday lives. In Chapter 9 we'll talk about common helpful homework assignments.

What Not to Do: The Four Sources of Resistance

As a way of summarizing and bringing into bolder relief your goals for the first session, let's look at the "ungoals," so to speak—what it is that you absolutely want to avoid doing in the first session and future sessions that breed resistance, resulting in clients dropping out or not following through on the treatment plan. While traditional psychodynamic approaches see resistance as a given of the therapeutic process as the client's defenses are challenged, in our brief therapy model resistance is seen as arising from one or more of four interrelated sources—all, unfortunately, connected to you.

No Agreement on the Problem

This can come at that the end of the first session when you present your treatment plan. You draw Minuchin's diagram of an ideal family structure and stress the need for Davon and Alicia to be on the same page, but Davon isn't buying it. Instead, he is holding onto his version of reality and that Alicia is the cause of problems. These become the objections you need to counter, but if you don't have the time to address them, or they remain silent and don't voice them, the couple or family drops out, feeling that you are describing a problem that they don't see.

But this lack of agreement can also come at the beginning of the session. Here is the court-order couple or family who has no investment in treatment, blame the community for misunderstanding them and are resistant from the start. Your challenge is to help them identify a problem that all can agree on—perhaps that of getting the community agencies to leave them alone—but if you fail or this is not possible, they drop out. Because there is no consensus on problems, there is no consensus to work on them.

Pacing: Too Fast or Too Slow

Too fast means that you give the couple or family a plan and homework that is too overwhelming for them. In an effort to emotionally move Linda and Brad along, you ask them to write love letters to each other. But Linda is still too entrenched in her hurt and can't summon the words and doesn't do the assignment. Or you ask a family to develop a bedtime routine or reward chart for the children, and, though they seem to understand, they really don't—they disagree about times or they don't fully understand how to break down chores for each child per day. They get frustrated and don't do the homework or, worse yet, decide this is all too difficult and drop out. You have moved too quickly, failed to fully have agreement when making your suggestions, failed to pick up on any non-verbal signs of hesitation.

But moving too slow is the more likely culprit that can surface in the early sessions with couples and families in crisis. Given their high emotional state, they are looking for answers, a clear plan, a change in the emotional climate. But if you didn't have clear treatment maps in mind to offer them, if you were not active enough in the session and didn't demonstrate leadership, or if the problem was replicated in the room and the emotional climate remained the same, they leave the first session feeling frustrated and don't return.

Faulty Expectations of the Process

Both lack of agreement on the problem and poor pacing are actually about failing to meet the couple's or family's expectations about therapy. But it can unfold within the process of the session itself: Davon imagined you would take his side against Alicia; Linda expected you to be more condemning of Brad; parents thought you would starting some type of play therapy with their 6-year-old, rather than spending the entire session as a family or asking them to bring in the other children to the next session.

Again, clients cannot not have expectations about what will unfold, but if you fail to ask about expectations or miss the non-verbal or verbal cues that you are not in lockstep, they wind up disgruntled and don't return, or half-heartedly participate.

Emotional Wounds Are Triggered

And maybe you didn't catch any of these issues because you missed transference cues and triggered emotional wounds, and the couple or family essentially shut down. Alicia sees you as another domineering male like Davon, Brad feels criticized the way he does with Linda. You inadvertently replicate the problem and the emotional climate stays, for them, the same; instead of feeling safe and hopeful, they feel unsafe and discouraged. While transference cues and emotional wounds can be difficult to pick up, especially when the process is emotional or you have many people in the room, your starting point for incorporating them into the session process is proactively looking for them. With practice and experience your awareness increases.

So to avoid falling into these therapeutic potholes you need to be clear and focused on the goals and tasks we've outlined: be active and demonstrate leadership, and build rapport and balance the system. Take the time to define and clarify expectations and emotional wounds, and look for transference cues. Skip doing the three-session assessment, the let's-pick-this-up-again-next-week last sentence, or filling the session by plowing through endless forms and intake questionnaires. Avoid replicating the problem in the room; be like your doctor and offer that initial assessment and plan. Make sure they agree and let them know that you and this process can help pull them out of this muck.

These goals hopefully provide you with focus for crafting a solid first-session structure. In the next chapter we'll look at process, drilling down and breaking down how to actually run the crucial first session.

References

Levinson, W., Roter, D. L., Mullooly, J. P., Dull, V. T. & Frankel, R. M. (1997). Physician-patient communication. The relationship with malpractice claims among primary care physicians and surgeons. *JAMA, 277*(7), 553–559.

6 First Session Process

So, we've mapped out the goals for that all-important first session. In this chapter, we'll look at the action steps you need to take to put all these goals in place. As mentioned in the last chapter, we can think of the first session as divided up into three sections, and that is the format we will follow here. As a way of illustrating the pacing of the session we'll follow two cases—one couple, one family—approaching the session from a cognitive-behavioral model; understandably, your own approach may be different. Try not to get caught up in the clinical aspects of these cases, but rather see the clinical material as a medium for describing the first session process.

But before we start, we need to underscore two points that we've mentioned before that are vital to successfully managing the process of the first session. One is the need to make sure that the clients are in lockstep with you through the process—that is, that you and they stay in agreement and on the same page each step along the way. You do this by tracking their reactions and not letting interpretations or suggestions go forward without solid buy-in. If you fail to notice resistance along the way, the climate will fail to change, and your closing—the presentation of your treatment plan and next steps—will be met with objections.

The other, equally important, is the need to watch the clock. As the one in charge of running the session, you want to make sure you have enough time to accomplish all that you need to. The only way to do this by paying close attention to the unfolding of the session. If you fail to leave enough time to present your treatment plan, the couple or family will likely leave feeling frustrated and question the helpfulness of you and your approach. To help you begin to think in this way, we'll map out approximate times for each of the sections and tasks.

Initial Contact

Isabel leaves you a voice mail saying that she would like to come in for couple therapy with her husband Luis as soon as possible. They had a "difficult weekend" and she sounds agitated.

Daniel sends you an email: He came across your website, noticed that you did family therapy and wondered if you had openings. He, too, would like to come in as soon as possible. While you notice that he doesn't leave a phone number, you do notice that the signature at the bottom of the email lists his title as president of a local manufacturing company.

Therapy starts now. What do you need to do? One is to respond to each of these clients as soon as possible. Couples and families in crisis are looking for immediate help and your quick reply sends an important message that you are responsive and sensitive to their needs. On the practical side, your delay in contacting them is likely to result in their finding someone else.

So you return Isabel's call. She thanks you for getting back to her so quickly and says that this is actually a good time to talk; though she is at work, she is on her break. You say that you received her message and are calling to see if she had any questions and to set an appointment time.

What you do want to do with Isabel at this initial contact is answer any important make-or-break questions. Here clients ask about insurance or the flexibility of your schedule, or whether they can bring their baby if they can't find a babysitter. You may not take the client's insurance or you don't have office hours on Saturday mornings, or no, you are not comfortable with them bringing the baby. These are important issues for the client and your asking about them before the first session clarifies expectations and avoids you both wasting your time. If you decide this is not a good fit, you need to be ready to refer her on to someone else.

What you don't want to do is start individual therapy on the phone. Why? Because this will unbalance the system. So, when Isabel says that she and Luis had such a horrible argument on Saturday that she wound up spending the night at a friend's house, you don't say, "Tell me more." Instead, you say that you are sorry to hear that, that that must have been frightening for both of them. And when she then says that while Luis said that he would come to therapy if she found someone, she is worried that he may back out. You then talk to her about how to talk to Luis—that she'd like him to come one time and see what happens—and you tell her that he is welcome to call you before the session if he has any questions. You refer her (and him) to your website, if you have one, to give them a better idea of you and your approach, and offer an appointment; throughout, you sound calm and attentive.

Because you don't have a phone number for Daniel, you respond to his email—again, as quickly as possible. You offer appointment times within the next couple of days, let him know that he is welcome to contact you by email or phone if he has any particular questions and refer him to your website for further information.

The aim here is to demonstrate responsiveness, concern and professionalism. Being deliberate in how you sound to Isabel or word your email to Daniel goes a long way in creating an initial impression, and your own website and profile do so even more. You cannot make an initial impression.

Preparing Ahead

Before you meet this couple or family you want to be mentally engaged and proactive. Rather than waiting to see what they present, you instead want to anticipate what they may expect and need most. Here your preliminary impressions and treatment maps come into play. We already know that Isabel is the "leaning in" partner, as is Daniel. We also know from Isabel's report that Luis may be ambivalent about therapy, and that he is "leaning out" and you may have to work harder to build rapport and soothe his concerns. The situation Isabel describes sounds like a "Big Fight" presenting problem, and we can already begin to map out the need to place this in its larger context, to assuage the emotional impact it may have had, to track with them why this confrontation was somehow different than others and to sort out what the underlying issues may be.

With Daniel, we obviously have less to work with. We don't know the precipitating event, his concern or even who may attend. That's fine. What we do know is that he is interested in family therapy, rather than individual or couple therapy and that he is president of a company. This lets us know that he is likely comfortable being in charge and directive; he may be interested in the bottom-line results. Perhaps—we'll have to see—but this gives us a bit of a clue to his possible expectations.

What's important here is to anticipate and plan. If someone calls up about domestic violence, a child with behavioral problems, a partner having an affair or a couple disagreeing about parenting or struggling with a teen who has an "attitude," you can begin to decide before the first session what it is you want to focus on in the session to confirm your initial impressions and thoughts, and begin to consider what it is you need to do and offer by the end of the session.

Part 1a: Opening (5–10 Minutes)

You meet Luis and Isabel in the waiting room, shake hands and lead them back to your office. They sit next to each other on the couch, Luis a bit stiffly. You thank him for coming, say that you and Isabel talked briefly on the phone, ask if they have looked at your website. Isabel says she has; Luis shakes his head. You then go on and tell them both about your background and experience and ask whether they have been in therapy before. Both shake their heads. You then go on and briefly explain your approach, that you want to provide a safe place for them to discuss their problems, help them see where they get stuck, help them learn other ways of communicating. They nod their heads as you are describing this, a good sign that they are so far in lockstep with you. You then go ahead and ask how long they have been married (two years), children (none), what they do for work. You ask Luis some details about his management job to begin to build rapport and see if he is able to open up; he does, and describes the team he has to supervise.

When you to out to the waiting room to meet Daniel, he stands, shakes hands and introduces you to his wife, Kim, and his daughter, Emma, who looks to be around 15 or 16 years old. Again, you shake hands, and notice that Emma doesn't make eye contact. You escort them back to your office. Daniel and Kim sit together on the couch, Emma on the chair closer to you. Again, you thank all for coming and ask if they have seen your website; Daniel and Kim have, Emma has not. You explain a bit about your background and ask if they have been in therapy before.

Daniel speaks up and says that he and Kim were in couple therapy many years ago and found it "moderately helpful." You ask what he means, and he says that they went for a few sessions and got some issues on the table but then stopped because they didn't feel like the therapist was giving them much in terms of feedback or suggestions. You ask Kim if that is true and she nods her head. You ask each about any experience with individual therapy and all say they haven't. You go to explain that you tend to use a cognitive-behavioral approach, that you tend to see problems in families coming from the way individuals bounce off of each other, that you look at where they may struggle solving problems and that you generally give suggestions and homework to help them change these patterns and learn skills. You notice Daniel and Kim nod their heads; you ask Emma if this makes sense to her and she quietly says yes.

As with Luis and Isabel, you ask basic questions—how long married (18 years), other children (Emma is their only child) and jobs—noticing that Daniel once again supplies the answers. You specifically ask Kim about her work and, like Luis, she seems to open up. You ask Emma her age (16), where she goes to school, whether she enjoys it (she does), what she hopes to do after high school (go to college and study architecture). Her voice is quiet; again, no eye contact.

What you are doing in these opening minutes is helping clients settle—give them an opportunity to get used to your voice, to get oriented to the room and you, and understand a bit about your approach in order to clarify expectations. Luis and Isabel seem to be on board with your approach. You deliberately pointed out to Daniel and his family that you take an active role, to offset the couple's criticism of their last therapy experience, and talk about patterns because you know it is easy for parents in crisis to view the problems stemming from the teen herself.

What you're also looking at and for is where you need to shore up the safety and rapport. Luis seems to be the one leaning out, but his stiffness may also reflect the awkwardness of being in therapy for the first time.

His opening up about his job is, again, a good sign. Similarly, you see how Daniel is taking the lead; as we suspected, he is probably used to being in charge, and as his therapy story possibly indicates, is looking for results. You need to make sure that he doesn't dominate the session but also doesn't feel sidelined. You need to create a balance between him and Kim.

But there is also Emma to be concerned about. She is clearly shy and may easily feel intimidated by having such a dominating dad, and we could imagine her being dragged here and feeling unsafe. You need to let her know you are in her corner and not let her parents gang up on her. That would only likely replicate what is already happening at home.

Part 1b: Client Story (10 Minutes)

"Tell me how I can help you." Not surprisingly, perhaps, Isabel speaks up: "We've been having a difficult time in the last few months, lots of arguments about little things—housework, bills—but Saturday we had a big fight." Isabel starts to tear up. "It just got so out of hand, both of us were yelling, I don't remember about what, but then Luis pushed me, hard against the kitchen counter." She is openly crying now. "I said I'm leaving, Luis yelled at me to come back, but I left and went to a friend's house. I came back the next day, but we really haven't talked since."

"You are sad," you say. "What upset you the most?" you ask in a gentle voice.

"That Luis got so angry. I've never seen him like this." You make eye contact and nod.

It's tempting to ask more about this, but you don't. Why? Because you don't want to fuel Isabel's sadness, have it dominate the session and leave you little time to connect with Luis and accomplish all the rest that you need to do, leaving him with the impression that you are taking Isabel's side. Instead, you turn to Luis: "Tell me what happened."

Luis takes a deep breath. "I'm sorry I pushed her," he says to you, then turns to her. She nods. "I think it got worse because I had had a couple of beers, but she had a couple too. But I guess what got me the most is that I'm fed up." His voice is getting louder. "She keeps running up these bills. I've talked to her about it, we sat down and I showed her the budget, she agrees, but then she goes off and spends another $200 on shoes." He's angry now. "She's out of control!"

"You're out of control," says Isabel. "You're the one always looking over my shoulder! I work too. You are always telling me what I can do and not do!" She's yelling too.

"No, I don't. I feel a responsibility that we don't go in debt, but you . . ."

"Hold on," you say, and hold up your hand. You don't want this to continue. To do so would only replicate the problem. You need to show leadership.

"I imagine that this is what your argument was like." They both nod. "So, it sounds like, Luis, that you have been feeling frustrated about money for a while." He nods. "And Isabel, you've been feeling a bit micromanaged—yes?" She nods. "So, tell me what happens when you try to have discussions about money when you're both not angry. Isabel, Luis says that he thinks you are agreeing with him when he brings this up. Are you?"

"I guess, sort of. I mean, I think I understand what he is worried about, but in the moment he seems . . . so controlling, and I just go along."

Daniel, not surprisingly, begins. "Kim and I have been worried about Emma. She seems to be struggling. Her school grades have been going down, she's quiet, spends a lot of time in her room, isn't doing much of anything with her friends. We think she's depressed. We've talked to her about it, but she sort of shrugs us off. And last week Kim noticed a cut on her arm and tried to talk to Emma about it, but Emma clammed up."

You turn to Kim; you need to bring her into the conversation. "Have you been worried about Emma?" Again, we don't want Daniel to speak for her.

"Well, I wasn't at first, not as worried as Daniel. I was a sulky teenager once, but when I saw that cut on her arm last week, that scared me." Kim is getting teary. "She just doesn't talk to us. We don't know what to do . . ."

"That's why we're here," says Daniel. His voice sounds firm. He turns to Emma. "What's wrong?" he says, sounding more demanding than concerned. Emma turns her head away. "See," Daniel says, "this is what she does." Now he's exasperated.

"You've heard this all before?" you ask Emma in a gentle voice. She nods. "So your parents say they are worried. Do you believe they are?"

"I guess." She shrugs.

"This is what we get all the time," says Daniel, now sounding even more frustrated.

As with Isabel and Luis we're at the verge of replicating the problem in the room. We can imagine that the more that Daniel pushes, the more Emma will shut down.

"Emma, is it okay for me to talk to you by yourself for a few minutes?" She shrugs, but says okay. "Okay folks, do you mind waiting in the waiting room for a few minutes?"

What we have been doing here is giving everyone—Luis and Isabel; Daniel, Kim and Emma—an opportunity to present their problems. We circle around the presenting problem and try to deepen the conversation a bit—by asking Luis and Isabel what happens when they talk about money. Ideally, we would want to have a similar conversation with Emma and her parents, to see where rational conversations possibly break down, but Emma is already moving to shutdown mode because Daniel is being so aggressive. She won't open up in the room with him being that way, and we don't have time to try to calm him down so the conversation can move forward. As with violent couples who cannot disengage, it's time to change the climate by changing the room dynamics.

Part 2: Assessment (15–20 Minutes)

Now that you have a rough idea of everyone's concerns, it's time to move to your assessment—moving away from the presenting problem and gathering the information that you need most to fully develop your preliminary plan.

Here you drill down to confirm your initial hypothesis and treatment map. If you are a psychodynamic therapist, you may ask about childhood and family of origin; if you are a solution-focused therapist, you may ask about successful problem-solving and positive experiences. Based on our more cognitive-behavioral model, here are some questions you might ask Luis and Isabel; in brackets are some of the rationales for asking the questions:

> *So, Luis, do you have a theory about why Isabel seems to have a hard time with money? Isabel, do you have a theory about why Luis seems so micromanaging and concerned about money? [Each's personal theories dictate where they each may think the solutions lie]*
>
> *How do you both make decisions about other issues besides money? Are there other issues you argue about? [Problem-solving skills, balance of power]*
>
> *Do you have good times together? Can you be intimate, both verbally and physically? [Able to have some positives to balance out negative]*
>
> *Can you each tell when you are beginning to get upset and realize that an argument is getting out of hand? Are you sometimes able to stop or calm yourself down? [Awareness of their own process and ability to emotionally self-regulate]*
>
> *Luis, do you ever feel like you are carrying more of the responsibilities than Isabel? Isabel, do you? Do you ever get resentful or angry about it? [Martyr role and moving to the persecutor in the relationship triangle]*
>
> *Luis, what is it that you feel Isabel doesn't fully understand about you? Isabel, what is it that Luis doesn't understand? [Deepening conversation, emotional wounds]*
>
> *Do you feel you both have the same vision of the future, about priorities and goals? [On the same page about vision]*
>
> *What are you each afraid will happen if things don't change between you? [Their anxieties and goals]*

Obviously, guided by your own clinical framework, you might have additional or different topics. What these questions are hoping to do is put the recent argument and struggle over money in a larger context—about triggering of each's emotional wounds—that Luis, perhaps, can't count on Isabel to be a responsible, equal partner, or that he feels constantly dismissed; or that Isabel feels micromanaged and treated like an acting-out teen—about communication and self-regulation, about priorities. Right now, there seems to be an imbalance of power—Luis, the martyr, Isabel the victim—and a power struggle over money, coupled with different styles and visions about priorities and how money is used. It's unclear right now how much Luis struggles to contain his anger and whether his recent behavior was an isolated incident or the tip of the iceberg of a bigger issue. By asking these questions we're also attempting to deepen the conversation by encouraging each to talk about what they normally do not and, hopefully, better understand how the other feels.

As you ask these questions, you want to make sure that each partner stays in lockstep with you, and that the conversation is balanced: that neither one feels as though you are ganging up on him or her, that if either one makes a face or seems awkward, that you pick up on it and explain why you are asking the question. Finally, you are looking for transference cues. You know that you need to not seem critical or micromanaging to Isabel and that you listen and not sound dismissive or unempathic to Luis. Throughout this section, you are aware of the time.

Emma's parents leave and Emma stays huddled in her chair. "Thanks for letting me talk to you by yourself," you say. She nods. "Your dad seemed to be getting pretty frustrated and it seemed to me that that was hard for you." Again, she nods. "Does this happen a lot?"

"Yeah, my dad can get that way. He gets worried and yells."

"And your mom?"

"She just gets flutters about, is always asking me if I'm okay, do I want to talk."

"Do you talk to her?"

"No, not really."

"Why not?"

"She'll just get more worried or go tell my dad and then he'll be coming down on me."

Emma's starting to open up and that's what you want. Our goals for her right now are clear—to build rapport, to have her feel safe and see that you are not like her parents. You want to find out about what she is struggling with, and why the cutting. But first you just spend time asking questions about everyday life—school, friends, what she likes, whether she dates. She is obviously bright; she does do well in school and feels pressure to get good grades. She briefly had a boyfriend who then dumped her for another girl. She doesn't talk to her parents about this.

"Was this hard for you?"

"Yeah, I guess. I didn't cry or anything, but I feel like it is my fault, that I didn't do something right somehow."

"Do you tend to give yourself a hard time?"

"I guess. I can be pretty critical of myself."

"Can you tell me about the cutting?"

And she does. She's only done it a few times. Once after the breakup, once because . . . she didn't know, she just felt so sad and lonely. She starts to cry. You give her the space.

"Your parents are worried that you are depressed. Do you think you are?" you ask gently.

"Yeah, I guess so. I feel like I don't fit in at school and feel pressure from my parents, especially my dad, all the time . . ."

"What is it you would want your parents to do most to help you feel better?"

"Back off, not make such a big deal about grades."

"Have you said that to them?"

"No."

"What do you feel would help you feel better?"

"I think it would help me to talk to somebody."

"Would you be willing to come back and meet with me?"

"Yeah, that would be a good idea."

"What about having family sessions to help your parents better understand what you need?"

"Hmmm . . . . I'm not sure I'm ready for that yet."

"Okay, we can play by ear and see how it goes."

You have a contract. You know that she is depressed, has been internalizing much of struggling within herself and with her parents. You talk a bit about your style, how you can mix family and individual therapy, that you'd like to help her feel less depressed and help her talk to her parents at some point to make things better at home. She nods. You say that you'd like to have her parents come back in and are wondering what she is comfortable with you saying. She's says she fine with your mentioning the depression and individual therapy. She is also okay with your talking with her parents so you can get to know them better, and you underscore the confidentiality between you. If she wants to share things with her parents (and you are hoping she will quickly get to that point), then you will have a family session.

Obviously, you're letting her set the pace at this point for two reasons: One is that she is clearly the one struggling and needs the support, and she is open to family therapy, which is important to help change family patterns and not replicate her withdrawal and internalization from her parents. The other reason you're not pushing a bit harder for family therapy is that she doesn't feel that she has a lot of control in her life and feels that her parents are dictating a lot of demands, and we don't want to replicate the problem. She needs to be more proactive and assertive to counter the withdrawal and only-child accommodation that she uses to cope.

Finally, you give her some homework.

"Just to help me, and you, better understand your depression, I wonder if you could track how you feel during this next week. What I mean is that I'd like you to check in with yourself every couple of hours and see how you are feeling on a scale of one to ten. If you notice that you are feeling down or anxious, notice what you are thinking about. That will help us see if there are particular things that your mind is circling around that are bothering you. If it helps, write them down. Does that make sense?"

"Sure, I can do that."

Part 3: Presenting the Treatment Plan and Next Steps (10 Minutes)

"I'd like to give you some feedback and let you know what I'm thinking," you say to Isabel and Luis.

You thank them again for coming in and that you realize how upsetting their argument was last weekend. You then go on to say that money is obviously a big issue for both of them—for Luis because he worries about the budget, and for Isabel because she feels micromanaged and doesn't share Luis's worries. You then talk about how money often becomes a power issue—whose way is going to win—and how it can trigger each one's emotional wounds. You explain to them how emotional wounds work—the learned sensitivity, the triggering of each other.

"It sounds like," you say, "that you, Luis, feel ignored when Isabel spends more than you thought you agreed on, and feel like you are the only one being responsible about this, and then you periodically get fed up and angry. And that you, Isabel, think that Luis worries too much, but you also feel pressured to conform, which you resent, and though you agree, you too get fed up, then go ahead and do what you planned, only making Luis angrier and seemingly controlling." You wait to see if they both non-verbally agree. They do.

"What we need to do," you say, "is a couple of things. We need to break this pattern of triggering each other. It also sounds like you both have a hard time sometimes not letting arguments get out of control—that is what happened over the weekend. And finally, we need to find a solution to the problem with money that you both can agree on. Does this make sense?" Again, you look for agreement and again they nod.

"So, what I'd like you to do over the next week is couple of things: One is to not talk about money at home—but think about it, especially you, Isabel, about how you would like you both to manage it differently—and we'll talk about it next time. I'd also like you to plan to spend some time together as couple doing something that you both would enjoy. The idea behind this is help you both regain your positive footing about each other. And finally, if anything comes up during the week that bothers you, write it down and we'll talk about it next time. How does this sound?" Again, they both nod.

What you have done here is tried to change the emotional climate in the room through education, reframing their problems in a new way, as not irresponsible vs. micromanaging, but as a triggering of wounds and dysfunctional patterns. You have also demonstrated leadership by showing that you understand how each feels, by linking their initial concerns to your assessment, and mapping out for them a path for change. And because you have monitored their being in lockstep with you, you can feel confident that they are likely to follow through.

You could, of course, have suggested that they have a conversation on their own, encouraging Isabel to be more honest and less accommodating, so they could possibly come up with a solution. But you are trying to move them toward success, and you are not sure whether Isabel can be assertive enough with Luis or whether he can, in fact, control his anger. To be successful, you decide, it would be better to provide support to her within the session process.

You invite Daniel and Kim back into the room with you and Emma. You thank them for coming and say that you appreciate their giving you the opportunity to talk with Emma by herself. "I realize," you say, "that I don't have more time to spend with you today. But let me briefly tell you what Emma and I discussed."

You then go on to talk about what you and Emma agreed on—that she is struggling with depression, that she is interested in individual therapy. You are taking the lead to reinforce to Emma that you are in her corner and leave her with a firm sense of safety. You say that next time you would actually like to split the session between Daniel and Kim and Emma. You ask Emma if that is okay with her—she says yes. You also mention that you and Emma talked about including family therapy at some point so Daniel and Kim don't feel left out and can better understand how to support Emma.

"How did I do?" you ask Emma.

"Fine," she says. Daniel and Kim nod their heads and both seem to breathe a sigh of relief.

Which isn't surprising. Despite their seeming frustration or anger, most parents are genuinely worried about their child. Seeing that their child is not resistant, in spite of her outward grumpiness, and is willing to accept professional help, relieves their worry and emotionally distributes their sense of responsibility. They, too, feel like they have someone in their corner, much like you might feel after seeing your doctor.

"What about medication?" Daniel asks. "I agree that Emma is depressed, but do you think she needs medication?"

You see out of the corner of your eye that Emma is pulling in. "We didn't have a chance to talk about this," you say. "That's something to think about, but I don't know if a referral for medication is necessary yet. That is something Emma and I can talk about next time." Daniel seems satisfied.

"Are there any other concerns you have right now?" Everyone is silent.

"So," you say, "we'll schedule a time for next week and split the session. Yes?" Everyone nods their heads.

What you are doing here is what you did with Isabel and Luis—laying out a plan, making sure there is agreement. For Daniel, Kim and Emma, the emotional climate changed by your tapping into soft emotions, but also through your strong rapport with Emma, as well as how you demonstrated leadership with the parents and matched Daniel's initial expectations. And although Daniel raised an objection, he wasn't insistent—a good sign that you have his support.

First-Session First-Aid

These two sessions went relatively smoothly, but obviously not all sessions will. Let's talk about what to do if things don't quite go so smoothly. Using our case examples, let's imagine places where the process may go off course, and map out clinical action steps you can take:

Luis and Isabel Escalate

Here we consider what to do if Luis's complaint about spending and Isabel's complaint about his micromanaging get out of control. Here you need to step up and ask them to stop and focus on each one at a time. But as we mentioned when we discussed violent couples, this can sometimes be difficult for them to do, and for you to rein in, because they so easily trigger each other. If that is the case, you need to call a strong halt and separate them—asking one to wait in the waiting room while you talk to the other. Just make sure you leave time to see the other partner individually as well.

Isabel Shuts Down

Here we imagine that Luis quickly escalates and, instead of pushing back, Isabel shuts down. Your first course of action is to ask Luis to stop, and then in a calm and gentle voice, focus on Isabel and try and draw her out. If this doesn't work (perhaps because she feels unsafe with Luis in the room), you can ask him to leave, much as you did with Emma's parents, and talk with her by herself.

There is some risk in doing this; Luis may feel resentful and anxious being excluded and worry that you may take Isabel's side. You will need to leave time and work hard to balance out the relationship, explain to them that this is something you sometimes do to better understand what each person wants and is feeling, and give him time to explain, and let you hear, his side of the story.

Kim Emotionally Melts Down

Kim begins talking about Emma's cutting and collapses into a heap of sadness. While you want to be empathic, just as you don't want Daniel to monopolize the session and climate, neither do you want Kim to do so. In clinical hypnosis, there is the concept of pacing and leading—at first matching the client's breathing pattern, for example—and then leading—gradually slowing your breath and having the client follow. You can do the same here. Begin by being empathic and actively listening, but gradually move Kim out of her emotional brain and into her rational one by asking more informational and intellectual questions. Rather than asking more about how she feels, for example, ask her instead what her theory is about Emma's cutting, or what behavioral solutions she has tried to help Emma. You can also bring Daniel and Emma into this conversation to help change the conversation's focus.

Daniel Is Too Domineering

Daniel, the company president, does try and take control. Unlike Kim's situation, which was about emotional regulation, this is about power. Here you need to take a calm but absolutely strong stand. Carl Whitaker, one of the grandfathers of family therapy, used to say that the first session is about establishing who is in control. If Daniel is dominating the session, you need to ask him to step down and give others a chance to speak. The challenge comes if you, too, feel intimidated by Daniel and abdicate your leadership. If you know that this is a danger for you, you need to anticipate, get supervisory support and have a clear game plan in mind ahead of time to offset this.

If you let Daniel go in this first session, you not only replicate the problem but also leave Kim and Emma feeling unsafe.

Emma Pushes Back

Instead of curling up on the chair, Emma actually gets angry when her parents start talking about her. This is not actually a derailment but is a sign of good mental health: She has the strength to speak up. Given her depression and cutting behavior, this is not likely (if she could, in fact, do this, she may not need to cut), but if she did, your role at this point is to shape the process so that she can say what she needs to say, help the parents hear her, help her understand the worry and anxiety they feel.

The challenge for you is that you may get caught up in the high emotion of it all and fail to take an active role, and they, again, only replicate the problem. If this is a challenge for you, once again, you need to receive supervisory support and have a game plan in place.

Luis Blames Isabel

Here you offer your explanation about emotional wounds and triggering of each other as part of your treatment plan, and Luis doesn't buy it. Instead, he continues to insist that, no, it is not his fault, that she is irresponsible, and begins stacking up evidence to make his case. He is playing courtroom. You need to manage his emotion and counter his objection to your feedback.

Take them one by one. Hold up your hand to help him stop and explain that you don't want to arbitrate their situation, but instead help them both learn to solve their own problems. Then drill down into his objection—what is it that he doesn't agree with regarding your explanation—and see if you can help him better understand what you are trying to convey, while still acknowledging his own frustration.

This can seem tricky, but you can say always say exactly that—that I understand how angry and frustrated you feel, that I am not taking Isabel's side, but I want to help you see (hear, feel) how to think about this differently so you both can solve this problem between you. I assume that that is why you are here and what you both want.

The same would apply if Daniel, for example, didn't agree with your response to his question about medication or even seeing Emma individually. These are objections that you need to counter with the same calm but firm voice while drilling down to find the source of the objection.

Emma Doesn't Open Up to You

This is the difficult one. Here, in spite of your efforts to be the ideal parent to offset her experience with her parents, she remains closed. She is untrusting of adults and, despite your efforts, sees you as one of them. You have a few options.

One is to say what you are thinking so she has a different context: "I know I'm asking you a lot of questions, but I want you to feel safe here and get to know you better."

You can also say what you think she may be thinking: "I know coming here feels pretty strange and you may be feeling ganged up on. I see my role as not taking sides, not like another adult giving you a hard time. I see myself as helping you say to your parents what you may have a hard time helping them understand." Again, how you sound is undoubtedly more important than what you actually say.

But what if neither of these approaches work? In spite of her silence, ask if she is willing to come back one more time and talk with you individually. Often teens and children will agree, much to your surprise, perhaps, because what seems to be resistance is in fact their own struggle to emotionally process what has unfolded. Emma does come back next week and, with the time to process and re-center, does open up.

Okay, you say, but what if she does not open up, does not agree to come back and actually walks out of the session? If Emma is not willing to engage, you need to shift gears. Here you bring the parents back in and focus on what they as parents can do to help Emma. Based on your assessment and treatment map, coach Daniel and Kim on how to be supportive without being intrusive. You may suggest their contacting the guidance counselor at school to check in with Emma and provide support. You may give information about cutting behaviors and the need to encourage Emma be more assertive at home, or even provide guidelines for when they may need to take more drastic steps and obtain an emergency custody order for a psychiatric evaluation.

Your goal here is to coach the parents on behaviorally changing the family dynamics so that the climate in the home changes, which, in turn, helps change Emma's behavior and provides information to help them feel more empowered and less anxious. They, and you, need to be clear about what is the best you and they can do.

Following Up

If, in spite of these first-aid efforts, you have lingering doubts later, reach out. If you worry that Isabel may have felt that you sided too strongly with Luis; that Luis didn't feel heard; that Daniel felt that you were being too authoritarian; or that Emma did, in fact, see you as yet another adult telling her what to do, then give them a call. Say what you think the client may be feeling. Through your voice and words of concern help show that you are sensitive to what unfolded, to what may have gone off course, what needs to be repaired. They may not respond, but often they will, because you are doing and providing what they normally do not receive.

And if they do not, you truly have done the best you can do.

Hopefully, this has provided you with some guidelines for navigating this all-important, yet often difficult, first session process. In the next chapter, we'll look at the focus of the second session and ways of handling the challenges these sessions can present.

7 Second Session and Beyond

You've done a good job in your first session. The crisis couple or family come back, and have done their homework. What to do next? In this chapter, we will look at the goals and tasks of this second session and subsequent opening sessions using our couple (Luis and Isabel) and family (Daniel, Kim and Emma) as our base. But first, let's step back and do a quick survey of the broader landscape of the therapy process.

Stages of Therapy

We can think of any course of treatment moving through beginning, middle and end stages, each with its own characteristics. Even if you are doing a brief therapy approach, these stages still apply, albeit in more concise form and with more limited goals. Keeping them in mind allows you to anticipate the changes ahead. Your understanding and perspective can also be passed along to the couple or family so that they, too, have a way of measuring progress as well as putting in a broader and more normalizing perspective the common challenges they may be facing.

Beginning Stage Characteristics

Here is summary, which we've covered earlier, of the common characteristics of the beginning stage:

- Playing courtroom—arguing over facts/content
- Arguing over right/wrong
- Using content to fuel emotions
- Easily falling into power struggles
- "You" statements: "I'll feel better when you change"
- Little awareness of process/patterns

For volatile couples and families, these characteristics may occupy several sessions. For those couples and families who are less volatile, less in crisis or have had past experience with therapy and/or are more self-aware, they may present with a few of these characteristics but quickly move beyond them. Your focus in this stage is to shape the communication, stop dysfunctional patterns, teach communication and self-regulation skills, uncover emotional wounds, help them become aware of process and facilitate problem-solving. You'll be taking an active role throughout the session.

Middle Stage Characteristics

You may begin to see these characteristics in the second session, but more likely at the beginning in the third or fourth:

- Inconsistent in applying new skills
- Arguing over means rather than being able to consistently focus on ends
- Seeming worsening of problems and/or greater awareness of individual problems
- Greater awareness of patterns/process
- Increased use of "I" statements
- Difficulty emotionally self-regulating and listening around "hot" topics

Some explanations are in order.

Inconsistent Skills

Any new skills you may teach a couple or family—communication, self-regulation—take time to be integrated into everyday life; gains are fragile, and often with minimal stress it is all too easy for them to fall back into old patterns. On good days Emma can be more mindful and assertive, and Luis less irritated and frustrated, but it doesn't take much at this stage for it all to fall apart.

Means vs. Ends

What this refers to is that in arguments or discussions the couple or family gets stuck in the weeds of means—Luis and Isabel are arguing over what should or should not have been purchased, rather than focusing on their larger goal of coming up with a plan that addresses both their views and values. Emma's parents are drilling down around specific grades at school and, in the process, are unaware of or are losing sight of their overall need of understanding why her grades are struggling at all and what they can do to support her. Over time and with practice, the couple or family can get better at communicating and being aware of process; they can tell when the conversational car is going off the road and going into the weeds of details. They are better able to stay focused on the ultimate goal, namely solving the problem.

Worsening Problems

Just when you thought everything was going well, now the couple or family throws you a curve—bringing up old issues from Christmas 2010, or now openly arguing, after they were quiet and polite, about issues that you've never heard about—steady heavy drinking, terrible childhood abuse or ongoing struggles with post-traumatic stress.

Here is where it is easy to panic—what did you miss, what is going wrong? Most likely, nothing. This is, in fact, a good sign. The opening sessions were about getting their foot in the door and checking you out. Now the couple or family are stepping up and talking about the secrets and problems under the problems because they now feel safe and trust you. You're doing a good job.

You're still very active in this middle stage, but you're intervening less. You're gradually helping the couple or family become more and more aware of and in charge of controlling the process, and helping them sidestep all the content. You point out when the conversational car is going off the road, you encourage them to move towards a solution rather than arguing over means, you help them see when the other person, or they themselves, are rolling their eyes or responding with the conversation killer "yes, but."

End Stage Characteristics

Finally, as you reach end stages, you'll notice more of these characteristics:

- Able to focus on ends and not get stuck on means
- Able to actively listen, even on difficult topics
- Ability to emotionally self-regulate
- Ability to compromise
- Aware of process and patterns and able to stop them
- More flexible—able to move against their grains and approach anxiety

Obviously, this is an ideal, with some couples and families coming closer to reaching these than others. While in longer-term therapy you will be looking for gains across a wider spectrum of behaviors in everyday life, in brief therapy you are more likely to see these characteristics in more specific and limited ways. Emma is more assertive with her parents, but will still struggle with intimidating teachers; Luis and Isabel are compromising around money, but you can imagine that if they have children, these old patterns and emotional wounds may arise again.

At this stage, you are less active; therapy has become a place of safety for more delicate topics; the couple or family is looking to you to gain your professional insights on a particular problem, such as parenting or dealing with extended family, and the emotional climate in the home is consistently positive.

Again, this is the map, not the terrain, and what actually unfolds will vary. But you can see the broad progression along two dimensions: moving from content to process, and from less self-responsibility to greater self-responsibility for each partner's own emotions and behaviors, resulting in the couple's or family's increased ability to set the agenda and essentially run, with your more minimal guidance, the sessions themselves.

Second Session Goals and Tasks

With this broader landscape in mind, let's look more closely at the second session. While the primary focus in the first session was on building safety, trust and agreement on a preliminary treatment plan, the goals of the second session are those of establishing momentum and completing any left-over tasks from the first session. Here are the most common goals and tasks that you'll want to consider.

Repair the Clinical Relationship

You felt that Luis may have left the first session feeling like you weren't taking his concern about Isabel's spending seriously. You tried to call him but were unable to reach him or leave a message. Or you're worried that Kim, due to your effort to control the clock, may have felt unsupported by you in her own sadness, or that Daniel may have lingering objections to your less-than-enthusiastic response to his question about medication for Emma. The second session is the time to mop up around these concerns.

This does not, obviously, mean that you need to accommodate and meet each client's expectations, but rather that you acknowledge each one's feelings and objections and explain your own thinking. You underscore to Luis his frustration about money; you say to Kim how aware you were of her own sadness in the last session; you wonder aloud to Daniel that he may still feel that medication needs to be considered more promptly. And then you explain again what you essentially said last time—about the couple and family patterns, about helping Emma define her own goals and needs. Here in the second session, each client's tunnel vision and anxiety are reduced; hopefully, they have had time to process what you said before and now. And if they once again raise objections, you again counter them. It is less about content and more about repairing the relationship with each partner or family member.

Check on Homework

You absolutely need to check on any homework that you may have prescribed. If you do not, you're teaching your clients that homework is not important after all. So, if you prescribe a violence prevention plan for Luis and Isabel, ask Emma to write a list of goals or ask parents to decide on a bedtime routine for the children, make sure you ask about it at the top of the hour.

If they don't do the assignment, the problem is less about them and more about you and a breakdown in the first session: that they didn't understand the connection between their problem and the assignment; that they didn't agree with your overall preliminary plan; that there were objections or failures of rapport that undermined the entire process; that the assignment was too overwhelming emotionally or intellectually and they could not carry it out; that their lives are too busy; that their concerns are overridden by other concerns (a common problem with couples and families in crisis) and the homework moved to the very bottom of their to-do list.

If they did do their homework, you want to find out about the process and results: whether Isabel and Luis were, in fact, able to call a halt to a potential argument; whether Emma struggled coming up with solid goals because she worried about doing it "right" or actually felt resentful when doing it because it felt like just more on her crowded plate; whether the parents could not only agree on a bedtime routine but also stick with the process, even though it took them much longer than they expected. This is all valuable information in fine-tuning your treatment plan. Not-doing is a bad solution to an underlying problem that prevents the doing, and you want to track just what this problem is. Tracking the results of homework helps you now begin to sort out the learning problems, and the problems about learning, that may hinder the couple or family from moving steadily forward.

When asking about homework, be aware of possible transference reactions and triggering of emotional wounds. You don't, for example, want to sound critical to Emma or micromanaging to Isabel, because you are likely to replicate the problem and trigger an emotional reaction that makes it difficult for them to hear your message. Be assertive and monitor your voice tone. When in doubt—when you suspect that your question is taken the wrong way—go ahead and say what they, and you, are thinking: "I'm not trying to be critical or micromanaging, the reason I'm asking about this is . . . ." And if they didn't do the homework, again ask gently what was the problem. Here you can offer options: did it seem too difficult or emotionally overwhelming or did they perhaps not understand how it related to their concerns, etc.

Second Session and Beyond 125

Continue With Your Assessment

You meet with Daniel and Kim to not only understand how they view their daughter but also because you suspect that they may be polarized in their parenting styles and are actually not working together as a team. Or you want to spend time in the second session drilling down with Emma to the thoughts and emotions that actually trigger her thoughts of cutting. Or Luis made a passing reference in the first session about having been hospitalized for depression several years ago that you want to better understand, or Isabel mentioned having a miscarriage last year and you are wondering how the loss has impacted her and the relationship. Whatever you didn't have time to explore, whatever topics were pushed aside because of time pressures, this second session is the time to gather whatever information you need to fully flesh out your perceptions of the couple or family and to fine-tune or confirm your preliminary treatment plan.

See Couple or Family Members Separately

We discussed in Chapter 3 the importance of separating violent couples if it appears that one partner is a bully and making it unsafe for the other to speak openly in front of him in the first session. But some couple therapists plan to see partners separately within in the opening sessions, not because of a serious imbalance in the system, but as a matter of course. In addition to providing an opportunity for any needed relationship repair, spending individual time with partners allows you to mentally separate out the individual personalities from the couple dynamics. Some therapists actually request two individual sessions after the first session or even before seeing the couple, but in our brief and crisis-focused approach, you can realistically just split one session between them.

If you plan on doing this for the second session, let the couple know your thinking at the end of the first session—that you'd like to split the session next time and see each individually, just so you can better sort out the individuals from the relationship. That said, you also want to say that if something comes up in the next week that they both feel that they need to talk about together with you in the next session, that is fine, and you can do the split session another time. If Luis and Isabel, for example, do come to the second session and say that they want to talk about the argument they had on Saturday night, go with that and do the session splitting later, when the crisis has settled. By following their more pressing agenda, you are underscoring for couples and families that this is indeed their therapy, that you are there to serve and that you want them to take an active role in setting the session agendas.

If you do see partners or family members individually, how do you want to use that time? Because you are the one initiating this individual conversation, it's a good idea to lay out your agenda at the start to focus and use the time efficiently. In addition to relationship repair and assessment topics, you may also ask for feedback on the first session and clarification of the partners' goals for therapy, and offer the opportunity for them to tell you anything that he or she didn't get a chance to say in the first session, or didn't feel comfortable saying in front of the other, that they think is important for you to know. You can explain that you want to pinpoint their individual goals because you view your role as advocating for both of them and that you want to be certain that you understand what it is that they most want changed. Drill down and make these goals as behavioral and concrete as possible so that you, and they, have a clear idea of exactly what they are looking for. If Isabel, for example, says she wants to be respected more by Luis, your next question is: what is it that Luis needs to concretely do for her to feel that he is respecting her?

Providing the opportunity for individuals to bring up topics that were not brought up in the first session can give you valuable information about issues and problems that, unaddressed, may undermine your treatment plan. Here Isabel, for example, may say that she worries that Luis drinks too much and fears that he is alcoholic. You ask if she has talked with him about her concerns and she says either yes, she has, but he dismissed it or got angry, or no, she has held back because she didn't feel safe bringing it up with him alone.

Since this is an important concern that could undermine treatment, your next step is asking if she is willing to bring it up in a couple session, assuring her that you would help her express her feelings and help him hear what she has to say. This type of confrontation with your support can usually work well—big concerns are now out in the open—and your clinical fork in the road next becomes that of deciding whether Luis needs further assessment for his drinking, and whether or not couple therapy should proceed.

If, on the other hand, Isabel balks at the idea of raising the topic even with your support because she worries that, though Luis may remain calm in the session, he may retaliate at home, her safety obviously becomes the priority. You may then decide to slow down the process, ask Luis as part of assessment about drug and alcohol use and see how open he is to talking about it, or focus instead on his anger, and assess whether this is an issue that requires his being referred out.

What often is disclosed, however, when you ask if there are topics that the partner did not feel comfortable sharing in the joint session is the controversial issue of secrets. Here Luis tells you in his individual session that he is in fact having an affair with a coworker on his job, or Isabel says that she actually had an abortion when they were dating that Luis doesn't know about and she doesn't want him to know.

This is controversial in that many clinicians have strong opinions about secrets and handle them in a variety of ways. Some, like John Gottman, for example, say at the very start of therapy (and actually state it on the paperwork that couples fill out before their first appointment) that the clinician will not hold any secrets and that anything said to him privately will be disclosed in the couple session, making it clear to the couple that they need to decide what they are in fact willing to say. Others believe that individual confidentiality is exactly that, and so the affair or the abortion will not be disclosed. But we can also imagine a middle ground that both upholds confidentiality and considers how the new information may impact the therapy process.

You may ask Luis or Isabel why they are deciding to share this information. Luis may say that he just wants to get this off his chest, or that he is essentially done with the relationship and is thinking of separating; Isabel may say that she just thought that you may think this is important to know or that the experience has made her fearful of getting pregnant again. You might say to Luis that while you will respect confidentiality, you are also uncomfortable continuing couple therapy. Based on your own clinical framework, you believe that the affair prevents the person from fully committing to couple therapy and undermines its purpose and focus. Until the affair is over, you say, you feel that couple therapy should be suspended.

You then go on to say the same to Isabel and Luis together—that, based on your assessment, you are not comfortable proceeding with couple therapy at this time. While this may leave Isabel with questions and leave Luis in a potentially awkward position that he may or may not address with her, you are being clear on your side that therapy stops. You have not violated confidentiality, you are not left holding the secret in the therapy process and you have upheld your clinical values.

Isabel's disclosure, on the other hand, is a bit different. The abortion was in the past and you want to respect confidentiality, but there is the lingering question that may signal a current relationship issue, namely why she didn't talk to Luis about this before. Again, she may say that she feared that he would get angry or that that he would have left her. This tells you something important about relationship dynamics—her belief that she needs to withhold rather than be assertive. In addition to her specific fears around pregnancy, Isabel's way of coping, undoubtedly tied to her own emotional wounds, is one that, if it goes unchecked, can permeate and derail the relationship both now and in the future.

So, you explain all this to her, and make sure that she is in lockstep with you and understands your concerns. If she is, you can then ask her if she is willing to talk to Luis, with your support, about the way his reactions affect her, as well as, without mentioning the abortion, to help him understand her fears about pregnancy. This is the middle ground—helping the couple repair important dysfunctional patterns that are undermining their presenting issues, while not needing to dredge up the past and risk confidentiality.

But this is one approach to the issue of secrets and confidentiality. It is important that you define your own bottom lines and clinical policies in advance—ones that are consistent with your clinical orientation, style and values about privacy—so that you are not caught off guard and forced to think and define in the moment.

While we've been focusing on couples, all that we've just discussed about separating the dyad holds true for family members as well. In the second or later sessions, you may want to see parents individually to assess the marital relationship and be assured that they are on the same page, gather needed information not covered in the first session, uncover issues that may undermine your treatment plan or define or better define individual goals so you have a clear path forward. But, depending on the family, you also may divide the family unit into various combinations for specific clinical goals. You realize that the shy 5-year-old who seems depressed may open up about how she feels about her stepfather if you meet with her and her two older brothers together, to support her and help her articulate emotions that they all may share. Or you may decide to see Emma and Kim together to better understand their dynamics without the more domineering input of Daniel. While you need to stay aware of balance, this "divide and conquer" way of gathering information and/or repairing relationship dynamics of the subsystems are often effective and efficient. They enable you to connect your own clinical dots and use time effectively to untangle potential snags.

Teach Skills

The second session is an excellent time to teach skills. It helps maintain momentum and gives crisis couples and families the tools they need to begin to resolve their learning problems and change dysfunctional patterns, and also moves them toward positive action and away from continuing to cycle around presenting complaints. Here you teach Emma anxiety-reduction techniques to use when she becomes emotionally overwhelmed. You help parents draw up the reward chart for chores or help the couple pull together a working budget. You role-play with a mother how to talk with her son about his failing grades, or Luis asking his supervisor about a raise. We'll discuss a variety of these skill-building techniques more fully in Chapter 9.

Deepen the Conversations

While the first session clearly requires you to keep a tight rein on the process in order to cover goals and tasks that need to be completed, from the second session on you are looking for the clients to take more and more responsibility for the session. As mentioned in our discussion of treatment stages, your control over time should become less as the couple or family understands process and is able to step up. Once your information gathering is completed, your focus can now shift towards shaping deeper conversations—those different, more honest and intimate conversations that they normally avoid—during the session hour. You ask hard questions; when they become defensive and fall back into old content, you stop the dysfunctional patterns and deliberately try to change the emotional climate. And when they are moving forward—speaking more honestly, more openly and being more vulnerable—you back off, give them the floor. You are, at this stage, like the rudder on the ship, helping them stay on course towards their goals.

These are some of the common goals and techniques of the second session. What you choose to actually focus upon will depend on your clinical orientation and your clinical needs, as well as the needs of the clients. For those couples and families in severe states of turmoil, all these goals and tasks may be pushed to later sessions simply because they need more time to vent their frustrations and are struggling with new iterations of their crises and problems; they still have emotional tunnel vision and are externally focused and reactive. You may find yourself listening and providing a safe place, repeating much of what you said in the first session because it wasn't fully heard or understood.

That's fine. The fact that they have returned lets you know that you've done a good job, that there is a therapeutic connection, that they value your leadership.

Drop-Outs and the Shift to the Individual

Or, to your surprise, they don't all return, or a partner or family member drops out. Luis and Isabel have another big argument and Isabel says she can't take it anymore and goes to stay with her sister in Michigan. Or Daniel, for all his being in charge, decides that he can't afford to take any time off from work, and departs, essentially handing Kim and Emma off to you to fix. The issue here is what to do if your initial plan for couple or family therapy collapses because one key member pulls out.

One of the beauties of thinking in terms of systems and patterns, as well as the dynamics of the relationship triangle, is that if one person changes his side of the dynamics, the other person, by deliberately changing his behavior, can generally come to do the same. Isabel, and Emma and Kim, have the power to shape Luis's and Daniel's behavior simply by changing their own. Even if Isabel runs off to Michigan, if she is more assertive with Luis or does her best to have a different conversation with him and doesn't emotionally overreact to his frustrations, over time, Luis may modify his behavior.

Similarly, if Emma learns to speak up and let her parents know what she needs and what bothers her, rather than internalizing her feelings, and then resorting to cutting, there is an opportunity for the parents to see her and treat her in a different way, thereby breaking the dysfunctional pattern. This is what you are trying to do when working with both partners or all of the family members—changing patterns—and you can do this even if you are seeing only one or two individuals.

So here you can coach Emma on doing exactly that: stepping up and telling her parents, with your guidance, what bothers her. If Luis returns after Isabel has left, you can suggest ways he can reach out to her in a way that doesn't replicate their interactions, but instead helps her better understand his underlying concerns and acknowledges her own frustrations rather than battling with her about them. When doing such coaching, however, you also need to let them know what to expect.

We're back to the relationship triangle, where the stepping of one partner out of her role and moving to the adult creates anxiety for the others, causing the others to increase their normal behavioral reactions. In spite of Luis's efforts, you let Luis know that Isabel may still not hear him or may try and pick a fight; similarly, Daniel may dismiss Emma's complaints. By helping them anticipate such reactions, and by offering your support as they hold steady in their attempts, you help the partners and family members get through these predictable transition periods.

Thinking in this way, namely that of having one individual become the change agent for the system, does not imply and should not be confused with manipulation. Luis or Isabel, Emma or Kim, are not acting to "get" the other to change in an indirect way. Rather, it's better to help them realize that this is about the bigger dynamic process—one person stepping out of the dysfunctional pattern and role, putting her head down, staying focused on what she needs to do to help others know what she needs, being the adult rather than the martyr, victim or bully—to ultimately better run her life. Your message is that by doing the best you can do, by taking responsibility for your actions and by controlling what you can control rather than focusing on what you want the other to do, you are always doing your best.

To summarize, the aims of the second session are to close any gaps left from the first in terms of solidifying relationships and assessment, to gather momentum by teaching skills, to check on and modify homework and to uncover areas of resistance.

Third Sessions

By the third session most couples and families have begun to settle and move away from their crisis state into middle stages of treatment. Simply by taking the step of seeking help, having an opportunity to be heard and understood, and seeing, with your help, a positive path forward towards solving their problems and making a commitment to action, the emotional climate has changed and dysfunctional patterns are beginning to unravel. Of course, some couple and families may still present with feelings of being overwhelmed or frustrated—because new environmental challenges have arisen, because their own expectations of changes in others have not been met or because their overall reactive and anxious states are continuing to be triggered.

If they are not settling, you want to look for and focus on the potential problems under the problem: Are there in fact new problems to address that are overwhelming them? Are they focusing more on the other, rather than focusing on themselves and what they can and need to do differently? Are they following through with the homework, and if not, why not? One of the key elements of therapy is accountability; their knowing that they are reporting back to you each week hopefully helps them stay focused. If they are not moving forward, you want to uncover the source of any obstacles.

Third Session Drop-Outs

But even as things seem to improve, the third session can also be a pivotal one where not just one partner or family member may drop out, but the entire couple or family stops therapy. Some of the common reasons for the third session drop-out follow.

The Crisis Is Over

Luis and Isabel are able to work out a budget plan and feel more confident than they ever had. Emma is feeling much better—she has been able to have some serious talks with her parents about their expectations—and has suddenly become involved with a new group of potential friends since she joined the field hockey team. There has been no more cutting, she and her parents are relieved and appointments are actually conflicting with her field hockey practices. They decide to stop for now.

While you think there is more work to do to firmly put the underlying problems to rest, you've helped the couple or family take enough of the edge off the problem and their worry to inspire them to move on. Once again, you call, and welcome them to come back anytime.

Anxiety Sets In

With the settling of the crisis or the telling of the story, the couple or family not only feel better by getting things off their chests, but one or several of them are now feeling anxious. You meet with Daniel and Kim in the second session and they begin talking about how they disagree not only about Emma but also about other issues, such as sex and extended family, and their honesty opens up an emotional can of worms that frightens them. Or Luis feels that he revealed too much about his past addiction history in the second session, and now worries not only about your judgement but also that you may try "going deeper" into this history the next time you meet. Rather than pressing forward, their anxiety causes them to drop out.

Your antidote to such increasing anxiety and potential drop-outs is to anticipate that any risk-taking by clients may increase their anxiety, and that you need to acknowledge and support them without judgment. But because their anxiety is also fueled by not knowing what you or they need to do with these issues, and how to integrate them into their presenting problems, they need your guidance.

You have two options: One is to fold their new concerns into the presenting ones by helping them see that though the issues seem separate in content, what they have in common is a dysfunctional process. Here you say to Daniel and Kim that you are happy to help them sort out these other marital issues, but that what you see as the underlying larger problem is their struggle to compromise, reach agreements and approach problems together as a team—the same problem fueling their differing approaches to Emma. If they make the connection, you can then offer to help them develop these skills as you address Emma's problems as a family.

You can also negotiate with the client whether a shift in focus is called for. As we mentioned earlier, if you feel that Luis has an active addiction problem or anger management issue that will interfere with his moving forward in couple therapy, you need to speak up and refer out. But on the heels of your second-session conversation, Luis may actually wonder if he needs help dealing with these issues. You both can now explore what may be the higher priority, what problems need to be tackled first.

Managing anxiety through the treatment process is, at its heart, about pacing and sensitivity—not moving too fast and leaving the client feeling overwhelmed, not stirring strong emotions without grounding them by offering a context in which the issues can be addressed. But if they don't return, again, call and say what you think they may be thinking—that you appreciate their opening up about their concerns and realize that discussing all this may have left them feeling anxious. Reassure them that you are willing to help them on these or other concerns and to move at their own pace.

Transference Issues Come to the Fore

You've done your best to uncover transference cues all along, but with the settling of the crisis and lifting of the emotional fog, Isabel realizes that she really does have a difficult time talking intimately with men and that they need to see a female therapist; or Daniel, in his own mind, is still having a power struggle with you over control of the session and makes an executive decision to stop. Reach out, say what you think and see if you can help allay fears, but then let go and respect their decision.

Sabotage by Family Members

A not-uncommon scenario is that Isabel comes in by herself for the first session to talk about her problems with Luis. She goes home, tells Luis that she met with you to talk about their relationship and that you suggested that they come back together as a couple. Luis is anxious about the whole notion of therapy, or now feels that you've bonded with Isabel and that he is already in the emotional doghouse. In either case, he promises Isabel that he will change, be kinder and gentler, and he is. Isabel, not wanting to risk disrupting a good thing, drops out.

If there's not a Luis, there may be his grandmother who lambastes therapy and talking to strangers about private business, or Emma's new field hockey friend convinces her that therapy is just for weirdos or that it's obvious that her father is the one who needs therapy, not her. Again, if they drop out, you do what you can—reach out, call and see who is willing to come in, say what you think they may be thinking. You say the door is always open.

Often you are not aware of just who may be undermining the therapy process, but sometimes you are—Luis mentions his grandmother, Emma her friend. The third session is a good time to bring in other family members or friends. They can be a resource of new information about the relationships, a potential source of support rather than sabotage.

Mandated Clients

Joel is ordered for therapy for anger management, and comes twice but then calls and says that he needs to work overtime for the next two months. He's talked to his attorney about it, who said that since he did come in twice and has a legitimate reason to not attend sessions, the judge will probably not sanction him. Joel drops out. Joel didn't want to come to begin with, but he's done enough to get the court off his back. You reach out, document, let him go.

Unexpected client drop-outs can be rattling for you, the clinician. But the reality check is that you can't control clients, and there are a host of issues that can lead to their withdrawal. The best you can do is anticipate, say what you think to get issues on the table, try and resolve the problem under the problem and then welcome them back so that guilt doesn't prevent their possible return in the future.

Maintaining Momentum

Some portion of your crisis clients will tend to drop away once the crisis is over and the climate has changed, but maintaining momentum, and keeping clients focused and engaged over the longer haul, is one of the challenges of any therapy and any client population. Clients can get bogged down in the middle stages of treatment because after the initial rush of commitment, the gaining of insights, the learning of new skills, and with them, the seeming rapid changes, the process now begins to slow down, as clients try and hold steady and integrate these changes into their everyday lives. They may get frustrated because they feel that they are working harder than their partners or family members, and begin to complain and apply the brakes to their own effort. In these middle stages, you may find yourself essentially saying the same things over and over in each session, hoping that by your repetition your suggestions will be heard and remain a priority.

Just as there are essential goals that you need to cover in the first session to make it successful, there are three essential elements that you need to keep on the front burner throughout the treatment process in order to maintain momentum and help you and your clients reach their destination.

Start Treatment Right Away

Our focus on the importance of offering a treatment plan and assigning homework in the first session underscores the need to build on the energy that the crisis brings. And even if you are continuing your assessment in the second or even third session, you still want to be proactive in assigning homework to put new skills and concepts into action. By doing this you will not only be staying in lockstep with their expectations, your hit-the-ground-running approach will prevent them from losing energy and focus and avoid their becoming discouraged and frustrated.

Track and Update Expectations and Goals

Again, to re-emphasize one of our essential tasks of brief therapy, you want to continue to track the process and stay in lockstep each and every session. Once treatment is underway, you want to check in periodically—say, every couple of sessions or even at the end of every session—to view the larger landscape. Is the therapeutic relationship still strong? Are you and the clients focused on the same goal, in step with the overall approach and process? Does what was covered in today's session help them feel that they are getting what they need and are moving forward?

You ask and see what they say next. If you get a less-than-solid yes, or if you notice a shift—cancellations of appointments, having little to say in the session or lack of a clear agenda—you raise your concerns. Maybe the clients are getting burned out on therapy or are distracted by other pressing outside concerns; you want to know.

The bigger danger, however, isn't that the client is somehow distracted or burned out, but that little progress is being made and expectations and goals are not being addressed because both you and the clients have fallen into a clinical rut, a treading of water. Though this is more likely to happen with individuals in longer-term therapy than couples and families in brief therapy, it is a dynamic that you want to stay alert to. Here we could imagine a situation, for example, where you and Emma, or you and Luis and Isabel, have fallen into a format where they present updates of their week, but the content only varies slightly and the process is essentially the same.

There are usually two sources for this condition. One is that therapy actually isn't working: you lack the skills or the right treatment plan to fix the clients' problems. Rather than realizing and admitting this to yourself, you instead falsely believe that you both need to just do more of what you're already doing, that something will "click" at some point and the clients will make gains. The clients may be unhappy, but either they have not been in therapy before, don't know what to expect, and are trusting you to lead the way, or they are hesitant to speak up and voice their concerns, often replicating some elements of the presenting problems.

The antidote to this wheel-spinning is self-reflection and honesty, and, more importantly, good consultation and supervision—an outsider view of what and how you are doing. You also want to have, as part of your treatment map, clear markers for concrete change. If no real ground is gained, albeit slowly, in spite of the clients doing the homework and actively participating in the session, you need to step back and question the viability of your plan and goals.

The other source also comes from a lack of an effective plan, but adds another and more subtle and powerful layer: Here we're talking about possible dependency—an ethical issue—where there is a good relationship but little real change. Though there is little progress, both the clinician and clients accept this because the relationship itself overrides the momentum of treatment. Here the therapist and clients are like an old married couple, both in their comfort zones of intimacy and safety; they even look forward to seeing the other: Emma, for example, is still cutting, but she looks forward to her sessions, as do you, and her positive feedback to you about the relationship draws you in. Though the spoken goal is to help reduce her self-injurious behavior, an unspoken one has really taken its place—maintaining the comfortable relationship. You and she are colluding—she saying she is trying, you deciding not to push or change gears—in order to not risk disrupting the relationship. Nothing is really changing, but it goes unaddressed.

Again, your antidote to this is supervision and/or colleague feedback, but also, more importantly, self-awareness, self-honesty, and planned and periodic evaluation of goals and process. This is part and parcel of clinical leadership.

Continue to Track and Explore Transference Issues

The third element that can kill momentum is the igniting of emotional wounds. No doubt you will at some point trigger strong emotional baggage in the client that you'll need to repair—this is part of most therapy—but your preventative strategy is having a clear map of "how to be" as part of your own treatment plan.

As mentioned earlier, you ideally want to know as quickly as possible what not to do with a particular client in order to avoid triggering these strong and distorted emotional reactions. The danger, most especially for less-experienced clinicians, is that they believe they've nailed down the major concerns, but then have stopped looking for the subtleties and variations as treatment progresses.

You may know, for example, that you need to be careful not to be like Kim and be too intrusive with Emma, or that you need to not sound critical and controlling with Isabel, if you are to gain rapport with them, but you may not know the subtleties of what it means to Emma or Isabel not to be intrusive or critical. While you think you are only asking for details to better understand a situation that Emma has described, she hears it as pressuring the way her mother does, and she drops out. Or worse, she doesn't drop out, but says nothing, continues to feel hurt and, as she does at home, takes what she gets. Rather than fixing the problem, you've inadvertently managed to only replicate it.

Your antidote is to draw out these subtleties—asking Emma, for example, what particularly bothered her about what her mother said—so you know exactly what the triggers are. Make this understanding the larger focus and explain why and how this is important to you so your actions are not inadvertently creating the problem. And as with dependency, it helps to gain an outside perspective from a supervisor or colleague, with a focus on unraveling this micro-process.

What each of these three tasks has in common is the need to closely track process as it unfolds in the room and in the session. The effectiveness and efficiency of brief work requires such a diligent and deliberate focus, and is the challenge of this type of work.

Beyond the Third Session

In most cases the emotional fire of the crisis has abated by the third session and if not, you and the couple or family are working hard to find out why. If the couple or family has not stopped therapy because the crisis, to them, appears to be over and their anxieties are reduced, you may see

Second Session and Beyond   137

a shift in content as they move into further sessions. Here are some of common changes to look for.

New Arguments, Old Process

Luis and Isabel have agreed on a plan for handling finances, but now, in the fifth session, bring up an argument that happened during the week over Isabel's mom coming for an extended visit. At her last extended stay, Luis grew resentful over his mother-in-law's making suggestions about decorating and rearranging furniture in the home, constantly offering advice about healthy cooking and actually making dinners while the couple was at work. Luis felt that she was being too controlling, while Isabel saw her mother as just trying to be helpful. Isabel wants Luis to relax and be more accepting; Luis wants Isabel to either talk to her mother about expectations before she comes or limit the length of her visit.

Though the content was different, the couple was essentially engaging in the same process that snarled their issues about money—polarization, Luis feeling dismissed, Isabel feeling controlled. We could imagine a similar situation with Emma and her parents, with the focus shifting away from school grades to their now pressuring her about helping out at home, and Emma withdrawing.

This is common for middle stages of treatment where the couple or family feels they are dealing with new issues but fall into the same dysfunctional process. They may have moved beyond seeing you as judge, but fail to see how the same dynamic is continuing, or even if they are aware of it, they don't yet have the skills to change it. You use the session to help them come to a resolution, not by getting caught up in and mediating the content—how much Isabel's mother actually takes over, what chores are Daniel and Kim asking Emma to take on—but, instead, by pointing out the process—the dismissiveness and control, the pressure and withdrawal. You guide them through the session to apply what they learned in dealing with the presenting problems to these seemingly new ones—that Luis and Isabel need to stop the power struggle and reach a compromise that both can agree on, that Emma needs to be assertive while understanding her parents' requests.

As the couple or family moves forward with your leadership, they will gradually be able to do this on their own. But it may take many rounds and successful experiences before they can. You let them know this is how change happens, that their experience is normal, and you support them in their progress.

Backsliding Into Presenting Problems

Even though Luis and Isabel seemed to put the money issues to rest, the same issue unexpectedly surfaces again when Isabel makes another large purchase without including Luis; or Emma does poorly on a final exam and her parents are again ramping up the pressure. When this happens, you want to wonder aloud, why now? Often it is triggered by stress creating a crack in the not-yet-firm new infrastructure, causing the underlying emotions and problems to resurface. The couple or family understandably feels discouraged or frustrated.

Your task, again, is to help the couple or family unravel and understand what may have triggered the falling back, while also helping them not to disasterize and, instead, regain momentum. Let them know that this two-steps-forward-one-step-back is normal and is still a moving forward. Reassure them that their progress will become more consistent as they gain skills and confidence.

Bringing Up Old Hurts

Middle stages are about repetition, and if finding presenting problems and dysfunctional patterns reoccurring doesn't make you wonder whether things are getting worse instead of better, the bringing up of old hurts easily can. Here Luis not only complains about Isabel's mom but also, seemingly out of the blue, mentions how her father made a slightly jabbing toast about him at their wedding. This is not so much about replaying of issues but more about the couple or family feeling safe enough with you and each other to speak up and clear out feelings that have been long swept under the rug.

You let them do this. That said, what you want to be careful of is any piling on—opening of the flood gates with the complaining partner heaping on hurt after hurt in a steady barrage, overwhelming the other. Control the clock and the content by saying exactly that—though you have a lot you want to get off your chest, I'm worried that you are overwhelming your wife. You also want to watch and help the other not slip into a defensive, fact-comparing fest. You help Luis and Isabel say that the point of bringing this up isn't to hurt back, but to help the other understand what has bothered them for a long time. The other partner needs only to listen and apologize for inadvertently creating the other's pain.

Bringing Up Sensitive Topics

Here Isabel tells her husband for the first time about her childhood sexual abuse, or Luis discloses his increasingly out-of-control pornography use. Or Daniel and Kim emotionally walk through the weeks before their first child died, or they both shift focus away from Emma and begin to talk about their marital concerns. This is about using therapy as a safe place to bring up such delicate topics. Having you there in the room to help them articulate what they want to say, as well as shape the reaction of the other, encourages them to take such risks. These can be powerfully intimate moments.

Goals of Subsequent Sessions

Driving these middle-stage shifts are both the still less-than-solid changes to the couple's or family's problem-solving process and an overall opening up of the system thanks to your leadership and support. In broader terms the post-crisis focus is one of circling and re-circling around key messages and skills, digging deeper into history or layers of problems, repairing and cementing into place the core skills that we initially outlined. A quick summary of common goals and tasks of this stage of treatment follows.

Move Towards the Adult

Or what we should probably say is help the partners move out of the rescuer, victim and persecutor roles. This is where you help Emma's parents take the acceptable risk of backing away from micromanaging Emma and her school work, or calm Isabel's resentments and curb her urge to act out against Luis. Here you constantly keep in mind the model of reasonable, adult behavior and find ways of closing the gap between that and what your clients present.

Repair Emotional Wounds

Focusing on emotional wounds is essentially moving away from the relationship triangle and defining the gap between the adult and what a client presents in a more detailed and deliberate way. Once you've moved beyond the fire of the crisis, this can often become the bulk of treatment, whether or not you spend time further exploring the past. With our more behavioral approach, you'll be helping a partner who withdraws to step forward and speak up, an angry partner to self-regulate and use anger as information about needs, a "good" partner to stop walking on eggshells and instead be assertive, particularly around his wants and needs. Each needs to move against his or her grain, say now what he couldn't say to his parents, while at the same time remaining sensitive to the other's wound.

What you'll need to map out in your own mind and negotiate with the couple or family members is the taking of small but successful baby steps towards changing their patterns. You'll need to encourage them to act in spite of the anxiety they feel. Again, what you'll see at this stage is inconsistency—Emma is able to speak up and be assertive with her parents a good deal of the time, but when her overall stress is high, she falls back on her older modes of coping.

You can use sessions to practice these more functional skills as well as design homework that zeros in on them—encouraging Emma to be assertive with her teachers when they misunderstand her, for example, even though it is still difficult for her to consistently do so at home. Help the client see that it is the new process that is important, and the goal, regardless of the changing content.

Continually Facilitate Good Communication

This is another core focus. You'll be continually pointing out to the couple or family when the conversational car is going off the road, when they are getting stuck in the weeds of the past, when they are heaping on content and their emotions are rising. You'll be challenging them to identify their emotions, talk about soft emotions and explain to the other the problem under the problem. As they progress, your voice will come into their minds and they will be able to self-correct more quickly.

Update the Relationship Contract

For couples who are likely going through the seven-year itch and need to update the relationship contract, helping them do this is a good use of couple sessions. Here you encourage them to talk about what they want to be different—more individual time, less advice, more help with the children, etc. Again, you want to help them make this as concrete as possible so the other knows exactly what to focus upon, and make it balanced so that both are getting what they need, not only the more dominant partner.

Clarify and Update the Couple's Vision

Luis wants to apply for the manager position at his job; Isabel wants to stop working once they decide to have children. Here you are helping the couple thread though their own needs as well as their individual priorities. Luis sees the job as a challenge and new chapter in his career, but he will be traveling more and will be less available to help at home. Isabel will take on the major responsibility for the children, but will still want time for herself. Or the loss of her income may require the couple to forgo future plans that they had considered.

Your focus in sessions will be to help the partners be as clear as possible. You will ask the hard questions to tease out reservations and underlying concerns. You will help them negotiate a balancing of needs—Isabel may rely on babysitters more to get the free time she wants while Luis is traveling—or they may use Luis's increased income to pay for a house-cleaning service. Your focus is on the process.

You want to resist jumping in with your solutions, but instead help them see their stuckpoints and the need for compromise, and encourage them to find their own joint path.

Daniel and Kim may have a similar challenge, namely that of envisioning their lives and relationship as the demands of parenting grow smaller over time. The looming empty nest can understandably create both anxiety and challenges for couples, particularly those who have been child-centered. Raise the issue, ask the hard questions. Help Daniel and Kim begin to imagine the future life that is to come.

It is easy to see how these foci and tasks are intertwined—rescuer and victim roles tapping into emotional wounds, emotional wounds affecting communication around visions and contracts. What you are essentially doing through these varying conversations is helping each of the partners and family members to individuate by speaking more clearly and approaching rather than avoiding their own anxiety; talking about what they have been withholding, often for a long time; and renegotiating old patterns and routines that no longer work in the present. You are moving them out of their comfort zones, towards their anxiety.

The End: Termination

You're fortunate if you are able to have a formal termination with couples and families in crisis; it is more likely that they have faded away, for both good and not-so-good reasons, before such conversations can come up. That said, that doesn't mean that you should ignore this important last stage. Some couples and families will be sticking around long enough for you or them to raise the question of: how do we know when we are done?

You can obviously begin to think of termination when the emotional fires and presenting problems are put to rest—and this is the case for a majority of couples and families in crisis. For those who stay and work longer, you'll know the end is near when they are able to solve more of their own problems on their own—because they are aware of their own process and can keep the conversational car on the road, because they are sensitive to each other's wounds and avoid stepping in those emotional potholes, because they are at least able to step out of the relationship triangle and be adult with some consistency. The emotional climate is calmer, more focused, less reactionary.

On a logistical level, couples and families ready for termination may begin to miss appointments or spread them out; in sessions, the content is more of about catching up, the topics more mundane. Once again, you need to take the lead. You ask how they feel about where they are at, whether they need to continue. If you are fully embracing a brief therapy model, your frame is likely one of both encouraging them to move along and encouraging them to return if needs arise.

Some couples and families will breathe a sigh of relief that the termination elephant in the room is finally being acknowledged, and will second your motion. Others, however, feeling not quite confident enough, may waver. Offer to simply spread sessions out—biweekly to monthly to bimonthly. If mini-emotional crises arise in between, do quick phone consults or email chats. If you feel confident in their ability to be on their own, your goal is to convey that confidence to them.

Finally, constantly reiterate to them that your door is always open, should they have a need to return. Your being clear about this reduces their anxiety and sense of cutoff, further enhancing their own success. Some will return should new crises arise, and your work will likely be more brief because the foundational skills are already in place. Others will return for help with the skills and support they need as they move through new developmental challenges. By your providing that leadership and safe relationship, you can feel confident that you will remain a trusted resource for them.

This concludes our journey through the opening sessions and stages of therapy. In the next chapter, we will look at specific techniques and tools you can use with couples and families to facilitate the treatment process.

8 Couple and Family Therapy Techniques and Tools

Each clinical approach has its own heart and soul of treatment—the unraveling of and shedding of new light on the past, the focus on language and self-talk of cognitive therapies, or our focus on patterns, process and behaviors in our brief approach. While the treatment maps for the common couple and family issues provide a blueprint and set the path for your overall treatment plan, it's valuable to have at the ready specific tools and techniques that you can use and clients can learn to enhance their own progress.

In this chapter, we are going to help you do exactly that—introduce you to a variety of tools and techniques that you can use to supplement your assessment, facilitate problem-solving, improve client communication, increase the client's own self-awareness and coping skills, and help clients move out of relationship roles and into the adult. We'll divide these into two types: those that you can use within the session to change the process, and those that you can teach and assign to clients to practice outside of sessions. Consider these as additional tools to fill your clinical toolbox; mix and match them as you choose.

Experiential Techniques Within Sessions

The beauty of experiential techniques is that they are . . . experiential. They shift the session process away from the comfort zones of reporting and stories, and put the clients on the spot and challenge them to behave and learn in new ways. Because they raise anxiety, you'll want to wait to try them until after rapport and safety have been created—generally, after the first session. Some clients find them particularly powerful, while for others the anxiety overrides the benefits and makes them feel too unsafe. The only way you'll find out whether these techniques are helpful is by actually trying them out fairly soon in the treatment process and seeing how the clients respond.

One of the maxims of couple and family therapy is experience before explanation. What this means is that you generally want to do as little introduction to a technique as possible. The point of experiential techniques is to get the clients out of their heads and into the experience itself. If you explain too much at the front end, you dilute the potential impact of the process. That said, you do want to explain afterwards—placing the experience in the larger context of your treatment plan, linking what they have just experienced to their presenting problems. You need to watch the clock and make sure you leave time to do this. If you don't, and leave them emotionally shaken, with no grounding, trust and safety are lost, and there is a good chance the clients will not return.

Sculpting

This exercise is one that you do once with any couple or family, probably in the second or third session, and after the emotional fires have died down. It is a powerful way of helping couple or families understand each other's perspectives; it can enhance your own assessment and help you and the couple or family more clearly define treatment goals. Finally, it helps cut through all the verbiage for talkative couples and families and dramatizes the core issues.

You begin by asking a couple, for example, if they are willing to do an exercise that they may find helpful. They are likely to say yes, though often a more tentative yes by one of the partners. Ask who wants to go first. Here are the instructions:

I'd like you to pretend that you are sculptor and you are going to make a sculpture of your relationship. You are not to talk, but instead, move your partner into a physical position that seems to represent how she emotionally seems to you most of the time. Don't forget to include an expression on her face. And then put yourself in the sculpture with your own body position; be aware of closeness and distance, and, again, shape a facial expression that represents how you feel in the relationship most of the time. Any questions? Okay, do it.

Here Luis, for example, has Isabel sitting in a chair, her arms crossed, pouting and ignoring him while he is standing behind her with arms outstretched and grimacing. Now you ask them to hold the position and ask Isabel how she feels sitting here: "Lonely; I can tell he is there and upset but I am afraid to turn around because I'm afraid he will only get worse." "And Luis, how do you feel?" "Like she is totally ignoring me. I'm angry and frustrated."

"Okay, Luis. Now change the sculpture and shape it into how you would ideally like it to be." Here Luis has Isabel stand up and give him a hug or stand next to him holding hands. Again, you ask how each feels. What you may hear at this point is Isabel saying that this feels good, or that the hugging feels a bit too suffocating. Good to know.

Now you allow Isabel to take her turn with both her present image and ideal future sculpture. Again, ask how each feels in those positions. Often the partners' future images are similar. You now can debrief and talk about the emotional climate that each perceives, as well as ways of behaviorally closing the gaps between the present and their ideals.

For families, the process is much the same. Here, it is best to start with the identified patient—Emma, for example. You can do this with younger children as well, say, aged 8 and up. Children younger than that often have a difficult time understanding the concept or tend to do behavioral sculptures—dad reading the paper or mom on the phone—rather than emotional ones, much like a kinetic family drawing. If you are working with a large family, there is no need, and it is not wise, to do everyone, because the repetition dilutes the emotional impact. Instead, pick the identified patient and one of the parents, and then ask for a volunteer or ask for the quietest of the group. Again, debrief, pointing out different perceptions, linking them to the presenting problems, talking about how to close the gap between now and the ideal.

Like most experiential techniques, this sidesteps the tit-for-tat defensiveness that comes with stories. There are no facts to argue over, no one is wrong and it goes to the heart of the problems. And the images can be used as metaphors that can be referred back to in later sessions. When Luis complains about Isabel tuning him out sometimes during the week, you can say that you remember his sculpture and wonder if once again they are both feeling this familiar way.

Life-Play Guided Image

This, too, is another exercise that you will do only once and when the emotional fires have cooled. It works well for couples, but you can also do it with individuals. In the spirit of experience before explanation, let's walk through the actual exercise, and debrief after. Try and do this as you read this, or have someone read it to you; the paragraph breaks indicate where to pause and allow the images to shape themselves:

Start by taking a few deep breaths just to help you settle. When you feel ready imagine yourself entering a theater. You walk into a lobby where there are a lot of people milling around. You walk through the lobby into the auditorium where you take the best seat in the house. In front of you is a large stage with a curtain drawn across it. You make yourself comfortable, and now the other people of the audience come in and take the seats around you. The house lights go dim and the stage lights go on. A play is about to start.

The curtain rises on the first act of the play. There we see your parents and the time is before you were born. Watch what happens, listen to what is said, see who else is there.

The curtain comes down . . . . The curtain rises on the next act and we you see on the stage, and you are a young child. Again, watch what happens, listen to what is said, see who else is there.

The curtain comes down again.... The curtain rises, you are on stage, but now you are a teenager and are with one or both of your parents. They are talking to you about growing up—about relationships and sex, careers and education. Listen to what they say, listen to what you say back.

The curtain comes down.... The curtain rises on the next act and you are on stage and now you are a bit older—it is the time in your life when you are leaving home for the first time, literally moving out of the house—to go to college, to get an apartment with friends, to get married. On stage with you are one or both of your parents. Watch what happens, listen to what is said, see if you can tell how you are feeling at that moment.

The curtain comes down.... The curtain rises on the next act and now you are a young adult and in a serious relationship—a boyfriend, a girlfriend, a partner—and that person is on stage with you. Watch what happens, listen to what is said.

The curtain comes down.... The curtain rises and the time is the present. You are on stage. Watch what happens.

The curtain comes down.... The curtain rises again and the time is five years from now, in the future; you are on stage. Watch what happens, see who is there, listen to what is said.

The curtain comes down.... The curtain rises again and the time is ten years from now, in the future. Again, you are on stage. Watch what happens, listen to what is said, see who is there.

The curtain comes down.... The time is the far-distant future, that time in your life when people not only see you as experienced but also wise. One or two people come to you and ask you for advice. They ask what it is that you've learned most from all your years of experiencing and living. Listen to what you say. Listen to what they say back.

The play is over now and the curtain comes down; the stage lights go off and the house lights go on. The audience gets up and begins to leave the theater. You follow them out and you overhear them talking about the play. Listen to what they say about the play....

Okay, how did you do? Did you see anything that surprised you?

The question to ask when you are doing any guided imagery is: Out of the things you could have seen, why did you see what you did, and what does it say about your life right now? What is the overall tone? Are there patterns that run through the scenes—conflict or loneliness, happiness or confusion?

What you do now is have each of the clients take turns describing his play. Walk through it scene-by-scene. Have each describe what he saw. Along the way you can ask more detailed questions to help you, in fact, visualize what the client saw: What exactly did your mother say? Could you tell how you felt? Were you surprised that your grandfather was standing towards the back of the room?

After each client has described his play, you now provide a framework for interpretation. Here are some guidelines.

The first scene of your parents is about early couple relationships—how did the parents get along, what were they doing? We all have an image of our parents' early marriage which can become our own subconscious model. How does this image mirror the clients' relationship in some way?

The second scene is of your childhood—out of all that the clients could have imagined, why this one—what does it say about their childhoods? Were you happy, sad? Alone, with sibs, with parents? What were they doing? How do these themes carry over to the present? What is the contrast between the first and second scene? What changed? That the parents were happy and close and now more distant and tense, for example. The change says something about the impact of their birth on the parents' marital relationship.

The third scene is a birds and bees talk about growing up—what did the parents say? While most teens did not get such a formal talk, teens generally receive a lot of ideas during these years about what makes a happy life, what are life's priorities. Often these parent-messages become the "shoulds" that drive our lives, and when we don't follow them, we feel guilty. Many mid-life crises are about the gap between the shoulds and wants. Finally, some clients will hear no advice in this scene because they didn't receive any in real life. They were then left to their own devices, or may have sought out other mentors, such as friend's parents, or teachers.

The next scene is leaving. What is pivotal about the scene is how they imagined themselves feeling at that time—excited, scared, depressed, guilty? Why? Even if they were excited, the question is why—is there something they were anxious to get away from? There is an idea that how you felt when you first left home becomes the bottom line for when you leave other things in your life—relationships, jobs. The question here for clients is when they look back over their lives, when they've left jobs or relationships, is there an emotional common denominator that they consistently hit—when I feel _____ I leave? This is often tied to emotional wounds, and differs for each partner. It also gives you a clue into what feeling-state in therapy might cause them to quit treatment.

An early relationship—what did they see, what was the tone? How was it like or unlike the first scene of parents? How does it mirror what the couple is struggling with now? Again, you are looking for themes and patterns.

The present—out of all that is going on in their lives right now, what did they see? How is it similar to or different from the other scenes? Sometimes the individuals will focus on their relationship and the image is like that of a sculpture, a summary of the state of the relationship. But at other times, the scene may be about work or the individual alone. What is important is the emotional tone.

Five years in the future—what did they see—how is it similar or different from what they consciously think about? How is it like or different from other scenes? Again, the content may vary—some may envision the relationship, but others being on the job. Some may have clear images, but those going through stressful transitions may have vague images or none at all. Reassure clients that not seeing a clear image only reflects their current level of stress.

Ten years in the future: What's changed from the previous scene? The image here may be more unclear. Tone is, again, important.

The final scene is a way of pulling together the moral of the story of the person's life. Again, those in transition may have a difficult time seeing this scene. If they did, what is the message they heard themselves saying to the others on stage? How is what they said similar to or different from what their parents may have advised?

Finally, the audience reaction is about our social sense, our natural tendency to wonder about what others think of us. What did the audience say about your play—exciting, boring, glad the character turned himself around, frustrated that he didn't? What's more important is how the clients reacted to the audience's impressions. How sensitive are they to others' opinions, or do they worry about what others may think?

This is the basic model. Feel free to add or adapt scenes. If you have a couple where both partners have been married before, for example, you may include scenes of their first marriages. If they are struggling over the role of extended family, you could include a childhood scene of a family activity that includes extended family, such as a holiday celebration. If you were to do this with Emma individually, most of your scenes would be about her future.

This can be emotionally powerful, stirring old memories and emotions. Because the individuals are self-selecting, they are not likely to imagine any new or terribly traumatic material unless they are extremely emotionally fragile, in which case you would skip doing this exercise. What this exercise provides is a sense of history for you, and a new view of each other for the partners. Because these are images and not facts, this is new content that they can't argue over. It changes the emotional climate.

Finally, as with the sculpture, make sure you watch the clock and leave time to debrief. If you decide to use this, mention the idea a week before—"When you come next week I'd like to do an exercise with you that may take up most of the session. But if something comes up that we need to talk about, we can save it for another time"—underscoring once again the clients' taking an active role in setting session agendas.

Enactments

Enactments were a mainstay of Minuchin's structural therapy approach. Essentially, you have the couple or family do in the session what they ideally need to do at home. You may ask Luis and Isabella, for example, to discuss their spending and then to work out a budget they both can agree on, or ask Emma and her parents to negotiate more realistic expectations about her school grades.

Your job is to help guide the process: Let them know when they are getting stuck in means and losing sight of the ends; facilitate their moving forward, rather than overstating their point or bringing up the past. Like the sideline coach, help them stay on track and move towards successful problem-solving and understanding. At the end of the exercise, give them positive feedback and highlight what you specifically saw them doing well, so they can hopefully replicate the process in the future.

Techniques and Tools to Use as Homework

Part of any good therapy, but particularly in brief therapy, where so much of work is not only short-term but also behavioral, is providing clients with tool and techniques that they can take away from treatment to help them better manage their anxiety, anger and depression, and change their roles and move towards the adult, and that, with practice, they can integrate into their everyday lives. By learning to more successfully navigate their lives on their own, clients feel empowered; their self-esteem increases. A smorgasbord of techniques and tools to teach and assign as you see fit follows.

Business Meetings

Couples and families who rarely talk or only talk when they are upset, and then argue and fail to circle back, quickly generate a stack of unsolved problems that either keep arising or are emotionally swept under the rug until tripped on. Often partners complement each other, with one partner more comfortable with talking but also apt to be more emotional, while the other struggles to speak up and tends to internalize emotions. The unfolding of the process in therapy results in the need for the quiet one to step up, and the other to step down in order to make it easier for the other to step up.

Business meetings are a way of helping couples and families change this process at home. It offers a structured exercise that moves the clients out of their emotional brains and into their rational ones, so they can be understood and problems can be solved. Here are the instructions for assigning this homework:

One of the things that I think would be helpful for you both to do this week is what I call a business meeting. Rather than trying to catch each other on the run, or bringing topics up when you're both tired and cranky, I'd like you instead to decide in advance on a time to meet that is good for both of you—say, Saturday morning after you've had a cup of coffee.

The idea here is to pretend you are at work. As you move through the week, make note of issues that you might want to bring up in the upcoming meeting, rather than tackling them in the moment—one or two items that you'd like to bring, either to help your partner understand how you feel, and/or to solve a problem. It might be as mundane as making plans together for the following weekend, or something more emotional, such as circling back to some comment on Tuesday that upset you. If you tend to be hesitant to speak up, you have time during the week to figure out how you feel and what you want to say so you don't have think on your feet. And if you tend to be more spontaneous and emotional, this gives you a chance to slow down, sort out your feelings and decide how important the issue is, and what is the problem that needs to get solved.

The meeting should only be about a half hour long. You want to take turns bringing up items. Again, sort out what the main point or problem is that you want to solve before you start, and, most important, you want to pretend you're at work—that is, stay in your rational brain and do not get overly emotional, just as you would do at a team meeting on your job. If the other guy starts to get upset, do your best to stay calm and focused. If you both get upset, see if you can calm yourselves down and get back on track. If this is too difficult, too emotional, stop, do not get into an argument. Just bring the topic to our next meeting and we will discuss here. Any questions?

The goal here is, as the instructions point out, to help the couple have a sane and reasonable conversation, and create a success-experience in communicating and problem-solving. The time limit and work state of mind help create this. Families can be asked to do the same: schedule a family meeting where everyone can bring up issues—planning outings, complaints about siblings, negotiating bedtimes or privileges. The parents need to be the ones to lay out the ground rules—no arguing, no snipping at one another, no having an agenda, setting a time limit. Coach them that their role is one of facilitation, not over-controlling the content, taking on the role as courtroom judge or double-teaming on any one child. Obviously, this is most effective for school-age children and teens.

Letter-Writing

This is a powerful exercise for helping clients reach closure and heal emotional wounds. It can be used to facilitate unresolved grief and loss, to relieve guilt or anger over a past relationship or to clarify emotions and needs in a current one. Emma might write letters to her parents about her own resentments and needs, or to a friend or teacher at school who she felt was not being supportive. If Luis was struggling with the loss of his father, he might write a letter laying out his thoughts and feelings; a partner projecting her old hurts from her ex-husband onto to her current one may write letters to her ex-partner to gain closure and help stop the projections. Most often the letters are not to be mailed, though we could imagine Emma, for example, reading or describing hers to her parents.

Here are the basic instructions:

I'd like you to write three letters. The purpose is to help you get things off your chest, get some emotional closure, discover how you feel and what you need. Imagine that this person were to come here for just an hour (point to an empty chair in your office); you were never going to see him again, but you wanted to have this one opportunity to express how you feel.

For the first letter just write down how you feel. Do this long-hand, pen and paper, no computer (computers make it seem more formal and move folks out the flow of thoughts). Just start writing and see what comes up. If you're not sure how to start, just write down that you don't know how to start. Do this as a stream of consciousness; don't worry about grammar and getting it right. It may be about things that made you feel angry or sad, things that you appreciate, whatever comes up. Write until you feel you have run out of things to say.

For the second letter, write down what you think that person might say, given his personality and your perception of him, if he received the first letter or heard you say what you wrote in it. He may be defensive or dismissive or curt or apologetic. Again, just see what comes out.

The third letter is probably the most important. Write down what it is that, ideally, you would like to hear the person say. Here he may say that he was sorry, or that he remembered an important time in your lives, or that he was proud of you. Again, just see what emerges.

You may find that though you start writing to one person, your thoughts shift mid-stream and you begin thinking of someone else (Luis's father, for example, suddenly also brings up memories of his mother or a former girlfriend). If you do, just switch and write about that person.

Take your time and do this when you have enough time and space; try to do all three letters at one sitting. Bring your letters in to our next session.

It's helpful for you to write the instructions down before they leave so they understand the difference among the three letters. And because this can create anxiety, you may find that clients will put this off and say they didn't have time this past week, forgot to do it, etc. Be gently persistent.

When they do bring the letters in, they will likely hand them to you. Hand them back and ask them to read them aloud. This is important. It is the reading that helps them express the emotions and provides both the information and experience to others in the room—they may easily cry or get angry. Just as you may do when hearing report about their guided imageries, ask for any specifics as they finish one letter and before they move onto the next—Emma, you wrote that your parents were not supportive; what does that mean, what you were specifically thinking about that felt unsupportive? The aim is to free up emotions by making language clearer.

After they finish, thank them for taking the risk. Ask if they were surprised by anything they wrote. Ask for feedback from partners or family members, steering them away from any defensiveness or attempts to soothe the other's feelings. Finally, as with the other exercises, place them in the larger context of the presenting problems—exploring, for example, what Emma's parents can now specifically begin doing to better support her, or underscoring for Luis and Isabel how Isabel's dismissiveness of Luis triggers old wounds associated with his father. Once again, leave plenty of time for the reading and debriefing.

Check-Ins

Check-ins are about helping clients monitor their emotional states, and are both proactive and preemptive. Clients who flare quickly with anger or are struggling with anxiety often have difficulty reining in their emotions because the anger or anxiety have reached too high a level. In order to have more emotional control, they need to become more attuned to their emotional states and then act before they reach an emotional point of no return; this is what the checking in does. It also helps them to step back from the feelings and see them more objectively.

Here are the basic instructions for assigning check-ins as homework:

Because, as we've discussed, you seem to go from 0 to 60 quickly with your anger (or seem to get quickly overwhelmed), it may be helpful for you to track your emotions so you can learn to catch and manage them sooner. During the next week, I'd like you to check in with yourself once an hour. If it helps, set your phone alarm to remind you. When the alarm goes, simply ask yourself: On a scale of 1 to 10, with 1 being perfectly calm, and 10 being enraged or overwhelmed, how am I doing?

When you find yourself getting up towards a 4 or 5 in terms of irritability or anxiety, the next question you want to ask yourself is what is going on: Is there a problem that I need to fix? You may realize that you are getting annoyed because your boss never responded to your email, or that you are worried that your partner might forget to call the electric company about that outstanding bill. If there is a real problem to fix, do something, take action—write another follow-up email to your boss or send your partner a text reminding her about the bill or, better yet, check into it yourself.

If, on the other hand, you have trouble defining a real problem, or if your problem is somewhat irrational—you're imagining that your boss is actually ignoring you because he's about ready to fire you, or that the electric company is likely to turn off your lights today—you don't want to get lost in those thoughts. Instead, say to yourself that you are upset, that your angry or anxious mind has, for some reason, fired up, and that you now need to do something to help you calm your mind. You may want to take some deep breaths, take a break and walk outside for a few minutes, listen to some music.

There are several processes at work here. One is that of stepping back and, through practice, helping clients become more attuned to their emotional states. You are also helping clients differentiate between rational and irrational anxiety and problems; sometimes the differences are obvious, others times murkier, and you can work with clients to help them learn to sort these out. You are also asking them to take action to address rational and real problems. This is important as a way of helping clients learn to use their emotions as information, rather than just being flooded by them or acting them out. Encouraging them to act quickly and decisively pushes them out of the quagmire of ruminating over what "right" action to take, which generally only feeds their heightened state. Finally, the taking of action is itself empowering and helps move them towards the adult.

As they report back to you about their experiences with this homework, help them identify their own particular indicators of stress, as well as possible triggers—why was Tuesday an emotionally more difficult day than Monday? It may be about lingering issues, but often it is about simple things like not getting enough sleep the night before. Understanding what makes them tick, identifying their own emotional patterns and stepping up and taking concrete action helps them and their partners not misinterpret and trigger each other, helping to break dysfunctional patterns before they get out of hand.

This same exercise can be assigned to those clients struggling with depressive moods that seem to fluctuate over the course of a day. Have them check in with themselves every hour, and when the scale starts to climb, see if there is a problem that needs to be fixed, and then, to offset the rumination and internalization, take some concrete action. This is particularly helpful in incidents of situational depression, where often the person feels trapped and his depressed voice says, why bother, it doesn't matter, you can't change it. The doing something is the antidote.

If no concrete problem can be identified, and it is just their current state of mind, they then need to attack their negative thoughts—just as anxious clients need to take steps to self-regulate—by writing down exactly what they are and countering them with rational thinking. (This is similar to dialectical behavior therapy, which instructs clients to move from their emotional to their "wise" mind.) Next, they should be instructed to make a list of good things that have occurred in the day and that they are grateful for—again, details and seemingly mundane things are important—the sun is out, my husband helped get the kids off to school, my cold is getting better.

And as with anxiety and anger, this taking of action helps the clients feel less like victims of their moods. By pushing back, and re-engaging their rational brain, they can, over time, rewire it.

First-Aid Plans for Acting Out Urges

If check-ins are about enhancing overall emotional awareness and emotional responsibility in order to keep emotions under a threshold level, first-aid plans are for those times when emotions have gone too high and are difficult to rein in. We talked earlier about assigning first-aid plans to help violent couples, who emotionally feed off each other and rapidly escalate, to disengage. But first-aid plans can also be assigned for those who are prone to being self-destructive—Emma and her cutting, for example, or clients who have cravings for drug use or disordered eating. Again, the instructions, using Emma as an example, are:

Here's something that I'd like to try to help you manage in case you have any urges to cut. It's a three-part plan that you do as soon as you start thinking of cutting. For the first part, I'd like to you write down whatever is going through your mind—what you are thinking and feeling at the moment. Don't worry about how it sounds or the grammar, just get your thoughts out. Set a timer and do this for ten minutes. (Writing longer can stir up too much emotional material and overwhelm the clients.) Next do some aerobic activity that gets your heart rate up—running or walking quickly around the block or jumping jacks in your room. Again, do this for ten minutes.

Finally, and this is the most important part, do something that feels to you like self-care. It might be taking a hot bath, listening to your favorite music, reading a great book, painting your nails. Again, do this for ten to 20 minutes. Actually, let's come up with a list right now of things you can do.

The idea here is helping calm your thoughts by getting them out. The exercise increases your endorphins, which helps you feel more positive; and, finally, the self-care is about exactly that, taking care of yourself, rather than being self-critical or resentful of others. Does this all this make sense?

Get a solid yes on this. Write out the instructions so the client doesn't have to try and remember them in the emotional heat of the moment. This strategy in dealing with any cravings is not about getting the person to stop following his urges, but having at the ready some substitute action to relieve the stress and break the compulsive pattern. This plan for Emma provides a period of time combined with activities to help calm the emotional mind. This can also be used for other forms of self-injury, drug or alcohol cravings, binge eating, pornography or video game addiction. Again, this is first-aid; the larger goals are addressing the underlying causes, solving the problems creating stress and increasing assertive behavior overall.

Emotional Freedom Technique

There is much on the internet on this, including YouTube videos and specific websites, as well as books under the category of tapping (see Evans,

2013; Ortner, 2014), and rather than trying to teach it here, it is easier to learn by viewing demonstrations. The technique is based upon Chinese acupressure and acupuncture, where the client taps on various meridian points on their body to help relieve emotional distress. It is simple to learn, safe (it does not create any abreactions), quick to do, and works well for various forms of anxiety, post-traumatic stress disorder and even physical pain. You can teach it to clients in the session and see how well it works for them; give them a handout of instructions, and then assign it as homework as a first-aid technique to practice when emotionally stressed. Again, having a technique to use in the moment empowers clients and helps them feel less at the mercy of their emotional states.

Assertiveness/Risk-Taking

Assertiveness is a foundational skill for success within couple and family relationships, and it is its absence that fuels the rescuer, victim and persecutor roles. Assertiveness is also a universal antidote to low self-esteem, anxiety and depression. Assertiveness is speaking up, saying what you want and need, being proactive rather than reactive, taking action rather than internalizing and ruminating. It is a skill that is essential for someone like Emma to learn to counter her feeling overwhelmed, as well for as those prone to anger, such as volatile couples, whose rational minds all too quickly go offline.

Being assertive in a specific situation and around a specific problem is a pin-point strategy for managing relationships in an adult way. But the larger underlying issue and its companion strategy are to encourage clients to expand their risk-taking experiences overall. Learning to approach rather than avoid anxiety and being willing to do new and difficult behaviors in spite of how you feel expand one's comfort zones, and counters the anxious and depressive voices that always say that disaster is always ready to happen, that you'll never succeed, that the world is unsafe, you are loser, why bother, stay put. It is only by going against the chant of these negative voices and finding out that what you fear would happen does not, that you find the path to no longer being so afraid in the world.

In assigning this as homework you may say something like this:

We talked last week about your anxiety (or depression or holding things in or blowing up), and one of the things that helps reduce these feelings (or behaviors) is learning to speak up and let others know what you need and want in a calm yet clear manner. This is a skill that you can practice. Now I realize that probably the hardest people to be assertive with are those close to you, like your partner, your parents or people in authority, like your supervisor at work. But you don't need to start there. The idea is stepping up anytime when your instincts are telling you to hold back.

So, if the staff person at Starbucks inadvertently gives you the wrong change and your head is saying it's only 50 cents, why bother, instead, speak up. If a colleague at work doesn't get back to you about a work question you asked, and you know in your gut that you're annoyed but your head is telling you that you shouldn't be so sensitive, try listening to your gut and do something to follow up. This is not about 50 cents or the answer to the question, it is about stepping outside your comfort zone and approaching, rather than avoiding, situations that make you anxious. The first few times you do this you will feel anxious or guilty—that's fine, that's because you're changing your patterns and your brain circuits haven't caught up yet. Those feelings will decrease with continued practice. Start with less threatening situations, and then move up towards those that feel more challenging.

But another part of this is learning to increase your comfort zone in general. This makes you more flexible in the world, increases your self-esteem and can make your happier in the long run because you are not afraid to try something new, grow and learn. Here it is about risk-taking in a more general and global way—doing something every day that feels a little bit uncomfortable. It doesn't have to be big—it could be as simple as ordering something new for lunch or driving a different way home. Again, it's not about the lunch or the drive, but pushing against your own habits and resistance, and experiencing the anxiety, yet moving forward and finding out that it turns out okay. Afterwards, ignore that self-critical voice that may say that it wasn't anything special or that you could have done better, but instead, make a conscious effort to congratulate yourself for taking the risk.

Helping clients, even in brief therapy, have success with such stepping-out behaviors begins to develop a life-long skill that they can continue to hone long after therapy is completed. Be sure to give plenty of positive feedback for any efforts, no matter how small.

Shoulds vs. Wants/Quick Decisions

These two related assignments are variations on risk-taking, but are geared primarily for those who tend to be martyrs. Where persecutors need to learn to self-regulate their anger and use it as information to let others know what they need, and victims need to learn to increase their self-confidence by both speaking up and tackling problems on their own, martyrs need to move out of over-responsibility and away from the "shoulds" that tend to dominate their thinking, their lives and their expectations of others. They need to stop living in their rule-bound heads, and shift their attention to gut reactions and wants in order to better understand what they need. These two exercises are aimed towards help shift and strengthen this focus; again, the instructions are:

I have a few things that I'd like you to try in the next week. The first is that I'd like you to pick a day—preferably a day you are not working. Before you do anything during that day—vacuum the rug, go to the grocery store, go on Facebook—ask yourself why you are doing this: because you should or because you want to. Just be aware of your inner response. You don't need to do anything different, just be more aware of what motivates you.

Similarly, if at any point during the week you have a gut sense that you want something, however faint the feeling may be—a desire to get pizza or call your brother—act on it: get the pizza, call your brother. Now what may happen is that you won't like the pizza, and your critical voice will scold you for being so impulsive. Expect it, but don't pay attention to it. It's not about pizza, but practicing recognizing and acting on your gut feelings. And if you have a sense that you don't want to do something, see if you can act on that—don't walk off your job, but don't be afraid to turn down that lunch invitation that you think you should accept, or skip cleaning out the kitty litter first thing Saturday morning if you don't want to do it right then. Again, it's not about lunch or kitty litter, but practicing acting on your gut reactions.

Finally, in conjunction with these or separately, experiment with making decisions quickly—the pizza, the kitty litter—or something else—sending off an email at work rather than laboring over it. Rather than managing your anxiety by being perfectionist, you are expanding your comfort zone by taking acceptable risks. Doing this at first will be a bit unsettling; your anxious mind will tell you that you are not thinking this through and may regret your decision—again, this is the lag between new behaviors and old reactions. But if you persist, making decisions quickly will increase your self-confidence and lower your anxiety as you come to realize that not everything is equally important, and that even if it doesn't turn out the way you hoped, you can still do something to repair or change it. Again, it is not about the content of the decision, but the doing and doing differently. Does all this make sense? Any questions?

Again, the assumption here is that clients are already in lockstep with you regarding the need to break out of the martyr role, become more flexible and move towards what they want as adults rather than being anxious and always walking on eggshells. Frame it as experiments to reduce performance pressure. Provide positive feedback on any attempts they make and help sort out those places where they got emotionally stuck.

Organizational Skill Training

What we're referring to here is helping clients be proactive in setting priorities and following through on everyday tasks. This is particularly helpful for both those clients with attention-deficit/hyperactivity disorder

(AD/HD), and those who are anxious and easily overwhelmed. They have several characteristics in common.

One is that they have a difficult time setting priorities—at any given time everything, to them, seems important or nothing really seems important, fueled by black-and-white thinking. Both types of clients tend to procrastinate—those with AD/HD because they have a difficult time focusing and actually are able to get more focused when they are facing a deadline, and those with anxiety because they feel overwhelmed, can't partialize the problem and avoid. They both are essentially emotionally driven; those with AD/HD tend to do the easy rather than the hard because the difficult feels too difficult for them; those with anxiety are wired to follow their emotions and their emotional, rather than their rational, brains, and these negative emotions both preoccupy them and derail them from moving forward.

It is no surprise that these learned ways of running their lives often spills over into their intimate relationships, creating a host of everyday problems: their partners and family members see them as unreliable, undermining trust and eroding caring; important tasks are not completed or are completed only with lots of stress and angst, spiking irritability and creating an ongoing negative climate within the relationship and household. Where martyrs are needing to move from the rational to the emotional, these clients need to move from the emotional to the rational. What they share is the need to break dysfunctional patterns by deliberately experimenting with new behaviors and learning new skills. Once again, the instructions are:

We've talked about your tendency to procrastinate (or get overwhelmed), which affects your ability to complete important tasks. I'd like to help you learn to change these patterns and I'd like you to try a new way of approaching these challenges in the next week.

On Sunday night, I'd like you to sit down and map out for yourself the three or four most important things that you want to accomplish in the next week. If you have a hard time deciding what are the most important ones, ask your partner (or your parent) to help you sort it out. They shouldn't tell you what to do, but should help you figure out what are the priorities. Write these tasks down.

Every night before you go to bed, think about or, better yet, write down the one or two things that are tied to your weekly goals and that you specifically want to accomplish in two hours the next day. So if, for example, it is writing a paper for school, you may decide on Monday that you need to make up an outline for the paper on Tuesday, or if you want to clean out and organize the garage over the weekend, you may use Friday evening to think about items you may want to give away or sell so you act on those the next day. Again, if you have a difficult time figuring this out, breaking down the bigger tasks into smaller ones and start to get a bit overwhelmed, settle yourself down and get some help from your partner (or parent). Thinking about this the night before will prime your brain for action, help you hit the ground running and help offset that feeling in the morning that you just don't feel like it, for whatever reason, which causes you to put it off. Finally, decide the day before what is the best time to do this—a time when you are most alert and focused.

The next day you want to hit the ground running and do this as you planned. What you don't want to do is get derailed. You're trying to train yourself to tackle harder things first rather than putting them off and opting for easier ones. Set to work but also set a timer—for an hour. Focus on the work for that time as best you can—avoid getting distracted by checking emails, having a snack, etc. After the hour, stop and take a break, but time the break—15 minutes, no longer. Go get a cup of coffee and do check your email, but only for the 15 minutes.

The break will help you emotionally and cognitively re-center; the timing helps keep you from physically and emotionally wandering off. After the break, reset the timer for another hour; stay focused. After the timer goes off, you can stop, but if you have some momentum, you can continue. Now you're done and you want to build in some reward—like make yourself a lunch on Saturday that you like, or do some exercise you enjoy, and then use the rest of the day to do easier things. Do this every day in the week.

Again, the goals here are helping you practice setting priorities, breaking big tasks into smaller ones so it is not so overwhelming and, most importantly, helping you accomplish things even if they do seem difficult and you emotionally don't want to, or you feel a bit overwhelmed. With practice, it will get easier. Does this make sense? Any questions?

It is helpful for these folks to have a sideline coach for rational problem-solving and emotional support. That said, it is also important, and you can stress this to clients, that they are the ones in charge and they need to say what type of support they need from the other. The danger here is that if they are more passive—if Isabel, for example, does not give Luis clear guidelines about how he can help her with budgeting, or Emma doesn't let her parents know what she needs from them when she struggles mapping out school assignments—they will, because of their own anxiety, take over. Rather than learning these important management skills, the clients will not, and will wind up feeling parentified rather than supported. When you check in with them on this homework, give positive feedback for gains and efforts, and then help break down where they may have emotionally gotten off track.

Sensate Focus Exercises

Let's shift focus. While we don't have the space to cover detailed treatment protocols for sexual problems, and sexual behavior issues do not generally put couples into crisis and bring them into therapy, it's helpful if you are working with couples to have in your clinical toolkit treatment protocols for working with the most common sexual issues. That said, one of the all-around best exercises for premature ejaculation, anxiety and performance issues, and even triggering from trauma, as well as just opening up a couple's overall communication about sex, is the classic sensate focus exercises originally developed by Masters and Johnson in the 1970s. It is a good starting point for most sexual problems.

There are small variations on the exercise that you can easily find online, but the basic format is a four-part approach. Here's how to present it:

I'd like you to try an exercise this next week which I think will be helpful in treating your _____ problem. It is called the sensate focus exercise and, basically, it is a four-step method of helping you both become more comfortable with each other physically and help you communicate to each other what you most enjoy and need. The first step, which I'd like you to do at least once this week, is what is essentially giving each other massages. Set aside a time when you are not hurried or distracted (the kids are in bed, the cell phones are off) and either start by being naked or, if that feels too uncomfortable, by staying loosely clothed together in bed. You are going to take turns. One person is the receiver, the other the doer; decide who wants to go first.

The person who is receiving the massage is in control and directs what the other person does. It is important that the doer just does what the other asks—this is important because it builds trust and reduces anxiety. You begin by simply massaging the person, but avoid any contact with genital, sexual areas—breasts, penis, etc. The person receiving the massage can say what they like, how hard to place pressure, where, etc. Take your time. Then switch roles. It's important that you avoid sexual areas and have no sexual intercourse during this week.

When they come in next week, follow up, see if they did the exercise, how they felt, were there any emotional triggers—strong reactions to certain types of touching, which is not uncommon for individuals who have a history of physical or sexual abuse. If the exercise was successful, both were able to relax and give feedback and move on to the next stage. If there were any stumbling blocks, see what the stuckpoints were, talk about how to offset them and reassign the exercise.

The second step is now doing the same, but without clothes, and include in the massage the touching of sexual/genital areas. Again, go slow; the person receiving is in control and gives feedback about what he likes and doesn't like.

Again, follow up, looking for points of anxiety or stress. Repeat the exercise if problem areas arose.

The third step is to move ahead, and this time include penetration, but simply that. Penetrate but do not thrust. This is important for reducing performance anxiety—especially for men struggling with erectile dysfunction or premature ejaculation—and increasing self-awareness of feeling emotional and physical feelings.

Finally, if all goes well, the last step gives the couple the green light to have intercourse. By moving slowly and successfully, each partner's own physical confidence has increased; they know what to do and not do to make it pleasurable for themselves and their partner.

What makes dealing with sexual issues difficult is often your discomfort, especially when countertransference rises up, such as when working with couples who remind you of your parents. Here your leadership and openness are especially important; if you fall into your own awkwardness, you are in danger of replicating the problem. You need to feel comfortable talking explicitly and asking hard questions to understand the details and stuckpoints, and if that is difficult, seek consultation and support. Only by your openness can couples come to do the same.

This concludes our chapter on techniques and tools. Undoubtedly, you already have a variety of techniques in your toolbox tied to your clinical models, and, hopefully, some of the ones we have discussed will add to them. What's important is seeing them as tools, not ends in their own right, which enables you and the couples and families to successfully implement their treatment plan.

What you want to avoid is feeling pressure, because of your own anxiety, to offer something new and exotic each week in order to keep the couple or family engaged. They are doing *your* style of therapy, but it is *their* therapy. The bulk of your work in a brief model will be on their agendas, helping them change their patterns and process around presenting problems, emotional wounds and stuckpoints to problem-solving. Techniques and tools should be in service to these goals.

References

Evans. J. (2013). *EFT: EFT tapping scripts and solutions to an abundant you.* New York: Speedy Publishing.

Ortner, N. (2014). *Tapping solution: A revolutionary system for stress free living* (8th ed.). New York: Hay House.

9 Integrating the Brief Approach Into Your Own Therapeutic Style

Maybe you are thinking of volunteering at a walk-in crisis clinic, or your supervisor is pressuring you to do more short-term work to counter the ever-present client waiting list. Maybe insurance plans are limiting the number of allowable sessions, or you are primarily a clinician who works with individuals on a longer-term basis and you are simply wanting to expand your clinical repertoire and flexibility. In this chapter we will highlight the concepts, skills and techniques of our crisis-oriented brief model and look at ways you can successfully integrate them into your own clinical style. We'll provide tips on how to apply this model to entire cases, as well as offer an à la carte approach—helping you choose and apply those concepts, techniques and models that most appeal to you.

But before we do that, let's talk about the challenges of moving from a longer-term model to a briefer, crisis-oriented one.

Shifting Gears

If you are showing up to the crisis clinic for the first time this week, making a clinical shift to working with this population and model can seem a bit disorienting and even uncomfortable. A crisis focus is going to not only require that you tolerate the likely high emotion, but also pressure you to put out the emotional fire, change the emotional climate and formulate and offer a clear and operative treatment plan before the clients leave the office—all the ground we covered in our discussions of the goals and processes of the first session.

If we add the elements of brief work to the mix, the challenges are compounded. If you are used to doing a multi-session assessment or see treatment as a slow peeling away of layers, for example, you are likely feeling that what you are offering clients is both incomplete in assessment and surface-skimming in treatment. The shorter timeframe and more narrow focus can cause you to feel there is too much valuable therapeutic and historical ground left unturned and potential life-changing insights left withering on the psychological vine. The pace will feel rushed, like pushing yourself to play a piece on the piano at a faster tempo than you feel capable of playing; you may get through it but not feel fully aware of what you just did.

And if the pace, which seems to turn the therapy into more of a sprint than a slow-but-steady marathon, doesn't unravel you, there is the change in process and your role to contend with—the directive stance, leadership, the shaping of the process rather than just letting it unfold. It's easy to feel that you are being too controlling, that you are pushing clients before they are ready, that you are not giving them the time and opportunity to voice their stories and define their own paths, that you are acting more like a hard-driving parent hustling the kids into the car to school than a supportive and kind grandparent or wise sage.

Finally, if you are not experienced with working with couples and families, you have another skill-set to throw on the pile. Here the dangers are those that we've repeatedly stressed—feeling overwhelmed by the flood of content and the belief that you need to sort it all out, the emotion and drama unfolding in the session, the triangle of seeing a couple. Your antidote is leadership, tracking the process rather than diving into the weeds of content and having a treatment map already in place so thinking on your feet doesn't become another source of anxiety.

All this is to be expected because you are stepping outside your comfort zone. But like the piano playing, you will likely find that it all turns out better than it feels, that what you fear might happen does not, and that, with practice, the initially frantic pace will become your (almost) new normal. By setting expectations with clients at the initial contact, getting ongoing feedback by tracking the process tightly and handling objections as they arise, your worry that you are dragging the client along, not getting the story straight or leaving someone out, will dissipate. When you see that there are indeed plenty of opportunities to adjust your impressions as you get feedback from clients and fine-tune their treatment, your feeling rattled by having an incomplete assessment before beginning treatment will abate. Rather than seeing them as two separate processes, you'll begin to see that assessment and treatment in brief therapy and crisis work are actually one circular path, each fueling the other.

Using the Brief, Crisis-Oriented Approach to New Cases

If you have some experience with doing brief therapy, either by choice or through job requirements, our model can offer you variations on the theme, and help you expand your perspective and skills. If you are trained to do long-term work and are considering applying our approach to one or two cases, think of the experience and learning as being similar to taking a language-immersion course. You may feel unsettled a good part of the time, not completely clear where you are headed, but if you follow the program, you may be surprised at the end how much you have really learned. Here are some guidelines to consider before stepping out.

Choose Appropriate Clients

A psychiatric social worker at the local hospital is doing discharge planning for a 16-year-old male, Tom Smith, who was admitted for a suicide attempt. She is wondering if you would provide the outpatient family therapy. The Smith family is struggling with many stressors, including unemployment by the father and medical issues for the mother. While they have participated in family sessions at the hospital, the parents' attitude has been one of mystification—not understanding why their son is struggling, and thinking that he just needs to change his attitude. Is a brief approach a good idea for this family? Not really.

The challenges for this family are several: The son needs support as he makes the transition back into everyday life. While individual therapy may help with this, the larger concern is that of the parents. Because of their own struggles, their struggle to fully understand what their son needs and what makes him tick, we could imagine family therapy needing to recognize a parallel process: The therapist and the therapy needs to treat the parents the way the parents need to treat the son. We could imagine sessions focusing on the parents' own struggles, educating and using the sessions as forums to help them come to understand their son's needs and helping them have the ongoing support they need in order to consistently support him. Seeing them only briefly could, we imagine, result in their falling back into old patterns, and the son once again sinking into depression.

As mentioned in the opening chapter, by and large, brief work should not be used with clients who need the longer-term support of a therapeutic relationship, whether it is due to their own isolation, their limited skills or learning abilities or the fragility of their mental states.

You have the responsibility to discern what might work best with clients and continually assess along the way whether the model is a good fit. This is part of your leadership and professionalism. If in doubt, seek consultation with a colleague.

Avoid Radical Shifts

You have been working with Jack and his depression for several months using an insight-oriented approach, but you're feeling stuck. While he seems to have occasional "Aha" moments, and is much more aware of the origin of his coping style, his overall level of depression isn't really much better. You're thinking that maybe a change to a more behavioral approach, with clear weekly goals and homework, may help him emotionally dig out.

You can, but you need to be cautious. While you have an ethical responsibility to not keep doing what you are doing if it doesn't seem to be working, you also need to be sensitive to radical shifts. This is too disorienting for clients and too easily misinterpreted. Given Jack's state of mind, we could easily imagine him misinterpreting your change of focus; he may feel that it is his fault that things aren't better, or that you are actually getting frustrated and trying to push him out the door. And, in a way, he is partially correct. There's a good chance this isn't about Jack, but about you and your frustration.

The problem in the room is the stuckness, and the stuckness is a symptom of an underlying problem. This is what you need to get on the table and explore with Jack and help him understand your thinking. If there is a sincere agreement that a change in focus is called for, then slowly begin to integrate it into your treatment plan or refer him to a different therapist, facilitating as smooth a transition as possible.

Map Out the Treatment Plan in Advance

While pragmatism and flexibility are at the heart of a brief, crisis-oriented approach, it's useful to think through your goals and tasks session by session for the first several ones. Map out for yourself, for example, what you need to cover in that first session so you can stay focused and move the process along. Since you know the presenting problem from your initial contact, think through your assessment questions and the homework assignments you may give. This type of preparation will not only help you reduce your own anxiety but also help you more clearly map out the terrain for clients, which, in turn, will help you stay on target.

Try to Stay Within Time Limits

Having a map for sessions can help you stay focused and active within the session, but you will undoubtedly feel rushed if your style is less directive. Again, while the session process is not a forced march, and you want to build rapport and make certain that clients stay in step with you, you may need to push yourself a bit to accomplish what you set out to do at the beginning of the session. It's back to the piano playing—feeling awkward at first, but finding it easier to move along as your skills become honed. Pushing yourself to stay within time limits will also help you not inadvertently slide back into your old style and approach.

Be Easy on Yourself

There is a parallel process unfolding as you apply a briefer model to specific cases. Just as you want to encourage and support clients in taking acceptable risks and breaking out of old patterns, you want to do the same yourself. The key here, as it is with clients, is doing it different rather than doing it right. You want to adopt an attitude of experimentation and even playfulness. There are no mistakes, just the learning of new skills. Pat yourself on the back for your efforts, just as you would do with clients.

Integrating Brief Therapy Concepts Into Your Session Process

If you don't want or don't need to adapt a complete brief, crisis-oriented model of practice, you can still experiment with applying some of the concepts into your approach as a way of expanding how you think and address the problems that clients present, as well as shape the session process. Here are some guidelines for integrating them into your current models.

Staying in Lockstep: Closely Tracking the Process

You undoubtedly are acutely aware of process. What is different about the brief therapy approach is making this a priority over content. Especially when working with couples and families, it is all too easy to, like them, get lost in the content of the clients' stories. You either get fascinated by the story itself or, like a detective, are hanging on to a client's every word, connecting dots, looking for gaps and instinctively starting to put together the pieces of a puzzle of the client's historical and situational landscape. Obviously, you need to be able to do this to some extent, but you don't want to get so caught up in it that you are overlooking what is happening there in the room, particularly non-verbal behaviors. If you feel you are weak in these skills, there are a couple of things you can do to ramp up your awareness.

One is just to practice focusing on non-verbal process in conversations in general. When you watch a movie, turn down the sound and watch facial expressions; when you see couples talking at a restaurant, see if you can tell whether they are in synch; when engaged in a casual conversation yourself, try focusing on the non-verbal interactions rather than focusing exclusively on the story, and see what you notice.

Next you want to train yourself to look for agreement, or lack of it, and the staying in and out of lockstep. Again, you can practice this in your own casual conversations, but a better way to become more sensitive to these breakpoints without the pressure of thinking on your feet is to watch videotapes of yourself or other clinicians, or even listen to audiotapes looking for agreement, hesitations or yes-buts following a clinician's comment. These are invaluable in training your eyes and ears to catch when clients are falling out of step.

The close tracking becomes essential at those critical breakpoints within a session when you make an interpretation, provide education or state your treatment plan. What is easy to do when hearing any negative reaction is to try and make your point stronger—repeating what you just said, adding more information, etc. Rather than trying to override their objections with more content, try focusing on the process—that is, the negativity itself. The mindset here is to say what you are going to say, and then take a breath and mentally stop. Watch carefully what happens next. Look for agreement. If it's not there, back up and clarify.

Leadership and the Active Role

Tracking the process is a matter of developing a focus and attuning your listening and observational skills. Shifting to a highly interactive role in the session is, as mentioned earlier, usually more difficult because, in addition to applying these skills, you simply feel uncomfortable. The key here is not worrying so much about content and what to say next, and when (having a map for the session will help you stay on course), but rather to allow yourself to be more spontaneous, less cautious.

Not getting lost in the content will certainly help give you the mental space to do this. But the other element is to take the risk of saying what comes to your mind rather than self-censoring or mentally deliberating about timing and correctness. This can feel a bit like doing trapeze without a net if this is not your style, but it helps to remember that you are using behavioral change as your primary tool, rather than insight. And if you are tracking the process closely, even if what you say confuses the client or creates some resistance right there in the room, you will be able to catch it and repair it.

That said, you don't want to dominate the conversation. You are leading and guiding, not pulling. If a client shuts down or their eyes begin to glaze over, you'll know that you're talking too much and the client is getting flooded. Stop, check in with the client—"I realize that I was just giving you a lot of information at one time. What are thinking?"—and see what happens next.

A good way of increasing your spontaneity in sessions is to practice outside of sessions with family and friends. Pay some attention to you when talking with others; notice ideas and images as they pop up in your mind. Rather than going on auto-pilot, letting the other shape the conversation, holding back or worrying what the other person may think, try speaking up and saying what is in your mind. If you feel a bit anxious when doing this, it is a good indicator that you are stepping outside your style and plowing new ground. Do it, see what happens and pat yourself on the back for the effort. Then try doing the same in sessions.

Working Within Session Time Limits

As we discussed in applying a brief crisis-oriented approach to new cases, it helps to clearly map out in advance what you want to cover in sessions if you want to stay within time limits, especially in the important first session. You likely already have some mental format in mind for first sessions, and in certain work settings the first-session material is prescribed, such as completing intake, Hippa or clinical assessment forms.

In a brief approach, it's important that you stay focused on the primary goals of building rapport, changing the emotional climate, tracking transference cues, assessment and presenting a clear treatment plan, while making certain the client is in step with you by tracking the process all along the way. You may need to manage required forms by mailing them to clients and having them fill them out before the session starts. Your goal is to cover the clinical material you need to cover by the end of the session, and to do this, you need to become more proactive, structured and efficient.

Think again about our physician analogy. What our physician does in 15 minutes, we want to do in 50. Think about the session in segments—opening, assessment, treatment plan, homework—and watch the clock as you move forward. Rather than being reactive and gathering information from the clients' stories (and risk getting lost in them), be proactive—shorten the stories and gather the information you need to confirm your treatment map by asking specific questions in your assessment.

Similarly, focus on changing the emotional climate by tapping into soft emotions, but watch the clock. Don't wait to do this until too late in the session—you need to leave time and room for the unfolding of these newer emotions—and you want to avoid intentionally exploring potentially emotion-laden topics such as trauma or abuse. Not only will stirring up such topics potentially derail the session process, but more concerning, it may derail the clinical relationship. Uncovering too much sensitive emotional material in the first session can leave the new client feeling overwhelmed, ungrounded and unsafe.

Our brief approach manages this by moving quickly through assessment material, but, that said, if a client does unexpectedly get emotionally overwhelmed—if Harold, for example, begins to break down and sob about his wife— your agenda goes out the window. You do your best to support him and then follow up to make certain that he is not, in fact, left overwhelmed or frightened by his own outpouring of emotion.

Training yourself to accomplish session goals within a timeframe is, like the other skills, one that improves with practice. As you become more familiar with pacing and with using treatment maps, as well as paying close attention to the clock, your running of the session, particularly of the first, will be easier.

Making Quick Assessments

This brings us to the related skill of making quick assessments and yet another potential source of initial discomfort. While our approach draws heavily on the relationship triangle and emotional wounds as a focus for assessments, any clinical model and map that is clear and able to help you confirm or deny your initial hypotheses about a client's problem and solution will work. What is important is that the assessment be concise, that you are once again able to thwart off any temptations to get bogged down in the back-story and content. Think of your physician with her pointed questions about symptoms and what has been tried, her checklist of family history. You want to do the same.

That said, don't be reckless. Take the time you need to assess the Smith family, for example; explore their resources, as well as their own expectations of therapy. Trust your instincts and be careful not to rationalize to yourself that they and their son are able to do what those less stressed and more engaged could do. But also, don't rationalize that every client requires the same degree of thoroughness because it fits within your own comfort zone. You can backfill with more details and history if and when clients get emotionally or behaviorally stuck in making progress. Experiment with moving ahead at a quicker pace than you may be used to, even if you feel less than certain and comfortable.

Recognizing Patterns

Our brief approach, like other systems-based models, looks at changing behavioral patterns. The focus is on the interactional rather than the intrapsychic; the core belief is that the DNA of dysfunction lies in the pattern between two people, rather than within the psychology of the one, and that the pattern is always more powerful than the people. This way of describing relationship problems helps offset client self-criticism, and because the initial goal is to simply stop the pattern, clients, particularly those who are perfectionistic, feel less pressure to do it right.

If this is new way of thinking for you, the starting point, like the focus on process, is to increase your awareness through practice. When observing a conversation between two people or watching a movie, avoid getting lost in the stories and don't worry about the internal psychology of each individual, but instead, focus on the tennis match of emotional exchange and non-verbal behaviors. Look at the way two individuals bounce off each other and the A to B, B to A sequences: Jack asks a question, Ann ignores him, Jack raises his voice, Ann ignores him, Jack yells, Ann screams back, Jack huffs and walks away. Though the content may change, it is the pattern that remains the same.

To map patterns in sessions with couples and families, ask "what happens next" questions: "So you ask your daughter to clean her room, and what happens next? So, she says that and then what do you do?" You want to be able to visualize in your own mind the sequence of actions. Once you identify it, present it to the client and see if that in fact is what he sees playing out. From there you can talk about the power of patterns in shaping relationships, and how by changing their steps in the dance, others will have to change as well.

Integrating Our Brief Clinical Concepts Into Your Approach

The concepts and skills we've mentioned so far help you shape the session process. Let's shift focus and now talk about some of the clinical concepts that we have been using throughout our approach.

Relationship Triangle

The relationship triangle is just a specific form of patterns and, as we've discussed, a quick and helpful tool to help couples and families understand their own dynamics and source of problems.

To use it as part of your assessment, visualize the triangle itself with its roles and dynamic shifts to the persecutor role as individuals, families or couples talk about their relationships. You can begin to map out roles in broad strokes—those who follow the rules, are nice and are over-responsible are martyrs; those who become overwhelmed and feel helpless are victims; those who are aggressive and angry are persecutors. Ask questions about the details of the personalities to assess roles and map dynamics: Does the client ever feel unappreciated for all he does, or have a difficult time with confrontation or making decisions, indicating martyr roles? Does the client sometimes get flooded with anxiety or feel besieged by problems, or feel criticized and controlled by those around him?

Then map out the move to the persecutor—does the martyr ever feel resentful that others aren't helping out, or the victim that others are micromanaging them at times? Once you can see a tight fit between the model and the client's relationship patterns, draw a picture of the triangle and run through the dynamics, including explaining the adult model, to help them understand and normalize their behaviors.

Being Adult

The model of the adult is part of your explanation of the relationship triangle. But because it also offers clients a better way of looking at how to run their lives and relationships overall, it's valuable to highlight the importance of the concept. Think of this as a proactive and preventative goal, similar to your physician's taking the time to educate you in broad strokes about the benefits and goals of developing good nutrition and exercise.

But the concept itself can also help you make assessments more quickly. In law, there is the concept of the reasonable man defense—what would we expect a reasonable man to do in this situation? This is essentially what the adult is about: thinking in terms of what a reasonable person would do—not emotional, yet assertive, clear but not controlling, responsible but not over-responsible or hypervigilant. Just as it is helpful to ask "what happens next" questions to map patterns, you can ask clients questions about their behaviors and the blocks that keep them from being adult: "So your boss said you couldn't have the weekend off. Why didn't you calmly say that you had already put in your request two months ago, rather than getting angry and stomping out of the office?" Or to a couple: "So you were talking about setting a new bedtime for your son. What caused this to turn into such a huge argument?"

What you are doing by asking these questions is mapping with the clients the gap between adult behavior and their response, and tracking the patterns that fuel the emotions. You are looking for what can't they do, where do they get stuck, what triggers old wounds. What is important when asking such questions is that you sound curious and gentle. You want to make sure that there is no hint of criticism in your voice suggesting that the clients should simply know better—this will only create resistance and potentially replicate the problem in the room. Watch their reactions to gauge if your comments were non-offensive. Once you and the clients have mapped these scenarios and their responses, you can show them the relationship triangle, describe the adult as a way of summarizing what's been discussed and present a model for new ways of behaving. With this model mentally in place for the client, you can continue to refer back to it through treatment.

Emotional Wounds

As we described earlier, the concept of emotional wounds—childhood-based learned sensitivities to the reactions of others—with our behavioral approach helps you in two ways. One is that it helps you define and explain to clients why and how they react so strongly to certain reactions of their partners, and how these reactions lead to negative emotional loops that lead to unsolved problems and violent arguments. The second is that the concept provides both a quick assessment tool and a treatment approach. Rather than spending many sessions unearthing childhood history and repairing wounds through awareness and insight, you can drill down in your assessment and uncover the trigger point for each partner; then, in sessions, help partners and family members learn how to recognize and override the impact of these wounds and heal them through concrete behavioral change in the present and within the relationship. This is what makes a briefer approach possible and more efficient.

To apply this in your own work, you can use the roles of the relationship triangle as a mental guide to ask pointed questions in your assessment—for example, when you look back over your childhood and important relationships, what is it that most upset you, most pushed your emotional buttons? How do you tend to cope when these situations happen—become quiet and withdraw; become anxious and walk on eggshells and try to accommodate; get angry and lash out?

Next, follow up by tracking where adult behavior breaks down—"So even though you were upset at your wife, what kept you from speaking up rather than keeping quiet? What were you most afraid of?" Look, once again, for what clients are not able to do—the holes (be assertive, control their anger, define their needs, approach potential confrontation)—and the gap between their coping styles and the adult.

This feedback is what helps you, and them, define their particular wounds. Your next step is to help them understand how this ties to their presenting problems, and you then encourage them to do the opposite of what they usually do when wounds are triggered—regulate their emotions, step up and be assertive about their wants and needs and take action rather than withdrawing or being accommodating.

Encourage them to mentally label past reactions from the reality of the present to help them tamp down their anxious minds. Assign them behavioral homework (speaking up even though they feel anxious and cautious, for example)—an acceptable risk that is likely to be successful.

As a byproduct of this process of defining their wounds, it helps you isolate possible transference cues and sidestep your unintentionally rewounding clients in the therapy process; you avoid the replication of the problem in the room. This is about knowing as quickly as possible what you don't want to do—not sounding critical, because Ann is particularly sensitive to criticism, or cutting Sam off, because he is sensitive to not being heard. By combining this with awareness of the process and by staying in lockstep, you can avoid triggering the client, which can easily lead to their dropping out.

The skill here, again, is detecting this as quickly as possible. Even in the initial phone contact, listen for client complaints about others. Ask in the first session about past therapy experiences and listen to how the client describes the therapist. Ask about breakpoints in past relationships, when clients have left or reached some emotional bottom line. The goal isn't to necessarily deconstruct each and every one of these past experiences, but rather to identify and behaviorally change the response to present triggers.

Working With Family and Friends

If you work primarily with individuals, the notion of bringing in family and friends to a session can feel overwhelming. But they can also be sources of support for clients who are anxious, angry or depressed; they can provide important information and perspectives that are difficult to get, otherwise; and they allow you to work directly with those individuals who are, in fact, part of the problems that need to be solved. Some tips for incorporating friends and family into sessions follow.

Define the Goal of the Session

Clients will often ask others to come in without giving them any clear idea of the focus. What family and friends are most fearful of is some verbal free-for-all where anything or everything will be dumped on the table, or the revelation of some dark secret. It's your job to assume leadership, and define the goals at the start of sessions to offset these fears; this creates safety. This doesn't mean you need to speak for the client, but you do want to make clear to everyone what is reasonable to accomplish with the session time: "Margaret and I were talking about ways you might be able to help her when she feels overwhelmed. I'm hoping that we can come up with some concrete steps in this session that you both can try at home."

Take a Few Minutes to Build Rapport

By engaging in small talk—about jobs and interests, thanking them for coming in, checking in on how they feel—you can, again, help the other relax and can convey safety by being gently in charge.

Get and Keep the Conversation Going

Your role is that of a facilitator, not an arbitrator. Ask the client to make an opening statement: "The reason why I invited you here is to understand what I need when I get overwhelmed. Though I know you are trying to be helpful, I realize that you're getting frustrated with me, and your taking over when I'm struggling doesn't really help me in the long run. I'd like us to do this differently."

Then let everyone have an opportunity to talk. Don't worry about content; help them, instead, to keep moving forward towards understanding, towards a solution. If they get derailed—if Margaret gets emotional or is being unclear, stop and clarify: "Margaret, you are sounding angry; what just happened?" or "Margaret, you said that you'd like Joe to just be supportive; what does that mean? How can he show support in a concrete way?"

Make Sure the Conversation Is Balanced

You are moving towards a goal; the session is not a stage for venting and ranting. Don't be afraid to interrupt and ask one to stop so the other can talk. Again, you are trying to create a dialogue where each person's intentions, needs and behaviors are understood.

Don't Be Afraid to Ask the Hard Questions

You want to guide the conversation but also take it to a more honest, deeper level. You do this by asking the hard questions, asking about what you think the other may be thinking or feeling: "Joe, Margaret doesn't understand why you get so frustrated. I'm wondering if you ever wish that she could deal with these things on her own, rather than always coming to you about them?" Joe may say yes or no, but that is not what's important. What is important is stirring the emotional pot, letting both know that this is the time and place to take the risk of being more open and honest.

Resist the Urge to Find a Solution

As an outsider to the story you may be able to see the blindspots that the individuals cannot. It is fine to make suggestions—"Have you ever thought of . . .?"—but be careful that you don't step in as the authority or judge because you are trying to quell your own anxiety or relieve the tension in the room. Your job is to help them come up with a solution to the presenting problem that they can emotionally agree on. It is their ability to talk and work through problems and emotions together—for Margaret to be assertive, for Joe to be able to listen—that, over the long haul, are what make relationships productive and healthy. If there is tension, talk about the tension to dismantle it and get them back on track, rather than jumping to quick solutions as a way of reducing the uncomfortable tension.

Take Care of Yourself

If Margaret feels it would be good for her entire family to come in at some point, it is up to you to decide whether this is an acceptable risk you are willing to take, or whether it is too overwhelming for you. If it is, either bring in a co-therapist to help you manage, or divide the family up into subgroups. Don't get hung up on means, but rather focus on ends. Give yourself the time and space you need to build up both your skills and confidence.

Integrating Techniques and Tools Into Your Approach

Many of the technique and tools described in our treatment maps and the last chapter are probably, in some form, already in your repertoire. But if there are some you want to add, here is a list of the major ones, along with tips for learning and incorporating them.

Changing the Emotional Climate

You probably instinctively shape the process during sessions in ways that do, in fact, change the emotional climate—asking a client to explain more about the "hurt" that they mentioned in the middle of a sentence, commenting on the sad look on a client's face. As with other aspects of brief therapy, these are only more deliberate because intentionally changing the climate is an important goal of the first session.

If you want to do this more proactively in your own practice, it begins, like other skills and techniques, by making the implementing of these skills a session goal, and then staying alert to opportunities to use them. Noticing and acting are the first step; some clinicians miss opportunities for changing the emotional climate because they do get caught up in the content and fail to notice the subtleties unfolding within the process. But some also fail to change the emotional climate because they don't use the full range and power of their voice.

Deliberating shaping your voice—paying attention to not what you say, but how you say it—is another important tool in your clinical toolbox. Some therapists get so caught up in focusing on what they want to say that they pay little attention to how they say it. You want to be conscious of and deliberate about how you sound, especially when confronting emotions. The general rule is to mirror the clients' emotions and sounds—quiet and reflective when they are, louder and more open when they are not.

That said, you always keep in mind any dangers of triggering rewounding. Here you want to consciously use your voice to convey safety and concern, to sound gentle when confronting a client so sensitive to criticism. When unsure, be gentle in order to tunnel under client defenses rather than strengthening them by inadvertently raising fear and anxiety. Like the other skills, this use of voice, too, is a matter of practice. Recording your sessions can help you become sensitive to how you sound, as can listening to or observing other clinicians.

Using Education

Naming, normalizing and defining problems help put to rest clients' distorted thinking and anxiety about their pressing problems. Successfully incorporating education into your sessions, especially in the opening sessions, is a matter of managing the time within the session and knowing what you want to say. Talking about genetics, brain functioning, and the limited ways children have to cope with their world can help counter a client's own assault on her personality and her feelings of inadequacy. Describing brain rewiring and upgrading of coping skills, and talking about increasing psychological flexibility, steers thinking away from right and wrong.

But don't put pressure on yourself to wing it. Instead, develop five-minute speeches on depression, anxiety and anger, child development, relationship dynamics, and so on, that fit into your clinical model. Track the process as you are talking—looking for any signs that a client's eyes are glazing over or that the client seems confused or negative. End your speech on implications for treatment of his presenting problem: "So even though you learned to be hypervigilant and walk on eggshells around others, it would be good if you now could learn to be more assertive, more adult and less fearful. Does this make sense? Is this something you and I can work on together?"

Homework

There is the now-cliché ending to therapy sessions often seen in movies—"It looks like our time is up for today; let's pick this up again next week"—showing therapy as one ongoing conversation, interspersed with daily life. Homework speeds up the treatment process by allowing clients to practice skills outside the office, and makes a clear statement to clients that therapy is more than talking about one's life; instead, it is about taking active steps to change it.

If you want to integrate homework assignments into your work, make sure your homework assignments are clear, concrete and achievable. We mentioned several types of homework assignments to try in the last chapter. First assignments are usually observational: notice how you feel when _____; pay attention to _____, with no request for change. These are warm-up exercises, so to speak, to help clients be proactive, and help you see if clients are on board with you and the treatment plan.

But subsequent assignments should focus on moving clients out of their comfort zones and into behavioral action, yet, at the same time, not be too overwhelming. This becomes the challenge—creating a psychological and behavioral stretch that also is one that the client can be successful doing. It's helpful to think in terms of having them apply broad, global individual skills—assertiveness, for example—in ever more challenging ways, moving up the anxiety hierarchy from strangers to friends or family members, rather than thinking in terms of challenging clients to resolve specific situations and problems—for example, talk to your husband about whether he wants to move to New Mexico or not. Focus your homework on helping them change their process (taking the risk of being assertive when they get the wrong change at Starbucks, because it is about assertiveness, not coffee) rather than helping them refine the content (whether or not to complain about the change and how to complain about it). You certainly want to help clients solve concrete problems, but you want to help them understand and override where they get stuck in solving those problems.

If, for example, 16-year-old Sam is conditioned to bite his tongue and is unable to tell his mother what is bothering him, creating depression and anxiety, it is better to think of his challenge as approaching his anxiety and being assertive—key to upgrading and developing a more flexible coping style—rather than immediately seeing this as merely a mother–child relationship issue. His response to his mother is only the current stuck-point in his ability to communicate his thoughts and needs. Pressuring him to move towards quickly changing his patterns with his mother not only can potentially replicate the problem (being another adult who seems intimidating) but also can overwhelm him and lead to failure.

Instead, give Sam the assignment of noticing social situations where he holds back—perhaps talking with friends at school—and ask him to try and go against his grain and take the risk of saying what he is thinking. If he does that successfully, his next assignment could be his doing the same with a low-risk adult—approaching one of his teachers, perhaps, who harshly graded one of his papers. With each success his self-confidence grows, and with your encouragement and support he will be ready to take on the biggest challenge, namely his mother.

Keep in mind that you can stack assignments so that clients can continue to work on several treatment goals at one time. Tanisha may be given the assignment one week to practice using Emotional Freedom Technique (EFT) when anxious, the following week to have a conversation with her supervisor about her work schedule and use EFT ahead of time if anxious, the third to offset her depressive mindset by writing out daily appreciations before she goes to bed while also following up with her supervisor and using EFT when needed. You are encouraging her to work on both new and old skills, short- and long-term goals. It is when clients don't follow through with an assignment that you need to regroup and determine the problem—that the conversation with her supervisor was too much of a challenge for Tanisha, she didn't use the EFT because she didn't fully understand how to do so, she didn't do the appreciations because she didn't see the link between them and her depression.

Experiential Techniques

EFT brings to mind the overall use of other experiential techniques such as sculpting, letter-writing, enactments, guided imagery and even sensate focus. Again, these are powerful tools that can help you with assessment, change the emotional climate and help you understand how clients learn best, as well as facilitate treatment. If you decide to use any of them, once again, be proactive. Consider in advance, before the start of treatment or before a specific session, where these may be helpful. Also keep in mind the mantra of experience before explanation—if you are explaining too much before initiating an exercise, it is likely due more to your own anxiety than that of the clients.

That said, you don't want your own anxiety to get in the way of offering or guiding the exercise. The best way to do this is to practice these in advance—do the guided imagery with your colleagues, role-play an enactment with your supervisor, try out the sensate focus exercises with your partner, use EFT to counter your own anxiety. Your own practice and experience will go a long way in not only helping you feel confident but also knowing what emotional reactions or objections to expect from clients.

Finis

This concludes our tips for integrating the elements of our brief, crisis-oriented approach into your own practice. This also concludes our journey together. It is hoped that these concepts and skills, this way of thinking about the problems of anxiety, anger and depression, have sparked a renewed reflection on your own assumptions, habits and methods of practice, and have stirred your own creativity. This, perhaps, is the ultimate purpose of approaching anything new—to shake up the ordinary, to ignite our questioning, to stimulate new ideas and to encourage us to experiment with something that we had not done before. This is how we grow. This is how we discover who we are, what we believe, what we need to do most.

Thank you for coming along.

Index

abandonment 35
abuse 17, 160; *see also* domestic violence
accommodation 33, 172
accountability 42, 131
acting out: children 22, 80, 85; first-aid plans 154; martyrs 15; taking responsibility 42–43; teenagers 86–88; victims 16
action-oriented approach 1, 3, 6
active listening 30–31, 38, 61, 92, 117, 122
AD/HD *see* attention deficit/hyperactivity disorder
addiction 21, 64–67, 132, 154; individual treatment 7, 46, 47, 55; taking responsibility 42–43; teenagers 86; *see also* alcohol; substance use
adult children 88–89
adult role 13–14, 170–171, 172; moving towards the 17–19, 26, 32, 100, 130, 139; techniques and tools 143
affairs 1, 21, 42–43, 50–57, 100, 126–127
age-appropriate parenting 79, 85
aggression 17, 86
agreement, lack of 102–103, 166, 167
alcohol 40–41, 64–65, 126; first-aid plans 154; individual treatment 46; sexual issues 68
ambivalence 52, 58, 107
anger 13, 27–28, 61–62, 114; affairs 54; alcohol use 126; as bad solution 41; bullies 17, 18, 45, 156; check-ins 152; childhood wounds 35, 36, 37; client stories 109; domestic violence 60; education on 176; escalation of emotions 29–30;

family and friends 172; grief turned to 66, 67; individual treatment 45–46, 55; letter-writing 150; parents 23; reframing 97–98; self-regulation 139; situational crises 72; taking responsibility 42–43; unresolved 34
anorexia 6–7, 47; *see also* eating disorders
anxiety 7, 13, 48; anxiety disorders 47; assertiveness 155; assessment 111; bullies 17, 18; check-ins 152, 153; children 80, 82, 83–84, 85; drop-outs 131–132; education on 176; emotional freedom technique 155, 177; experiential techniques 143; family and friends 172; martyrs 14, 15, 17, 18; middle stages of therapy 139, 141; money issues 70; organizational skill training 157–158; quick decisions 157; risk-taking 37; separation 89, 90; sexual issues 68–69; situational crises 72, 89; termination of therapy 142; therapist's own 66, 69–70, 90, 161, 165, 174, 177–178; victims 16
arguments 4, 61–62, 95, 111, 114, 120, 137
assertiveness 19, 27, 139, 176; adult model 13; domestic violence 60; homework assignments 155–156; martyrs 18
assessment 5, 9, 12, 162–163, 168; communication skills 34; emotional wounds 37, 171–172; first session 22, 91, 96–97, 104, 111–114; foundation for 43; making quick assessments 169; second session 125, 130; starting point for 39

attention deficit/hyperactivity disorder (AD/HD) 47, 76, 157–158
attention seeking 78, 85

balance 48, 51–52, 54–55, 116–117, 173–174
behavioral change 4, 41, 48, 119, 167, 171
behaviors, focus on 3
bias 48, 51
Big Six skills 40–43
bipolar disorder 7, 46, 47
blame 45–46, 58, 60, 62, 70, 89–90
boundaries: clinical 6, 93; martyrs 18
Bowen, M. 13
bulimia 47; *see also* eating disorders
bullies (persecutors) 16–17, 28, 156; assessment 111; domestic violence 60, 63, 125; emotions 27; individual treatment 45–46; moving towards adult role 18; relationship triangle 170
business meetings 149–150

calmness 13, 32, 61, 62, 84; business meetings 150; check-ins 152–153; countering objections 101
change 42, 135; behavioral 4, 41, 48, 167, 171; domestic violence 62; families in transition 81–83; family dynamics 119; motivation for 59
check-ins 152–153
childhood wounds 35–38, 63; *see also* emotional wounds
children 73; business meetings 150; common behavioral problems 83–84; families in transition 81–83; format options 75–76; individual treatment 128; parenting guidelines 77–80; sculpting technique 145; structural family model 19–23; *see also* families; teenagers
client stories 109–111
clients, choosing appropriate 164
clinical relationship 123
cognitive-behavioral approach 108, 111
comfort zone 29, 42, 135; behavioral change 4; children 78; expanding 155, 156; experiential techniques 143; homework assignments 176; middle stages of therapy 141; quick decisions 157; therapists 163; victims 18

common ground 9
communication 1, 26–34; affairs 57; assessment 112; behavioral change 4; business meetings 150; differing visions 39; domestic violence 58, 61, 62; middle stages of therapy 121, 140; parents 80; role-modeling 99; sexual issues 67, 68, 69; situational crises 71, 90; techniques and tools 143
compassion 28
compliments 33–34
compromise 32–33, 39, 63, 70, 122, 132, 137, 141
confidence: children 84; homework assignments 177; quick decisions 157; therapist's 174, 178; victims 16, 18, 156
confidentiality 127–128
connection 54–55, 92, 94
consensus 101
content 8, 40, 43, 163, 166; affairs 51; domestic violence 62, 63, 64; stages of therapy 120, 123
coping styles 37, 63, 81, 139, 143, 172, 177
countertransference 93, 161
couples: addictions 64–67; affairs 50–57; characteristics of couples in crisis 7–9; communication skills 27–34; domestic violence 57–64; drop-outs 131–133; emotional wounds 35–38; emotions 42; enactments 148–149; family dynamics 23; first session 105–119; homework assignments 103, 149–150; individual treatment 45–49, 125–128; learning problems vs. problems about learning 40; life-play guided imagery 147, 148; linking problems 100; middle stages of therapy 136–141; model for 13–19; money issues 70–71; relationship rollercoaster 23–26; sculpting technique 144–145; second session 123–129; sexual issues 67–70, 159–161; shift to the individual 129–130; situational crises 71–72; treatment maps 45–72
crisis-oriented approach 162, 163–166
criticism 34, 35, 36–37, 124, 172, 175

de-escalation 61–62
decision-making 13, 157
deconstructing relationships 55–56, 57
defenses 14, 102, 175
defensiveness 13, 30, 95, 129, 145
dependency 135
depression 41, 47, 48–49; affairs 56; assertiveness 155; check-ins 153; daily appreciations 177; education on 176; family and friends 172; individual treatment 55; situational crises 72; teenage 113, 114, 115–116, 117, 164, 177
diagnosis 1, 12
dialectical behavior therapy 153
differing visions 38–39, 65, 90, 96
divorce 23, 25, 53, 58, 81
Doherty, William 9
domestic violence 57–64, 125
dredging up the past 30, 127–128
drop-outs 102, 103, 129, 131–133, 172
Dull, V. T. 92

eating disorders 6–7, 46, 47, 76, 86, 154
education 99, 115, 167, 175–176
Ekstein, R. 39
emotional climate 6, 22, 72, 168, 175; crisis focus 162; domestic violence 59; experiential techniques 177; first session 91, 97–99, 103, 115, 116; positive 34, 123; sculpting technique 144–145; second and subsequent sessions 129, 131; termination of therapy 141
emotional freedom technique (EFT) 154–155, 177, 178
emotional wounds 14, 35–38, 141, 171–172; addictions 65; affairs 56; assessment 111, 112, 169; differing visions 39; domestic violence 63; first session 96, 104, 114, 115, 118; homework assignments 124; letter-writing 150; life-play guided imagery 147; maintaining momentum 136; parents 80, 81; repairing 139–140; sexual issues 67, 68, 69; situational crises 90; stages of therapy 121; transference cues 98
emotions 1, 2, 4, 120; ability to use as information 27–28, 62; affairs 54, 56; bullies 18, 27; changing 41; check-ins 152–153; crisis focus 162; empathizing with 42–43; escalation of 29–30; families 84; first-aid plans 154; grounding 132; high 7; honesty 29; letter-writing 150, 151–152; life-play guided imagery 148; martyrs 18; middle stages of therapy 140; mirroring 175; negative 158; problems about learning 39, 40; responsibility for 29, 32, 42–43; sculpting technique 144–145; self-regulation 27, 60–62, 111; situational crises 71; soft 97–98, 116, 140, 168
empathy 42–43, 117
empty nests 25, 141
enactments 148–149, 178
ending therapy 141–142
erectile dysfunction 67, 68, 160–161
escalation 8, 29–30, 60, 63, 84, 86, 116
ethical issues 46, 135
expectations 2, 3, 8, 45, 163; addictions 64; affairs 53, 54; differing visions 38–39; domestic violence 58; family assessment 22; faulty 103–104; first session 91, 94–96, 106, 108; maintaining momentum 134–135; parents 73; third session 131
experiential techniques 143–149, 177–178
expertise 94
experts 47

facts 8
families: adult children 88–89; choosing appropriate clients 164; common behavioral problems in young children 83–84; drop-outs 131–133; emotions 42; enactments 148–149; first session 105–119; format options 74–76; homework assignments 103, 149–150; individual treatment 45, 47, 48; life-play guided imagery 148; linking problems 100; middle stages of therapy 136–141; parenting guidelines 77–80; polarized parents 80; sculpting technique 144, 145; second session 123–129; shift to the individual 129–130; sibling rivalry 84–85; situational crises 89–90; structural family model 19–23, 74,

Index

80, 100; teen acting out 86–88; teen oppositional behavior 85–86; in transition 81–83; treatment maps 73–90; working with family and friends 172–174; *see also* children; parents

feedback 5, 6, 9, 163; from colleagues 136; enactments 149; on first session 126; letter-writing 152; parenting 78, 85; positive 33–34, 78, 149, 157, 159

first-aid plans 154

first session 6, 105–119, 134; affairs 53, 55–56; assessment 22, 96–97, 111–114; building rapport 92–94; client stories 109–111; countering objections 100–102; defining problems and expectations 94–96; domestic violence 58; emotional climate 97–99, 115, 116, 175; feedback on 126; first-aid 116–119; following up 119; goals 91–104; initial contact 105–107; linking problems 99–100; openings 107–109; preparation 107; presentation of treatment plan and next steps 114–116; resistance 102–104; time limits 168

flexibility 122

floor-time 79–80

focus, change in 164–165

following up 119

Frankel, R. M. 92

gender issues 68

goals 5, 9; affairs 57; assessment 111; first session 91–104; individual 126; maintaining momentum 134–135; middle stages of therapy 139–141; organizational skill training 158–159; second session 123–129; working with family and friends 173

Gottman, John 30, 31, 33, 127

Greenspan, Stanley 79

grief: affairs 50–51, 54, 56, 57, 100; domestic violence 59; letter-writing 150; marijuana use 66–67; parental separation 83

guided imagery 145–148, 177, 178

guilt 15, 16, 150

healing 35, 36, 37, 57, 150

Hendrix, Harville 30–31, 35

homework assignments 4, 149–161, 172, 176–177; affairs 54; assertiveness/risk-taking 155–156; behavioral change 41; business meetings 149–150; check-ins 152–153; domestic violence 58, 63; emotional freedom technique 154–155; emotional skills 28; first-aid plans 154; first session 102, 108, 114; letter-writing 150–152; maintaining momentum 134; middle stages of therapy 140; organizational skill training 157–159; pacing 103; positive comments 34; second session 124, 130; sensate focus exercises 159–161

honesty 14, 29, 43, 174

house metaphor 25–26, 31

hypervigilance 7, 176; affairs 56; bullies 17, 18; grief turned to 66, 67

individual treatment 7, 45–49, 55; children 76; domestic violence 60; second session 125–128; teenagers 88, 113

individuation 85, 88, 141

instincts 3

interpretations 42, 105, 167

intimacy 14, 135; communication skills 29; healing wounds 35; honesty 43; identifying emotions 27; sexual issues 67

language 4, 92–93, 97

leadership 9, 136, 163; active role 167; choosing appropriate clients 164; crisis work 53; domestic violence 59, 60; first session 93–94, 103, 104, 109, 116; second and subsequent sessions 129; sexual issues 161; termination of therapy 142

"leaning in, leaning out" 9, 107

learning problems 39–40, 70, 96, 124

letter-writing 150–152, 177

Levinson, W. 92

libido 69

life-play guided imagery 145–148

listening 4; active 30–31, 38, 61, 92, 117, 122; building rapport 92

lockstep, staying in 5, 37, 104, 172; close tracking of process 166–167; first session 94, 96, 105, 107–108, 112, 115; maintaining momentum 134

magical thinking 14, 17, 36, 38, 60
mandated clients 133
maps *see* treatment maps
marijuana 46–47, 64, 66–67
marriage 24
martyrs 14–16, 25, 28, 42, 100, 158; assessment 96, 111, 112; domestic violence 63; homework assignments 156–157; money issues 70; moving towards adult role 17–18; relationship triangle 170
massage 160
matching 93
McCarthy, B. 69
means vs. ends 121–122
medication 47, 48, 100, 101, 115–116
micromanagement: adult children and parent issues 88, 89; assessment 111, 112; homework assignments 124; loss of trust 51; money issues 70, 110, 114; relationship triangle 170
middle stages of therapy 121–122, 130–141
mind rewiring 34, 38
Minuchin, S. 19, 74, 80, 86, 100, 148
mirroring 92–93, 175
miscommunication 31, 53
momentum 134–136
money issues 70–71, 109–110, 111, 112, 114, 137–138
moving forward 56–57, 72
Mullooly, J. P. 92

name-calling 30
negative comments 33–34
Nichols, Michael 31
non-verbal signals 62, 98, 103, 104, 166

objections: close tracking of process 167; first session 100–102, 103, 105, 116, 118; handling as they arise 163; second session 123, 124
obsessive-compulsive disorder (OCD) 47
old wounds 30, 35–38, 68, 138, 171; *see also* emotional wounds
openness 14, 174
organizational skill training 157–159

pacing 103, 117, 132, 162–163, 168
parents 73–74; adult children 88–89; assessment 96–97; awareness of who has the problem 28; business meetings 150; childhood wounds 35; choosing appropriate clients 164; common behavioral problems in young children 83–84; countering objections 100, 101, 102; families in transition 81–83; format options 74–75; learning problems vs. problems about learning 40; life-play guided imagery 147; parenting guidelines 77–80; polarized 80; sibling rivalry 84–85; situational crises 89–90; structural family model 19–23; teen acting out 86–88; teen oppositional behavior 85–86; *see also* families
patterns 3, 29; changing 41, 130, 139, 169, 170, 177; recognizing 169–170; repairing dysfunctional 4, 127–128, 131, 153; stages of therapy 120, 121, 122
perfectionism 42, 157, 169
persecutors *see* bullies
personal responsibility *see* responsibility
"playing courtroom" 8, 47, 120; affairs 51, 53; first session 95, 118; polarized parents 80
polarization 80, 100, 137
pornography addiction 64, 65–66, 154
positive comments 33–34
post-traumatic stress 47, 85, 122, 155
power issues: addictions 65; assessment 112; domestic violence 59; families 21, 22, 73–74; first session 117; money issues 70, 114; problem-solving 32; sexual issues 67–68, 69; stages of therapy 120; teen oppositional behavior 86
"pre-compromise" 33
preparation 107, 165
present, focusing on the 3, 9, 36
priorities, setting 157–159
problem-solving 4, 5, 8, 18–19, 32–33; business meetings 150; communication skills 29; countering objections 101; domestic violence 62; families 79; focus on 122; healing emotional wounds 38; homework assignments 176; honesty 43; money issues 70, 71; parents 23; sexual issues 68, 69; solution-focused therapy 111; stages of therapy 121; techniques

and tools 143; teen oppositional behavior 86
problems: awareness of who has the problem 28–29; as bad solutions 40–41, 54; education 175; first session 91, 94–96, 99–100; learning problems vs. problems about learning 39–40, 96, 124; middle stages of therapy 131, 137–138; situational crises 71–72; willingness to return and repair 31–32; worsening 121, 122
process-oriented approach 1, 4, 40, 43, 123; awareness of process 29–30, 121, 122; close tracking of process 163, 166–167; domestic violence 63, 64
procrastination 158
professionalism 106–107, 164
psychodynamic approach 3, 102, 111
psychotic disorders 7

quality time 79–80
quick decisions 157

rapport 7, 9, 49, 168; children 73, 75; families 74; first session 91, 92–94, 104, 108, 112, 116; sexual issues 68; similarities 93; working with family and friends 173
reasonable man defense 171
referrals 46, 48, 55, 76
reframing 97–98, 99, 115
relationship contract 24, 26, 140
relationship repair 123, 128
relationship rollercoaster 23–26, 38, 99
relationship triangle 100, 170, 171; addictions 65; assessment 111, 169, 172; balance 51, 54; dynamics 129; education 99; emotional wounds 139; family therapy 73, 75, 80; money issues 70; role transitions 130; termination of therapy 141
reparation 31
reparenting 98
resentment 15, 16, 25, 100, 170
resistance 94, 102–104, 105, 118–119, 130, 167, 171
responsibility 13–14, 28, 130; for actions 42–43; assessment 111; bullies 17, 18, 28; de-escalation 62; for emotions 29, 32, 42–43; individual treatment 60; over-responsibility 15–16, 28, 156; second and subsequent sessions 128–129; stages of therapy 123; under-responsibility 16, 28; victims 18
responsiveness 106–107
rewounding 35–36, 38, 63, 172, 175
risk-taking 37, 43, 57, 132; children 78, 84; homework assignments 155, 156, 177; honesty 29, 174; quick decisions 157; sensitive topics 138–139; by therapist 165–166; victims 18
role-modeling 99
role-play 84, 128, 178
Roter, D. L. 92
routines 77–78, 84; families in transition 81, 82, 83; relationship rollercoaster 24, 26
rules 31, 60; breaking 84; childhood wounds 35; families in transition 81, 82, 83; parenting 77, 85; relationship rollercoaster 24, 26; separation 53
rumination 51, 153

sabotage 133
sadness 98, 109, 117
safety 7, 93; children 100; comfort zones 135; domestic violence 59, 63; first session 98, 108, 115; working with family and friends 173
scope of treatment 6
sculpting 144–145, 177
second session 123–129, 130
secrecy 65, 126–128
self-awareness 62, 120–121, 143, 160–161
self-care 154
self-criticism 89–90, 99, 156, 169
self-differentiation 13
self-disclosure 93
self-esteem 60, 78, 149, 155, 156
self-harm/cutting 7, 86–88, 110, 112–113, 117, 135, 154
self-reflection 135
self-regulation 18, 27, 139; assessment 111, 112; children 84; domestic violence 60–62, 63; individual treatment 45–46, 60; parents 20; stages of therapy 121, 122; teen oppositional behavior 86

sensate focus exercises 159–161, 177, 178
sensitive topics 138–139
separation 53, 82–83; anxiety 89, 90
seven-year itch 23, 26, 140
sex 57, 67–70, 97, 159–161
shame 65–66
"shoulds" vs. "wants" 42, 156–157
siblings: adult 89; childhood wounds 35; format options 76; sibling rivalry 84–85
Silver, N. 30
similarities, highlighting 93
single parents 81
situational crises 71–72, 89–90
skills: Big Six 40–43; communication 1, 26–34, 39, 58, 61, 62, 63, 80; emotional 1, 27–28; homework assignments 108, 176; inconsistent 121; learning problems 39–40, 70; middle stages of therapy 139–140; money issues 71; organizational skill training 157–159; sexual issues 69–70; teaching 128, 130; termination of therapy 142; therapist's 174
solution-focused therapy 111
spontaneity 167
stages of therapy 120–123
stepparents 81, 82
stress 72, 153
structural family model 19–23, 74, 80, 100
stuckpoints 26, 43, 57; middle stages of therapy 141; sexual issues 69, 160, 161; stuckness in therapy 164–165
substance use 46–47, 55, 64, 66–67, 154; see also addiction
suicidality 86, 164
supervision 66, 70, 76, 90, 117, 118, 135–136

tapping technique 154–155
techniques and tools 143–161, 174–178; experiential 143–149, 177–178; homework 149–161, 176–177
teenagers 73, 164–165; business meetings 150; families in transition 81; first session 108, 109, 110–111, 112–114, 115–116, 117–119; format options 75; homework assignments 177; individual treatment 76; oppositional behavior 85–86; parenting guidelines 79

termination of therapy 141–142
therapy, stages of 120–123
third session 130–136
time limits 165, 168
time management 105
time-outs 62
transference 14, 132–133, 136; emotional wounds 172; first session 98–99, 104, 112; homework 124; tracking transference cues 168
transitions 78–79, 81–83
treatment maps 5–6, 9, 143, 163; addictions 64–67; affairs 50–57; couples 45–72; domestic violence 57–64; families 73–90; first session 91, 96, 103, 107, 111; individual treatment 45–49; information gathering 168; markers for change 135; money issues 70–71; preparation 165; sexual issues 67–70; situational crises 71–72
treatment plans 12, 143, 168; close tracking of process 167; crisis focus 162; first session 91, 105, 114–116; maintaining momentum 134; preparation 165; second session 125
triggers 35–36, 116; assessment 171; check-ins 153; domestic violence 63; first session 104, 118; money issues 70; sensate focus exercises 160; transference issues 98, 136
trust: affairs 50, 51, 54, 56, 100; building 98; domestic violence 59; mirroring 92; parenting 78; similarities 93
"try it and see" approach 42, 48

victims 16, 17, 28, 141, 156; assessment 112; domestic violence 63; money issues 70; moving towards adult role 18; relationship triangle 170
violence 57–64, 125
visions: clarifying and updating 140–141; differing 38–39, 65, 90, 96
voice, therapist's 175
vulnerability 14, 67, 68

Wallerstein, R. 39
warnings 78–79
Whitaker, Carl 117
withdrawal 35, 37, 114, 172

Taylor & Francis eBooks

Helping you to choose the right eBooks for your Library

Add Routledge titles to your library's digital collection today. Taylor and Francis ebooks contains over 50,000 titles in the Humanities, Social Sciences, Behavioural Sciences, Built Environment and Law.

Choose from a range of subject packages or create your own!

Benefits for you
- Free MARC records
- COUNTER-compliant usage statistics
- Flexible purchase and pricing options
- All titles DRM-free.

Benefits for your user
- Off-site, anytime access via Athens or referring URL
- Print or copy pages or chapters
- Full content search
- Bookmark, highlight and annotate text
- Access to thousands of pages of quality research at the click of a button.

 REQUEST YOUR FREE INSTITUTIONAL TRIAL TODAY — **Free Trials Available** We offer free trials to qualifying academic, corporate and government customers.

eCollections – Choose from over 30 subject eCollections, including:

Archaeology	Language Learning
Architecture	Law
Asian Studies	Literature
Business & Management	Media & Communication
Classical Studies	Middle East Studies
Construction	Music
Creative & Media Arts	Philosophy
Criminology & Criminal Justice	Planning
Economics	Politics
Education	Psychology & Mental Health
Energy	Religion
Engineering	Security
English Language & Linguistics	Social Work
Environment & Sustainability	Sociology
Geography	Sport
Health Studies	Theatre & Performance
History	Tourism, Hospitality & Events

For more information, pricing enquiries or to order a free trial, please contact your local sales team: www.tandfebooks.com/page/sales

 Routledge Taylor & Francis Group | The home of Routledge books

www.tandfebooks.com